The English Radical Imagination

Culture, Religion, and Revolution, 1630–1660

NICHOLAS McDOWELL

CLARENDON PRESS · OXFORD

OXFORD
UNIVERSITY PRESS

Great Clarendon Street, Oxford OX2 6DP

Oxford University Press is a department of the University of Oxford.
It furthers the University's objective of excellence in research, scholarship,
and education by publishing worldwide in

Oxford   New York

Auckland Bangkok Buenos Aires Cape Town Chennai
Dar es Salaam Delhi Hong Kong Istanbul Karachi Kolkata
Kuala Lumpur Madrid Melbourne Mexico City Mumbai Nairobi
São Paulo Shanghai Taipei Tokyo Toronto

Oxford is a registered trade mark of Oxford University Press
in the UK and in certain other countries

Published in the United States
by Oxford University Press Inc., New York

© Nicholas McDowell 2003

The moral rights of the author have been asserted
Database right Oxford University Press (maker)

First published 2003

British Library Cataloguing in Publication Data

Data available

Library of Congress Cataloging in Publication Data

Data applied for

ISBN 0–19–926051–6

1 3 5 7 9 10 8 6 4 2

Typeset in Minion
by Regent Typesetting, London
Printed in Great Britain
on acid-free paper by
Biddles Ltd,
Guildford and King's Lynn

OXFORD ENGLISH MONOGRAPHS

General Editors

TO MY PARENTS

Preface and Acknowledgements

THIS BOOK SEEKS to build on the many advances in interdisciplinary study in recent years by developing our historical knowledge through the application of literary techniques of textual analysis. At the same time I am influenced by theories of cultural history that have questioned the value of rigid distinctions between elite and popular cultures in the early modern period. Finally, and more specifically, I seek to revise long-standing assumptions about the nature of radicalism in the English revolution: about where radical beliefs came from, who held them, and how they were expressed.

The English Radical Imagination is a much revised version of a D.Phil. thesis submitted to the University of Oxford in 2000. My research between 1996 and 1998 was funded by the Arts and Humanities Research Board. Latterly I am grateful to the Master and Fellows of Fitzwilliam College, Cambridge, for electing me to the post of Research Fellow and for providing an ideal environment in which to complete and then revise my work. I was supervised at Oxford by Nigel Smith, now of Princeton University. I was fortunate indeed to work with such an inspiring and generous scholar, who has become a good friend. Many thanks also to Tom Keymer for his kind and helpful interest in my work while at Oxford. My examiners, A. D. Nuttall and Thomas N. Corns, were characteristically acute and constructive in their criticism. Most of my research was undertaken in the Bodleian, and I should like to thank in particular the staff of Duke Humfrey's Library. Others who helped by reading my work, suggesting ideas, or locating references include Philip Grover, Meiling Hazelton, Dan Hedley, and Michael Long. At Cambridge, Richard Serjeantson was a scrupulous critic of Chapter 5. Hero Chalmers and Claire Preston also provided encouragement. The School of English at the University of Exeter has proved a supportive environment in which to begin an academic career; thanks in particular to Andrew McCrae and Karen Edwards for sharing their wide knowledge of the seventeenth century. My greatest debt is acknowledged by the dedication. Sally Faulkner is mentioned last but should always be put first.

N. McDowell

Contents

Note on Texts/Abbreviations

IN ALL QUOTATIONS punctuation, spelling, and italicization remain as in the originals, apart from the modernization of the long s, i/j, and u/v. Where a modern edition of a text has been used, quotations have been compared with the original where possible and corrected where necessary. Where a work is named and discussed at length, page references are given parenthetically in the text.

Unless otherwise stated, the place of publication for early modern texts is London. Dates of publication are given as on the original title pages. Unless otherwise stated, all biblical citations are from the Authorized Version. The following abbreviations have been used throughout.

BDBR	R. L. Greaves and R. Zaller (eds.), *A Biographical Dictionary of British Radicals in the Seventeenth Century*, 3 vols. (Brighton, 1982–4)
CPWM	*Complete Prose Works of John Milton*, ed. D. M. Wolfe et al., 8 vols. (New Haven, Conn., 1953–82)
CRW	*A Collection of Ranter Writings from the Seventeenth Century*, ed. Nigel Smith (London, 1983)
DNB	*Dictionary of National Biography*
LT	*The Leveller Tracts, 1649–1653*, ed. William Haller and Godfrey Davies (New York, 1944)
OED	*Oxford English Dictionary*
WWW	*The Writings of William Walwyn*, ed. J. R. McMichael and B. Taft (Athens, Ga., 1989)

Never did the human mind attain such a magnificent height of self-assertiveness as in England about the year 1650.

Lytton Strachey, 'Muggleton', in *Portraits in Miniature* (1931)

1

'Illiterate Mechanick Persons': Writing, Radicalism, and the Dominant Culture

My object in this book is to revise our understanding of radicalism in the English revolution and to make new claims for its social, cultural, and literary diversity. My method can be broadly defined as literary in that I proceed in Chapters 3–5 by analysing the rhetorical strategies, stylistic devices, and discursive contexts of some of the most significant radical writing published in the 1640–60 period. My central argument, which I explain here and elaborate on in Chapter 2, is that such analysis involves a reconstruction of the various relationships between the orthodox intellectual and literary culture of early modern England and the development and expression of heterodox belief in the mid-seventeenth century. This reconstruction raises methodological and conceptual issues concerning the formation of cultural history. Yet it may initially appear to be an unfruitful, one-dimensional subject for a book-length study, for the radicals themselves, their seventeenth-century enemies, and their twentieth-century friends all represent the relationship between radical belief and elite culture as starkly adversarial. In his voluminous heresiography *Gangraena* (1646), the Presbyterian cleric Thomas Edwards blamed the 'Errours, Heresies, Blasphemies and pernicious Practices' infecting England in the 1640s on the failure to prevent 'illiterate Mechanick persons' from engaging in public discussion of religious matters. He claimed that 'the confusion and disorder in Church matters both of opinions and practises' was due to 'all sorts of Mechanicks taking upon themselves to preach and baptize, as Smiths, Taylors, Shoomakers, Pedlars, Weavers &c. there are also some women Preachers in our times'. The ignorant heretics who populate *Gangraena* and threaten to overwhelm godly order in England believe there to be 'no need of learning, nor for reading of Authors for Preachers, but all books and learning must go down, it comes from want of the Spirit, that men write such great volumes, and make such adoe of learning'.[1] The radicals' own words, as quoted in influential works of history and criticism, seem to confirm this characterization. The Leveller leader Richard Overton was 'confident that it must be the poor, the simple and the mean things of this earth that must confound the mighty and the strong'. William Dell, New Model Army chaplain and exponent of 'free grace' or the doctrine—termed 'antinomianism' by its opponents—that the elect are set free from the moral law, insisted that 'a poor plain countryman, by the spirit which he hath received, is better able to judge of truth and error touching the things of God than the greatest philosopher, scholar or doctor in the world that is destitute of it'. Paraphrasing Acts 17: 6, Dell cited the example of the Apostles as his authority for the inversion of social, religious, and educational hierarchies: 'Poor illiterate men turned the world upside down'. The Fifth Monarchist Christopher Feake mocked those who refused to accept 'that a company of illiterate men and silly women should pretend to have any skill in dark prophecies, and to a foresight of future events, which the most learned Rabbis, and most knowing politicians have not presumed to hope for'. Isaac Pennington described the early Quakers as 'young country lads, of no deep understanding or ready expression, but very fit to be despised every where by the wisdom of man'.[2] Overton, Dell, Feake, and Pennington apparently agreed with Edwards on this issue at least: the radicals emerged from the ranks of the formally uneducated or illiterate laity and believed this very lack of education and book learning to testify to their spiritual authority.

Christopher Hill, the most influential scholar of radicalism in the English Revolution, also agrees with Edwards about the social and cultural origins of radical ideas. In *The World Turned Upside Down* (1972) and numerous other books and essays over the latter half of the twentieth century Hill argues that with the collapse of traditional structures of political and religious authority in the early 1640s a 'lower-class heretical culture burst into the open'. While the evidence before the 1640s is necessarily sketchy, this popular heretical culture probably had a 'continuous

---

[1] Thomas Edwards, *Gangraena; Or a Catalogue and Discovery of many of the Errours, Heresies, Blasphemies and pernicious Practices of the Sectaries of this time, vented and acted in England in the last four years*, 3 pts. (1646), i. sig. A5ᵛ, 130–1.

[2] Overton and Dell quoted in Christopher Hill, *The World Turned Upside Down: Radical Ideas during the English Revolution* (1972; repr. Harmondsworth, 1991), 38, 94, 100; Dell is also quoted in Barry Coward, *The Stuart Age: A History of England 1603–1714* (London, 1980), 208; Feake quoted in Keith Thomas, *Religion and the Decline of Magic: Popular Beliefs in Sixteenth and Seventeenth Century England*, (1971; repr. Harmondsworth, 1991), 178; Pennington quoted in N. H. Keeble, *The Literary Culture of Nonconformity in Later Seventeenth Century England* (Leicester, 1987), 163.

underground existence' stretching back at least to the Lollards of the later Middle Ages. In the absence of effective State censorship, 'unorthodox men and women of the lower classes' were free to print for the first time views that had previously circulated orally in the radical underground. Writings of the 1640s and 1650s by those who were categorized by their enemies as 'Levellers', 'Diggers', 'Seekers', 'Ranters', and 'Quakers' provide the outline of 'another revolution which never happened', 'the revolt within the Revolution' which 'might have established communal property, a far wider democracy in political and legal institutions, might have disestablished the state church and rejected the protestant ethic'.[3] Although this was a period of 'glorious flux and intellectual excitement', characterized by the 'overturning, questioning, revaluing of everything in England', the radical ideas surveyed by Hill were articulated by common people who had no experience of or contact with the intellectual culture of the educated elite: 'the eloquence, the power, of the simple artisans who took part in these disputes is staggering'. Nonetheless these unbookish lay people were inspired by a book. They drew their confidence from the Reformation principle that the biblical Word was accessible to all, and extended this principle to its logical anticlerical and democratic conclusions by 'asserting the possibility of any individual receiving the spirit, the inner experience which enabled him to understand God's Word as well as, better than, mere scholars who lacked this inner grace'. Emphasizing 'reliance on the holy spirit within one, on one's own experienced truth as against traditional truths handed down by others', the radicals violently rejected the notion that a university education and a facility in Latin, Greek, and Hebrew conferred superior spiritual knowledge upon a separate clerical caste.[4]

Hill repeats the claims of hostile contemporaries such as Thomas Edwards about the lowly intellectual background of the radicals, but from a positive and sympathetic Marxist perspective. Edwards uses the charge of ignorance to disqualify radical voices from being heard, whereas Hill celebrates the conditions in which ordinary people were free to engage openly in religious and political speculation. Like Edwards, however, Hill sees radical ideas and writings as an expression of a popular culture that evolved outside the institutional educational and cultural structures of

---

[3] Christopher Hill, *Milton and the English Revolution* (London, 1977), 69–71 (69, 71); Hill, *The World Turned Upside Down*, 13–15; see also 'From Lollards to Levellers' and 'God and the English Revolution', in *Collected Essays of Christopher Hill*, ii. *Religion and Politics in Seventeenth Century England* (Brighton, 1986; repr. 1988), 89–116, 321–42.

[4] Hill, *The World Turned Upside Down*, 14, 95, 362, 368; Hill, *The English Bible and the Seventeenth Century Revolution* (1993; repr. Harmondsworth, 1994), esp. 196–252.

early modern England. Popular culture in the early modern period has usually been regarded as the 'culture of the illiterate, a culture transmitted orally by customs and practice, not through the printed word'. The obvious problem in retrieving the beliefs and values of the illiterate is the necessary reliance of the historian on textual sources. Consequently it is difficult to 'discern the extent to which the historical record of this culture has been contaminated by elite commentators' and was in fact 'designed to persuade, shape, or even re-direct opinion'. Scholars have nonetheless sought to 'uncover the values of popular culture through the growing mass of "popular literature", notably ballads, chapbooks, and other ephemeral publications but also the radical and other writings of the minority of working people who recorded their views and experiences in print'.[5] Since *The World Turned Upside Down*, the great quantity of radical literature that survives amongst the 22,000 books and pamphlets collected by George Thomason between 1641 and 1660 has provided a focus for those seeking to write 'history from below'. This literature has been valued by both historians and literary critics for providing access to the culture of the common people that is not mediated through sources produced by the elite, the 'learned and educated few at the top of society'.[6]

Yet the status of radical texts as authentic artefacts of seventeenth-century popular culture becomes problematic when we check the biographical details of the writers quoted at the beginning of this chapter. Richard Overton matriculated as a sizar at Queens' College, Cambridge, in 1631 and acted in Latin plays at the university. William Dell graduated with an MA from Emmanuel College, Cambridge, in 1631 and may briefly have held a fellowship there before becoming an Independent minister; he was Master of Gonville and Caius College, Cambridge, from 1649 until the Restoration. Christopher Feake graduated with an MA from Emmanuel College in 1635 and owned a considerable amount of property in London. Isaac Pennington matriculated at Catherine Hall, Cambridge, in 1637 and was the son of a rich merchant who became Lord Mayor of London in the early 1640s.[7] As the following chapters demonstrate, many

---

[5] Tim Harris, 'Problematizing Popular Culture', in Harris (ed.), *Popular Culture in England, 1500–1850* (London, 1995), 1–27, (6, 8, 10); Jonathan Barry, 'Literacy and Literature in Popular Culture: Reading and Writing in Historical Perspective', in Harris (ed.), *Popular Culture in England, 1500–1850*, 69–94 (69).

[6] For examples of historical and literary claims that radical writing of the English revolution provides authentic access to popular belief see respectively Barry Reay, 'Laurence Clarkson: An Artisan and the English Revolution', in Christopher Hill, Barry Reay, and William Lamont (eds.), *The World of the Muggletonians* (London, 1983), ch. 6; James Holstun, 'Ranting at the New Historicism', *English Literary Renaissance*, 19 (1989), 189–225.

[7] See *BDBR* for biographical details.

of those who made important contributions to the extraordinary radical ferment of these years possessed a considerable degree of formal education. One of the central concerns of this book is to demonstrate the range of intellectual resources employed in some of the most powerful radical writing of the English revolution. Another is to account for the disjunction between this range and the images of the radicals as 'simple artisans' and 'illiterate Mechanick persons' projected by themselves, in contemporary polemical literature, and in twentieth-century scholarship. In the process some fundamental challenges will be made to deeply embedded preconceptions about the cultural identity of radical writers, the literary sophistication of their prose, and the social composition of their intended audience. By accepting at face value contemporary claims about the ignorance or simplicity of these writers, we run the risk of failing to appreciate both the complexity of their ideas and the artistry of their writing. My point is not simply that there was a far greater diversity of culture and education amongst radical groups than has previously been appreciated; more significant is the interpretative advantage to be gained from this insight for the textual analysis of radical belief. Nonetheless the series of close readings of radical writers in Chapters 3–5 questions the axiomatic identification of the 'radical' and the 'popular'—'popular' in the sense of being 'produced by the people', rather than commonly held—and has wider implications for our approach to the writing of cultural history.[8]

RADICALISM AND CULTURAL HISTORY

William Dell frequently appears in both *Gangraena* and *The World Turned Upside Down* as a representative of the sudden effusion of artisanal radicalism condemned by Thomas Edwards and admired by Christopher Hill. In sermons preached and published in the early 1650s Dell declared that 'the throne of the Beast in these Nations, are the Universities, as the fountaine of the ministry'. Attacking the application of 'fleshly wisdome, Rhetorical Eloquence, and Philosophical Learning' to spiritual matters, he maintained that 'all divinity is wrapped up in human learning to deter the common people from the study and enquiry after it, and to cause them still to expect all divinity from the clergy, who

---

[8] Barry Reay, 'Popular Religion', in Barry Reay (ed.), *Popular Culture in Seventeenth Century England* (London, 1985), 91–128 (91); preface to J. F. McGregor and Reay (eds.), *Radical Religion in the English Revolution* (Oxford, 1984), p. v. See also the definitions of 'popular' in Raymond Williams, *Keywords: A Vocabulary of Culture and Society* (London, 1976), 199.

by their education have attained to that human learning which the plain people are destitute of'.[9] By the 1630s the clerical profession in England was basically graduate.[10] Dell's anticlericalism is based on his substitution of inner spiritual experience for formal education as the prerequisite of religious knowledge, and the anti-intellectual rhetoric that he derives from this substitution is characteristic of radical attacks on the institutional structures of education, in particular the universities.[11] Yet Dell's rousing rejections of the relevance of formal education to spiritual knowledge rang out around the cloisters of St Mary's, the university church in Cambridge, and were delivered during his time as Master of Gonville and Caius College. In a brief discussion of Dell's virulent attacks on the principle of theological education Peter Burke has noted that 'it is ironic, to say the least, that [Dell] should have given learned references in a criticism of the function of learning in the study of divinity'. Burke is puzzled by the apparently anomalous presence of these references, mainly to patristic, medieval, and contemporary authorities: are they, he asks, important to Dell and his argument, or does he use them because he believes the reader thinks they are important?[12]

It is appropriate that Burke should point out the apparent contradiction between popular message and elite medium in Dell's argument in a contribution to a collection of essays in honour of Christopher Hill. Six years before Burke's _Popular Culture in Early Modern Europe_ (1978), a ground-breaking study of the developing antagonisms between the cultural worlds of the educated and the humbler ranks of society, Hill presented _The World Turned Upside Down_ as the story of how various groups amongst 'the lower fifty per cent of the population' sought 'to impose their own solutions to the problems of their time, in opposition to the wishes of their betters'. In recent years students of popular culture, including Burke himself, have become increasingly aware of the limitations of a bipolar model of cultural division and conflict, which tends to structure cultural history in terms of a series of preconceived binary divisions: 'elite and popular; patrician and plebeian; high and low; rulers and ruled; learned and unlearned; literate and illiterate; godly and

⁹ William Dell, _Several Sermons and Discourses_ (1709), 142, 144, 585. Dell's sermons in St Mary's, Cambridge, were published in _The Stumbling Stone_ (1653) and _The Trial of Spirits_ (1653).

¹⁰ Helen M. Jewell, _Education in Early Modern England_ (London, 1998), 62.

¹¹ L. F. Solt, 'Anti-intellectualism in the Puritan Revolution', _Church History_, 25 (1956), 306–16; Hill, _The World Turned Upside Down_, 300–5.

¹² Peter Burke, 'William Dell, the Universities, and the Radical Tradition', in Geoff Eley and William Hunt (eds.), _Reviving the English Revolution: Reflections and Elaborations on the Work of Christopher Hill_ (London, 1988), 181–9.

ungodly'. These dichotomies have been found to be insufficiently flexible to do justice to the complexities of early modern society: first, to instances of 'vertical' rather than 'horizontal' cultural division, exemplified in England by the evidence for Puritan varieties of faith amongst both the highest and lowest ranks of the population or by the promotion of traditional festive culture by the royalist nobility; secondly, to the role of the 'middling sort' of people, who accounted for at least thirty per cent of the population.[13] The middling sort were able to read, buy, and, increasingly, write books and pamphlets. While there has been much debate about levels of literacy in the early modern period and over the methods by which these levels can be ascertained, historians have become accustomed to thinking in terms of a 'literate world of yeoman, tradesmen and craftsmen' in seventeenth-century England.[14] Research into the social composition of separatist congregations and larger radical movements such as the Fifth Monarchists and the Quakers indicates that the rank and file membership did not come from the bottom 50 per cent of the population, who were 'the labourers, cottagers, paupers'. Rather they were 'independent craftsmen and small tradesmen . . . husbandmen and yeoman . . . the "middle" sort of people; the less illiterate sections of the population; those who would have been included in a Leveller franchise'. The links between the separatist and gathered Churches of London and the Leveller movement are unsurprising in that the Levellers not only pressed for religious toleration but spoke for this socio-economic constituency of small tradesmen and merchants. Only the small groups of labourers who followed Gerrard Winstanley's call to dig the common land in 1649–50 support the argument that organized radical religion flourished amongst the bottom half of the population.[15] In his prophetic and intensely millenarian writings of 1650 George Foster, about whom virtually nothing is known, recounts how God—'that Mighty Leveller'— spoke to him and interpreted his visions. One of Foster's visions is strikingly suggestive of the socio-economic base of radicalism in this period: he saw a man on a white horse 'cutting down all men and women

---

[13] Harris, 'Problematizing Popular Culture', 15–16, 19.

[14] Margaret Spufford, 'First Steps in Literacy: The Reading and Writing Experiences of the Humblest Seventeenth Century Autobiographers', *Social History*, 4 (1979), 407–35 (430); Keith Wrightson, *English Society, 1580–1680* (London, 1982), 183–98; Keith Thomas, 'The Meaning of Literacy in Early Modern England', in Gerd Baumann (ed.), *The Written Word: Literacy in Transition* (Oxford, 1986), 97–131.

[15] Barry Reay, 'Radicalism and Religion in the English Revolution', in McGregor and Reay (eds.), *Radicalism in the English Revolution*, 1–22 (18); F. D. Dow, *Radicalism in the English Revolution 1640–1660* (Oxford, 1985), 33; John Gurney, 'Gerrard Winstanley and the Digger Movement in Walton and Cobham', *Historical Journal*, 37 (1994), 775–802.

that he met with that were higher than the middle sort, and raised up those that were lower than the middle sort, and made them all equal'. In one of his first pamphlets the tailor and itinerant preacher Laurence Clarkson, who was associated with a variety of radical religious groups between 1645 and 1660 and was briefly imprisoned on the charge of being a 'Ranter', defined the 'oppressors' as the 'nobility and gentry' and the 'oppressed' as the 'yeoman, farmer, the tradesman and the like'.[16]

The boundaries defining popular culture in the early modern period have been extended in recent years. The predominately literate middling sort have been studied within the context of a culture of the non-elite that was marked at most levels (including, if to a much lesser extent, semi-literate sections of the poorer sort) by an increasing familiarity with the world of writing and print.[17] This incorporation of the literate middling sort into the category of the popular can be seen as an attempt to maintain the status of popular culture as a distinct area of study in the light of arguments that our necessary reliance on textual sources precludes any direct contact with the mentalities of the common people. According to these arguments, since our sources 'tell us about the interaction of elite and popular cultures', that interaction should become the focus of research. Scholars should thus be less concerned with 'the false problem' of establishing what is and what is not popular culture than with identifying how 'differing cultural configurations criss-cross and dovetail in practices, representations, or cultural products'.[18] William Dell's anticlerical and anti-intellectual sermons from the pulpit of St Mary's, Cambridge, exemplify this interaction of 'differing cultural configurations'. Dell, as a university graduate, minister, and academic, is unquestionably one of the 'learned and educated few at the top of society', yet he voices the arguments of popular lay radicalism by attacking the clergy and the universities as structures of power designed to keep the 'plain people' in ignorance and subjection. At the same time this populist rhetoric is structured by a series of learned textual references and allusions that are only comprehensible to an elite audience or readership. Dell's sermons resist categorization as either 'elite' or 'popular', even in terms of an expanded

[16] George Foster, *The Sounding of the Last Trumpet* (1650), 17–18; Laurence Clarkson, *A General Charge, or Impeachment of High-Treason, in the name of Justice, Equity, against the Communality of England* (1647), 10.

[17] Reay, 'Popular Culture in Early Modern England', in Reay (ed.), *Popular Culture in Seventeenth Century England*, 1–30 (1–2).

[18] Harris, 'Problematizing Popular Culture', 10; Roger Chartier, *Cultural History: Between Practices and Representations*, trans. Lydia C. Cochrane (Cambridge, 1988), 37–40 (38). Cf. Bob Scribner, 'Is a History of Popular Culture Possible?', *History of European Ideas*, 10 (1989), 175–91.

concept of popular culture that encompasses those 'middle sort of plain-hearted people', as one artisan radical put it, who were literate but yet 'destitute of school learning and human arts and sciences'.[19]

My contention in this book is that to understand the culture of radicalism in the English revolution we need to develop a greater understanding of how that culture was shaped not simply by conflict between the cultural worlds of the high and the low, of the learned and the unlearned, but by their interaction. I show how university-educated radicals draw on their knowledge of learned culture and their experience of institutional education to expose those systems and structures of knowledge as a means of preserving hierarchical and antichristian relations of power. Recent studies have argued that the history of orthodox ideologies and cultural practices in England needs to be understood in terms of a dynamic process of dialogue with heterodoxy.[20] Orthodoxy, after all, can only be defined in relation to what is deemed heterodox by those in positions of power and authority in a society. In my discussions of the Leveller Richard Overton (Ch. 3), the 'Ranter' Abiezer Coppe (Ch. 4), the Quaker Samuel Fisher (Ch. 5), and the Fifth Monarchist John Rogers (Epilogue) the articulation of radical belief is also revealed to be the product of dialogue between orthodoxy and heterodoxy. Heterodox ideas are expressed through satirical application of the cultural resources provided by an orthodox education, or through the heterodox interpretation of texts—whether Latin grammars, academic plays, or works of biblical philology—usually considered representative of orthodox values. The languages of the dominant culture are frequently scrambled and misapplied for the purposes of parody and subversion, but also to develop and articulate new and radical modes of thought.

This focus distinguishes *The English Radical Imagination* from previous literary-oriented work on radical literature of the English revolution, such as Nigel Smith's study of the influence of Continental spiritualist writing on radical religious belief and expression. Smith defines the context for his study as the 'gap between orthodox university education and the ways in which the unlearned came by what they knew . . . the extent to which extreme sectarian knowledge systems were produced by men who were unlearned if literate'.[21] In my discussion of the

---

[19] Clement Writer, *An Apologetical Declaration* (2nd edn., 1658), 78–9.

[20] Roger D. Lund, 'Introduction', and J. G. A. Pocock, 'Within the Margins: The Definitions of Heterodoxy', in Lund (ed.), *The Margins of Orthodoxy: Heterodox Writing and Cultural Response, 1660–1750* (Cambridge, 1995), 1–32, 33–53.

[21] Nigel Smith, *Perfection Proclaimed: Language and Literature in English Radical Religion, 1640–1660* (Oxford, 1989), 267.

intellectual origins of Leveller ideas in Chapter 3, however, I examine how William Walwyn, who came from a comparatively prosperous background but did not go to university, used translations of classical and humanist texts that he bought in London in the 1630s to develop theories about the uncertainty of knowledge and the consequent necessity of religious toleration. This is a different instance of how heterodox ideas were formed from an interaction between elite and popular cultures. Yet, as with my case studies of university-educated writers, the example of Walwyn questions the theory that these heterodox ideas had previously circulated orally for generations in a lower-class radical underground, bursting into public view in the 1640s with the greater publishing freedoms brought about by the breakdown of centralized authority during the civil wars. The role of Walwyn's reading during the 1630s in shaping the religious and political views that he expressed in print during the 1640s illustrates how literacy begot heresy rather than vice versa.

This point is related to my decision to choose 1630–60 as the period covered by this study rather than to begin in 1640. Other than Walwyn, the radical writers who are discussed in detail in the following chapters were at university in the 1630s. In demonstrating how these writers use their access to elite discourses of cultural authority to shape the development and expression of their heterodox ideas, I am suggesting a continuity between their cultural experiences during the 1630s and their radical visions of the 1640s and 1650s. It is significant in the context of this study that the 1630s was the peak period for university entry in early modern England after the highpoint of the 1580s; indeed in terms of proportion of the male year-group university entry in the 1630s was higher than at any time until the twentieth century.[22] The sudden surge of admissions in the late sixteenth century led to some concern about the potentially subversive activities of unemployed and discontented graduates, who have been described as the 'alienated intellectuals' of early Stuart England. In *The Anatomy of Absurdity* (1589), Thomas Nashe warned of the dangers to the stability of Church and State posed by disaffected scholars: 'This green fruit, being gathered before it be ripe, is rotten before it be mellow, and infected with schisms before they have learnt to bridle their affections, affecting innovations as newfangled, and enterprising alterations whereby the Church is mangled'. The increase in admissions in the 1630s seems to have led in the 1640s to something like the situation envisaged by Nashe. Amidst the unprecedented turbulence of the civil wars there were more new graduates than for several generations; these

---

[22] Jewell, *Education in Early Modern England*, 112.

men had gone to university in preparation for a clerical career but found the established Church system and their own career structures in disarray. Some of these alienated intellectuals—the sons of merchants and yeoman 'who had become learned in vain and could only blame society for their personal disappointment'—were doubtless attracted to the 'innovations' and 'alterations' of radical ideas, as well as to the financial support offered by itinerant preaching or the role of pastor to sectarian congregations.[23]

The radicals discussed in Chapters 3–5 also emerged in the 1640s from mostly orthodox religious contexts. It is now widely accepted that until the rise of Laudianism in the 1630s Calvinism was the doctrinal orthodoxy of the Church of England. 'Puritan' in the Elizabethan and Jacobean periods was used as a term of abuse for those few who pressed for a transformation from an episcopalian to a Presbyterian form of Church government, or, more ambiguously, to denote the most zealous Calvinists, who were distinguished by their zeal rather than their Calvinism. These 'hotter type of Protestants' sought reform from within the established Church.[24] There does seem to be some consistency in what has been called the 'lay religious impulse' in early modern Europe, centred around the rejection of mediating forms—ceremonial, clerical, educational—between the individual and the divine.[25] However, the Puritan backgrounds of the writers who provide the focus for this study indicate that their radical beliefs are better explained as a reaction to or a development of the ambiguities and contradictions of Calvinist theology than as an expression of heretical ideas which circulated in a timeless 'radical underground'. They are the product of a specific cultural and historical context rather than the efflorescence of an autochthonous folk irreligion, welling up from the depths of popular culture.

[23] Mark H. Curtis, 'The Alienated Intellectuals of Early Stuart England', *Past and Present*, 23 (1962), 25–43; Thomas Nashe, *The Unfortunate Traveller and Other Works*, ed. J. B. Steane (Harmondsworth, 1985), 472; Roger Chartier, *Cultural History: Between Practices and Representations*, 139.

[24] Influential essays on this topic are Nicholas Tyacke, 'Puritanism, Arminianism and Counter Revolution', in Conrad Russell (ed.), *The Origins of the English Civil War* (London, 1973), 119–43; Peter Lake, 'Calvinism and the English Church', *Past and Present*, 114 (1987), 32–76. Both are reprinted in Margo Todd (ed.), *Reformation to Revolution: Politics and Religion in Early Modern England* (London, 1995), 53–70, 179–207.

[25] For an attempt to summarize the 'lay religious impulse' see Michael Mullett, *Radical Religious Movements in Early Modern Europe* (London, 1980), 65. The most comprehensive discussion of 'radical spiritualism' in sixteenth-century Europe remains G. H. Williams, *The Radical Reformation* (Phila., 1962). In *England's Troubles: Seventeenth Century Political Instability in a European Context* (Cambridge, 2000), 247–68, Jonathan Scott seeks to place English radical religious belief in the intellectual contexts of the European radical Reformation.

THE RHETORIC OF ENTHUSIASM

In combining biographical detail and literary analysis to relate the radical beliefs expressed by writers in the 1640s and 1650s to their cultural experiences in the 1630s my approach bears some comparison with that adopted by David Norbrook in his important recent study of the republican imagination as an evolving element within the dominant culture rather than a sudden response to regicide or a counter-cultural phenomenon. Norbrook 'concentrates on writers from the elite' in order to 'trace republican elements not just on the extreme margins of pre-1649 literary culture but close to its centre'. He argues that these ' "middle of the road" republicans may not have caught the modern imagination as much as the Levellers, Diggers and radical prophets, but they deserve attention'.[26] The distinction here rests on the assumption that these more extreme radicals were unfamiliar with the intellectual and literary culture of their day. I seek to dispel this assumption and in so doing revise the critical commonplace that claims to prophetic inspiration—pejoratively termed 'enthusiasm' in the seventeenth century—were a means of escape from social, educational, and cultural disenfranchisement. According to Keith Thomas, the point about religious prophecy and inspiration is that they were 'potentially open to everyone'. For 'artisans and petty tradesmen' who lacked the education to engage in biblical exegesis or political philosophy 'prophecy was an easy way of gaining attention'. In *The Puritan Experience* (1972) Owen Watkins refers to figures such as Abiezer Coppe as 'vulgar prophets', who claimed divine inspiration because 'lacking both educational background and identification with an established denomination, they could invoke only the authority of personal experience'. Barry Reay describes the Quaker elevation of the spiritual authority of the 'inner light' above that of the Scriptures as 'the uneducated man's and woman's way of rejecting the hegemony of a learned elite'. A literary critic has recently argued that radical writers in this period adopted the 'manic' persona of the prophet in their writings because there was 'no other available language of self-authorization' for 'uneducated lay people'. In this reading the rhetoric of enthusiasm 'is a particular strategy for speaking and writing with an authority otherwise unavailable to those assigned a lowly social identity'.[27]

[26] David Norbrook, *Writing the English Republic: Poetry, Rhetoric, and Politics, 1627–1660* (Cambridge, 1999), 14–15.

[27] Thomas, *Religion and the Decline of Magic*, 177; Owen C. Watkins, *The Puritan Experience* (London, 1972), 61; Barry Reay, 'Quakerism and Society', in McGregor and Reay

The language of these critical representations echoes that of hostile contemporary commentators such as Thomas Edwards who were 'convinced that the subversive attitudes of the unlettered and ungodly multitude could find expression in the doctrines of enthusiasm'.[28] Edwards's warnings about 'swarms' of 'all sorts of illiterate Mechanick preachers, yea of Women and Boy preachers' invading the towns of England in the continued absence of a Presbyterian Church government are evidently designed to play upon elite anxieties about the collapse of social hierarchy. 'Mechanick' and 'mechanical' were familiar terms of class distinction in early modern culture. They explicitly designated an artisan, a person who engaged in manual labour, but were pejorative in their association with the 'mean', the 'vulgar', and the uneducated. References to 'mechanicals' in Shakespeare are 'most often the embodiment of a distinct class voice, tied to the attempt to . . . distinguish high from low'— as in York's 'base dunghill villain and mechanical' in 2 *Henry VI* (I. i. 193) or Cleopatra's 'Mechanic slaves | With greasy aprons, rules and hammers' (V. ii. 209–10).[29] However, the claim in *Gangraena* that radical movements were composed of 'all sorts of Mechanicks' has been substantiated, as we have seen, by research into the social composition of the Baptists, the Levellers, the Fifth Monarchists, and the Quakers, which has found the rank and file to have come from the lower-middling sort in both urban and rural areas. There are also numerous examples of radical writing which appear to confirm the claim that enthusiasm was a means for those previously cast in the role of cultural dependants to assert their authority and autonomy. An instance of the 'Mechanick Enthusiast' frequently cited by contemporaries and critics is the cobbler Samuel How, pastor of a separatist church in pre-war London. In the posthumously published *Sufficiencie of the Spirits Teaching without Humane Learning* (1640) How condemned the notion that 'knowledge of arts and sciences, diverse tongues, much reading' in any way increased a person's ability 'to understand the mind of God in his word'. The humanist curriculum had rather imported heathen corruptions into the primitive Christian faith. Study of classical languages and literature was 'the means

(eds.), *Radical Religion in the English Revolution*, 141–64 (146); Clement Hawes, *Mania and Literary Style: The Rhetoric of Enthusiasm from the Ranters to Christopher Smart* (Cambridge, 1996), 28, 37, 41.

28 J. F. McGregor, 'Seekers and Ranters', in McGregor and Reay (eds.), *Radical Religion in the English Revolution*, 137.

29 Patricia Parker, ' "Rude Mechanicals" ', in Margreta De Grazia, Maureen Quilligan, and Peter Stallybrass (eds.), *Subject and Object in Renaissance Culture* (Cambridge, 1996), 43–82 (45–7). The text used for quotations from Shakespeare is *The Riverside Shakespeare*, ed. G. Blakemore Evans (Boston, Mass., 1974).

of bringing in all those abominable errors that the earth hath drunk in, both in doctrine and practice'. Indeed he declared that 'such as are taught by the Spirit, destitute of human learning, are the learned ones who truly understand the Scriptures' for 'the wisdom of the world is foolishness with God (1 Cor. 3: 19)'.[30] A more flamboyant example is the London goldsmith Thomas Tany, who issued a 'Disputative challenge to the Universities of *Oxford* and *Cambridge*, and the whole Hierarch of *Roms* Clargical Priests', in which he declared: 'know I was and am the Gold-Smith, and God hath made me the refiner's fire, to refine the Gold from the dross, which is, but thus much to separate ye Priests from your trade of lies'. Tany's profession becomes symbolic of his prophetic status, so raising the divine authority of the 'mechanic' above that of the university-trained cleric. He repeatedly emphasizes that 'I am not learned in what I declare'. This lack of learning and his persecution by the authorities testify to his divinely sanctioned role as prophet and martyr: 'I am in Prison at the writing hereof, and the Prisons were always the Prophets schooles, we read true lectures in the empty walls, in our restraint, without *Baals* Books, in which ye learned Priests so much glory'. Tany has taken his 'Degrees' in spiritual learning not at Oxford and Cambridge but in 'them two Land-Colledges', Newgate and the King's Bench. Having undergone an alchemical process of spiritual transmutation which has burnt away his carnal knowledge—'the power of my God did overpower my understanding, and manhood and wisdom; which is indeed the very Devil in man'—his language ironically confounds the interpretation of the learned, providing a divine rationale for the solipsism of his prose: 'I know what I write, though it be dark unto you'.[31]

More celebrated examples of the 'Mechanick Enthusiast' are Gerrard Winstanley and George Fox. A good deal is now known about Winstanley's failed career as a cloth merchant in London in the early 1640s and his subsequent life as a corn chandler in Surrey, before prophetic visions later in the decade inspired him to identify the Fall with economic, political, legal, and educational monopolies and to establish agricultural communes which would restore men to their Edenic state of perfection.[32] For Winstanley, the 'preaching clergy, or universative

[30] The phrase 'Mechanick Enthusiast' is from Daniel Featley, *The Dippers Dipt* (1645; 5th edn. 1647), sig. B3ʳ; Samuel How, *The Sufficiencie of the Spirits Teaching without Humane Learning* (1640), 12–13, 24–6.

[31] Thomas Tany, *Theauraujohn High Priest To the Jewes* (1652), in *The Writings of Thomas Tany*, ed. Andrew Hopton (London, 1988), 26–30.

[32] J. D. Alsop, 'Gerrard Winstanley: Religion and Respectability', *Historical Journal*, 28 (1985), 705–9.

power' sought to monopolize scriptural interpretation and religious knowledge for their own financial gain. The minister claims superior spiritual authority by dint of his education but only to 'force people to maintain him from the earth by their labours for his sayings, by the laws of the kingly power. He says some are elected to salvation and others are reprobated; he puts some into heaven, thrusts others into hell never to come out, and so he is not a universal saviour'. The clergy strive to distinguish themselves from the common people on the grounds of their formal education because 'the light of truth that springs up out of the earth, which the scholars tread under feet, will shine so clear, as it will put out the candle of those wicked deceivers'. In line with his belief in the potential for universal salvation, Winstanley outlined a scheme for universal education in *The Law of Freedom* (1652) which has been described as exhibiting 'a kind of intuitive Baconianism'. Arguing that 'the secrets of the creation have been locked up under the traditional, parrot-like speaking from the universities and colleges for scholars', he advocated vocational training in the various manual trades and liberal education by means of discussion groups in each 'digging' commune. These forms of education were, however, merely a supplement to the spiritually pedagogic act of cultivating the land, through which all men 'may learn the inward knowledge of things which are, and find out the secrets of Nature'.[33]

Winstanley may have ended his life as a Quaker. The Quaker doctrine of the inner light or 'internalized apocalypse' developed the enthusiastic conviction that the Spirit speaks to man apart from the Word in Scripture into an enduring sectarian ideology. One of the best-known statements of the sufficiency of the Spirit's teaching comes from Fox, foremost of the early Quakers and one-time apprentice to a shoemaker and sheep grazier, in his journal entry for 1646:

At another time, as I was walking in a field on a First-day morning, the Lord opened unto me, 'that being bred at Oxford and Cambridge was not enough to fit and qualify men to be ministers of Christ': and I stranged at it, because it was the common belief of people. But I saw clearly, as the Lord opened it to me, and I was satisfied . . . But my relations were much troubled at me, that I would not go with them to hear the priest: for I would get into the orchard, or the fields, with my Bible, by myself . . . And I saw that being bred at Oxford or Cambridge, did not

---

[33] Gerrard Winstanley, *A New-Yeeres Gift for the Parliament and Armie* (1650), in *Divine Right and Democracy: An Anthology of Political Writings in Stuart England*, ed. David Wootton (Harmondsworth, 1986), 234; Winstanley, *The Law of Freedom and Other Writings*, ed. Christopher Hill (Cambridge, 1983), 102, 351–4, 361–5; Charles Webster, *The Great Instauration: Science, Medicine, and Reform, 1626–1660* (London, 1975), 367–9.

qualify or fit a man to be a minister of Christ; and what then should I follow such
for? So neither them, nor any of the Dissenting people, could I join with: but was
as a stranger to all, relying wholly upon the Lord Jesus Christ.

For Fox, divine revelation, or 'opening', did not end with the Apostles but
was an ongoing possibility, potentially available to anyone. In 1658 he had
a meeting with a representative of the Protectorate despatched to
Durham to investigate the possibility of establishing 'a college there to
make ministers of Christ'. Fox 'went to the man and reasoned with him
and let him see that this was not the way to make them Christ's ministers
by Hebrew, Greek and Latin and the seven arts which was all but the
teachings of the natural man'. Fox cited the examples of Peter and John,
who 'could not read letters' but 'preached the word Christ Jesus, which
was in the beginning before Babel was'. He maintained that the Holy
Spirit was 'the saints' teacher in the Apostles' days and so it was now'; only
those who have 'the same pouring out of the Holy Ghost as the Apostles
had' are possessed of religious truth, regardless of their degree of formal
education.[34]

Enthusiasm evidently licenses a disruption of the ordering social
principle of decorum, according to which discussion of religious matters
is a function of education, ordination, and office. The claim to prophecy
can be used to invert the relationship between sign and signified, between
exterior power and interior glory, between formal 'human' learning and
personal spiritual knowledge. For Thomas Edwards, as we have seen, the
dangers of popular sectarianism and heresy were constituted in terms of
gender as well as class; the collapse of both public and domestic order was
exemplified by the appearance of women preachers who had rejected
their subordinate place within society and the family. The opportunity
for public expression granted to women by the conviction that the simple
and the weak were more likely to be subject to prophetic visions has been
illuminated by a considerable amount of scholarship in recent years.[35]

[34] The term 'internalized apocalypse' is taken from M. H. Abrams, 'Apocalypse: Themes
and Variations', in C. A. Patrides and Joseph Wittreich (eds.), *The Apocalypse in English
Renaissance Thought and Literature* (Ithaca, NY, 1984), 353–6 (see also G. F. Nuttall, *The Holy
Spirit in Puritan Faith and Experience* (Oxford, 1946), 26); George Fox, *The Journal* (1694),
ed. Nigel Smith (Harmondsworth, 1998), 10, 255–9.

[35] Some of the most notable studies are Keith Thomas, 'Women and the Civil War Sects',
Past and Present, 13 (1958), 42–62; Elaine Hobby, *Virtue of Necessity: English Women's
Writing 1649–88* (London, 1988), 25–53; Smith, *Perfection Proclaimed*, 45–53; Rachael
Trubowitz, 'Female Preachers and Male Wives: Gender and Authority in Civil War
England', in James Holstun (ed.), *Pamphlet Wars: Rhetoric in the English Revolution*
(London, 1992), 112–33; Phyllis Mack, *Visionary Women: Ecstatic Prophecy in Seventeenth
Century England* (Berkeley, Calif., 1992); Hilary Hinds, *God's Englishwomen: Seventeenth
Century Radical Sectarian Writing and Feminist Criticism* (Manchester, 1996).

The Fifth Monarchist prophet Anna Trapnell is one of the most striking examples of those women who justified their authority to speak publicly on religious and political matters by opposing revelatory experience to the academic qualifications denied to women in the period:

the creature can never learn the lesson of humiliation and self-denial, till it hath been in the School of free grace, that is, the free School where the best learning is to be had, the poor and fatherless here finds mercy . . . oh what a manner of love is this! that makes no difference between fools and learned ones, preferring ideots before the wisdom of the world, making the ignorant and erring Spirit to have the greatest understanding?

The language in which Trapnell celebrates her assurance of salvation suggests that the doctrine of 'free grace', or 'antinomianism', was felt by its adherents to provide a release not only from the guilt of sin and the bondage of religious formalism but from the Puritan tendency to regard ignorance as a sign of damnation.[36] While prominent heresiographers such as Edwards represented antinomianism as a belief in universal salvation and thus as a subversion of the Calvinist doctrine of election, free grace more usually involved an extension of Calvinist theology to its logical conclusions by denying the relevance of moral and religious law to the always-already-saved elect. Despite this retention of the Calvinist division of elect and reprobate, 'free grace had democratic implications'; for if works are irrelevant to salvation and some have been predestined to be saved whether they are sinners in this life or not, then anyone, no matter their status in society or their level of education, could be one of God's saints.[37] Both enthusiasm and antinomianism were thus potential constituents of a revolutionary ideology in that they offered immense spiritual power to those who felt themselves to be in a powerless social position. Just as free grace is fundamentally Pauline in its opposition of the dead, fleshly letter of the Mosaic law to the redeemed life of the Spirit in Christ (see e.g. Romans 7: 5–6), so an authorizing biblical text for both 'Mechanick' preachers such as Samuel How and female prophets such as Trapnell was 1 Cor. 1: 27: 'God hath chosen the weak things of the world to confound the things that are mighty'. The Pauline language of inversion and paradox provided radicals of the English revolution

[36] Anna Trapnell, *A Legacy for Saints* (1654), 15–16; John Stachniewski, *The Persecutory Imagination: English Puritanism and the Literature of Religious Despair* (Oxford, 1991), 143–5, 153, 250–1.

[37] David Wootton, 'Leveller Democracy and the Puritan Revolution', in J. H. Burns (ed.), with the assistance of Mark Goldie, *The Cambridge History of Political Thought 1450–1700* (Cambridge, 1991; paperback edn. 1996), 412–42 (441); A. D. Nuttall, *The Alternative Trinity: Gnostic Heresy in Marlowe, Milton, and Blake* (Oxford, 1998), 201–6.

with divine sanction for the reversal of seventeenth-century hierarchies of social status, education, and gender that had been regarded as God-given.

Richard Coppin, an itinerant Berkshire lay preacher, also looked to Galatians 1: 12 to justify his public intervention in religion and politics: 'For I neither received it of men, neither was I taught it by men, but by the revelation of Jesus Christ'. Coppin declared that his commission to preach came from the divine presence within, not from 'Oxford and Cambridge, or the schools of Anti-Christ, by the laying on of hands of the Bishops or presbytery'. The main theme of Coppin's *Divine Teachings* (1649) is that all learning in 'so far as it is human' is false: as 'the life of a Saint is even the life of God himself' it 'cannot be said to . . . learn of, or be taught, anything but what is itself'. The elect 'Saint', in other words, is made absolutely self-sufficient by inner revelation. The 'Ranter' Abiezer Coppe, the most notorious radical prophet of the 1640s, supplied a preface to *Divine Teachings* in which he introduces this concept of the pedagogic sufficiency of the indwelling spirit. Coppe emphasizes his lowly social and educational identity but only to magnify his prophetic identity as the mouthpiece of God: 'To the (nominal) Author is given the tongue of the learned, though he knoweth not letters'.[38] These examples again seem to confirm the ascription in *Gangraena* to unlearned (though evidently literate) 'Mechanick persons' of the heretical belief that 'there is a perfect way in this life, not by Word, Sacraments, Prayer, and other Ordinances, but by the experience of the Spirit in a mans self' (i: 24). Yet while Coppin appears to have had little experience of institutional education Coppe was a star pupil at Warwick School in the early 1630s and went on to Merton and All Souls Colleges in Oxford. At one point in Coppe's first publication under his name alone, *Some Sweet Sips, of Some Spiritual Wine* (1649), he addresses at some length his former 'Cronies', the 'Scholars of Oxford' (*CRW*, 51). So Coppe had in fact attended one of Coppin's 'Schools of Anti-Christ'. As I show in Chapter 4, Coppe's knowledge of institutional education is central to the elaborate rhetorical strategies of his prose. Despite the explicit rejection of any authority but the indwelling Spirit in both *Divine Teachings* and *Some Sweet Sips, of Some Spiritual Wine*, and the similarities between their anti-intellectual, anti-formalist language and argument, Coppe structures his polemic around a sophisticated parody of his experience of being taught Latin

[38] Richard Coppin, *Truths Testimony and a Testimony of Truths Appearing* (1655), 16; Coppin, *Divine Teachings* (1649; 2nd edn. 1653), 16, 19, 22–3; Abiezer Coppe, 'An Additional and Preambular Hint' to Coppin, *Divine Teachings*, in *CRW*, 74.

grammar which provides a stark contrast to the plain, scriptural style of the formally uneducated Coppin.

The rhetoric of enthusiasm as manifest in the prophetic texts discussed in this book emerges less as a discursive escape from educational and cultural disempowerment than a complex, allusive, and exuberant satirical mode which has affinities with the ludic 'folly' tradition of Erasmian humanism. The 'popular' language of prophetic inspiration is fused with the 'elite' language of humanist play. More confusingly, the claim of ignorance is combined with the display of learning. As I explain in Chapter 2, this apparently contradictory construction of discursive identity may be explained by locating radical strategies of self-representation in relation to long-established cultural stereotypes of the heretic that were circulating in print in the 1640s. The radical fusion of popular and elite languages that I identify in these writings may be contrary to expectation but it bears comparison with the notion of 'bricolage' that has been used to illuminate the nature of radical belief and expression in England in the aftermath of the French revolution. In his study of William Blake and the culture of radicalism in the 1790s Jon Mee shows how Blake, in common with other 'radical bricoleurs' of his time, combines 'elements from across discourse boundaries such that the antecedent discourses are fundamentally altered in the process'. While these seemingly disparate rhetorical resources 'might seem to the modern reader to be mutually exclusive', they are fused to effect the 'disruption and transformation of hegemonic discourses'. This breaking down of cultural authority facilitates the creation of 'new languages of liberation'.[39] The subversive rhetorical strategies identified by Mee are also evident in the radical writing of the English revolution—even if liberation for the religious radicals of this earlier period is mostly defined in terms of greater obedience to the will of God.[40] Yet where Mee finds bricolage to be typical in the 1790s of 'artisan radicals' and those 'barred from orthodox channels of knowledge and its transmission', in the 1640s and 1650s it seems to be more characteristic of those who had previously passed through those orthodox channels. Effective parody depends, after all, on familiarity with the forms of language and behaviour which are the object of ridicule or subversion.

The interaction of popular and elite in the radical culture of the English

[39] Jon Mee, *Dangerous Enthusiasm: William Blake and the Culture of Radicalism in the 1790s* (Oxford, 1992), 8–10.

[40] A point strongly made in J. C. Davis, 'Religion and the Struggle for Freedom in the English Revolution', *Historical Journal*, 35 (1992), 501–30.

revolution was evidently not a purely textual phenomenon. As I discuss in more detail in Chapter 4, Abiezer Coppe's preface to Richard Coppin's *Divine Teachings* indicates that individuals from different cultural backgrounds moved in the same social milieu, held similar opinions, and must therefore have influenced the development of each others' religious and political beliefs. While this study is primarily concerned with the textual expression of radical belief, its findings suggest that more historical work needs to be done on how radicalism flourished in the social interface between the learned and the merely literate. Chapter 5, for instance, concentrates on the rejection of the Bible as a rule of faith by Samuel Fisher, one of the few early Quakers with a university education. Yet the intellectual basis on which Fisher sets Quaker belief will be shown to illuminate the nature of that belief as it was expressed by 'mechanick' Quakers who also ventured into print. Nigel Smith has previously shown how translations of mystical, occult, and Neoplatonic texts circulated in unlearned lay culture in the mid-seventeenth century. The translators of these texts were necessarily educated men: John Everard, who had a doctorate in divinity from Clare College, Cambridge, explicitly sought to disseminate spiritualist ideas and beliefs associated with the radical Reformation amongst '*Tinkers, Cobblers, Weavers, Poor sleight Fellows*'.[41] Everard, who died in 1641, caused problems for the Caroline authorities because heresies espoused by 'a scholar of [his] undeniable achievement could not be dismissed so easily' as those spread by 'ill-bred laymen'.[42] The example of the Elizabethan separatist Churches provides a model of how religious dissent had previously developed in early modern England in a situation where university graduates interacted with the middling sort. The rank and file separatists were merchants, craftsmen, and artisans. The separatist leadership was 'provided very largely by the University of Cambridge'. From the pen of men such as Robert Browne and Henry Barrow came attacks on the forms of grammar, rhetoric, and logic in which they themselves had been trained.[43]

The culture of radicalism in the English revolution encompassed the perspectives not only of artisans such as Richard Coppin, Gerrard Winstanley, and George Fox, but of university men such as John Biddle,

---

[41] Smith, *Perfection Proclaimed*, chs. 3–5; John Everard, *The Gospel-Treasury Opened*, 2 pts. (1657), i: 86.

[42] T. Wilson Hayes, 'John Everard and the Familist Tradition', in Margaret Jacob and James Jacob (eds.), *The Origins of Anglo-American Radicalism* (London, 1984), 60–9 (66).

[43] Michael R. Watts, *The Dissenters: From the Reformation to the French Revolution* (Oxford, 1978), 72–4 (72); Robert Browne, *A Treatise upon the 23. of Matthewe* (Middelburg, 1582), 182–9.

the antitrinitarian often cited to illustrate the limits of Cromwellian toleration. Biddle had briefly been a fellow at Magdalen Hall, Oxford, after taking his MA at the College in 1641; in 1634 he had published verse translations of Virgil's *Eclogues* and Juvenal's *Satires*. Biddle put his skill in Latin to heterodox use after the regicide. He was behind the 1652 translation from the Latin of the antitrinitarian *Racovian Catechism*—the translation seems to have been licensed by Milton and was then suppressed by Parliament—and worked on the proofs of a new edition of the Septuagint Bible while in prison awaiting sentence for refusing to recant his views.[44] The diversity of educational and cultural background amongst the radicals of the English revolution substantiates Roger Chartier's rejection of the assumption that 'it is possible to establish exclusive relationships between specific cultural forms and particular social groups'. This assumption, Chartier believes, leads scholars to work deductively rather than inductively; to mould the evidence to fit certain predefined notions of cultural division.[45] One charge that might be made against my method in this book is that I myself in acting as heresiographer valorize those with education and culture and exclude the many unlettered men and women amongst the clamour of radical voices during the 1640s and 1650s. My point though is not to conclude that the 'Ranter' Laurence Clarkson is a less interesting writer than the 'Ranter' Abiezer Coppe because Coppe went to Oxford and his writings satirize humanist pedagogy while Clarkson was a tailor whose early pamphlets display a shaky literacy. My point is that to treat Coppe as if he were Clarkson is to do a disservice to them both and to impede our appreciation of the diversity and complexity of the English radical imagination.

[44] On Biddle's authorship of the translation see H. J. McLachlan, *Socinianism in Seventeenth Century England* (Oxford, 1951), 193; on the issues surrounding its licensing, possibly by Milton, see Stephen B. Dobranski, 'Licensing Milton's Heresy', in Dobranski and John P. Rumrich (eds.), *Milton and Heresy* (Cambridge, 1998), 139–58.

[45] Roger Chartier, *The Cultural Uses of Print in Early Modern France*, trans. Lydia C. Cochrane (Princeton, NJ, 1987), 3; see also Chartier, *Cultural History*, 30.

2

'Named and Printed Heretics': Literacy, Heterodoxy, and the Cultural Construction of Identity

POLEMIC AND REALITY

If we are 'to understand both the [English] revolution and its power', according to a recent historical study, we need to recover the 'intellectual and practical contexts' of radical belief. Insisting that the revolution should be approached as 'not a constitutional phenomenon, but a process of belief', Jonathan Scott provocatively states that 'English radicalism . . . *was* the English revolution'.[1] Such claims for the centrality of radicalism indicate a reversal in its historiographical fortunes. During the 1980s 'revisionist' historians reacted to what they regarded as the exaggerated claims of earlier scholars, in particular Christopher Hill, by seeking to demonstrate the marginality of radical belief or even to deny its existence outside contemporary polemical literature. Their central objection to previous representations of popular radicalism was the 'reliance, indeed the total reliance, on printed sources'.[2] They argued that the naive use of polemical and heresiographical texts—such as Thomas Edwards's *Gangraena*, which was designed to scare the men of property away from the Independents, generally more tolerant of sectarianism, and into the arms of the 'godly orthodox Presbyterians'—led Hill and others to repeat contemporary exaggerations of the scale of popular revolt and heterodox belief.[3] While the destruction of 'most of the landmarks of

---

[1] Scott, *England's Troubles*, 33, 35.

[2] John Morrill, 'Christopher Hill's Revolution', in *The Nature of the English Revolution: Essays by John Morrill* (Oxford, 1993), 273–84 (279). For a brief and cogent overview of revisionist objections to earlier histories of radicalism see Dow, *Radicalism in the English Revolution 1640–1660*, 1–9. See also Richard Cust and Ann Hughes, 'After Revisionism', in Cust and Hughes (eds.), *Conflict in Early Stuart England: Studies in Religion and Politics 1603–42* (Harlow, 1989), 1–46.

[3] *Gangraena*, i. 56; the best discussion of the polemical contexts of *Gangraena* is Tolmie, *The Triumph of the Saints: The Separate Churches of England, 1616–49* (Cambridge, 1977),

an ordered society', in particular the established Church, created a sense of acute anxiety, uncertainty, and 'moral panic' amongst elite groups, the 'actual disorder and the perceived imminence of the total collapse of order are quite different' in the period between 1640 and 1660. The failure to take account of the transmission of polemical myths and distortions in printed sources, combined with a neglect of popular royalism, neutralism, and Anglican 'survivalism', led historians to produce consummate studies of the rhetoric of disorder rather than its actual history.[4]

The most controversial application of revisionist arguments was the attempt by J. C. Davis to abolish the 'Ranters', considered by contemporaries to be the most extreme of the radical groups which emerged in the 1640s. The behaviour alleged of the Ranters in a flurry of sensational pamphlets in 1649–50 is exemplified by this extract from *The Ranters Religion* (1650):

these Monsters come short of the very Heathen, while they make the Almighty not only the Countenancer, which but to imagine is damnable blasphemy, but the efficient cause of sin, and dare impiously to affirm, that that man who tipples deepest, swears the frequentest, commits Adultery, Incest, or Buggary, the oftenest, Blasphemes the Impudentest, and perpetrates the most notorious crimes with the highest hand, and rigidest resolution, is the dearest Darling to Heaven.

The Ranters' outrageous subversion of the divine economy of sin, heaven, and hell through 'practical antinomianism'—the committing of acts commonly thought to be sinful to demonstrate the transcendence of moral and religious law—was depicted by Hill as the most vigorous instance of plebeian opposition to the Puritan ethic.[5] For Davis, however, there was no such thing as a Ranter sect or Ranter theology. The Ranters were a media fiction, a 'projection of the fears and anxieties of a broader society'. Constructed from mythic stereotypes of deviance such as the atheist, the witch, and the plotting papist, the Ranters represented an inverted religion and morality, an inversion required by English society to define orthodox values through their most extreme contraries in a

130–8. The Independents conceived of the true Church of 'visible saints' as composed of autonomous 'gathered Churches' but maintained the need for a national ecclesiastical structure for the unregenerate (ibid. 93–4).

[4] John Morrill and John Walters, 'Order and Disorder in the English Revolution', in A. Fletcher and J. Stevenson (eds.), *Order and Disorder in Early Modern Britain* (London, 1985), repr. in Morrill, *The Nature of the English Revolution*, 359–91. See also John Walter, 'The Impact on Society: The World Turned Upside Down?', in John Morrill (ed.), *The Impact of the English Civil War* (London, 1991), 104–22.

[5] Anon., *The Ranters Religion* (1650), repr. in app. to J. C. Davis, *Fear, Myth and History: the Ranters and the Historians* (Cambridge, 1986), 158; Hill, *The World Turned Upside Down*, esp. 151–230.

period of profound uncertainty. Davis's arguments provoked much discussion and not a little acrimony, fuelled by his contention that Marxist
historians had transformed a polemical fiction into historical reality in
their eagerness to 'create the history of a popular democratic tradition in
English history and culture'.[6]

The concern of revisionism with the exaggeration, distortion, or invention of popular radicalism by contemporary commentators is evidently
related to the developing awareness amongst cultural historians of the
methodological difficulties involved in defining and recovering popular
belief when access to that belief is mediated through textual sources.
Davis's arguments are salutary in demonstrating the tendency of even (or
especially) the sympathetic critic, in acting as heresiographer, to employ
categories and definitions which are products of contemporary polemical
literature. Hostile observers of radical religion in this period were, as
J. F. McGregor points out, 'prone to assume that a doctrine required a
sect to propagate it'.[7] Some of those accused by the heresiographers
made the point themselves, as illustrated by William Walwyn's sardonic
impersonation of Thomas Edwards: 'I have most presumptiously and
arrogantly assumed to myself, a power of judging and censuring all judgements, opinions and wayes of worship (except my own) to be either
damnable, heretical, schismatical or dangerous [under] the common
nick-names of Brownists, Independents, Anabaptists, Antinomians,
Seekers and the like'. Walwyn was amused by the charge that he had
founded his own sect: 'tell all men these Walwynites everywhere, turn the
world upside down; breathing strange, and unwelcome doctrines, such as
your Churches and people cannot bear'.[8] He recognized that scare stories
about popular revolt, such as the recurring references in antisectarian

---

[6] Davis, *Fear, Myth and History*, pp. x, 130. Davis took issue with the historiographical
tradition represented in particular by the work of Hill and A. L. Morton's *The World of the
Ranters: Religious Radicalism in the English Revolution* (London, 1970), and also with the
assumptions of J. F. McGregor's 'The Ranters: A Study in the Free Spirit in English Sectarian
Religion, 1648–1660', B.Litt. thesis (Oxford University, 1968). For a selection of arguments
in the Ranter debate see Barry Reay, 'The World Turned Upside Down: A Retrospect', in
Eley and Hunt (eds.), *Reviving the English Revolution*, 53–72; Christopher Hill, 'Abolishing
the Ranters', in Hill, *A Nation of Change and Novelty: Radical Politics, Religion and Literature
in Seventeenth Century England* (1990; repr. 1993), 172–218; J. C. Davis, 'Fear, Myth and
Furore: Reappraising the "Ranters"', *Past and Present*, 129 (1990), 79–103; J. F. McGregor et
al., 'Debate. Fear, Myth and Furore: Reappraising the Ranters', *Past and Present*, 140
(August, 1993), 155–210.

[7] J. F. McGregor, 'Seekers and Ranters', 121; see also J. C. Davis, 'Puritanism and
Revolution: Themes, Methods, Categories, and Conclusions', *Historical Journal*, 33 (1990),
693–7.

[8] William Walwyn, *A Prediction of Mr. Edwards His Conversion and Recantation* (1646),
in *WWW*, 231; Walwyn, *Walwyns Just Defence* (1649), in *WWW*, 415.

literature of the 1640s to the bloody Anabaptist uprisings in Germany in the 1520s, served specific ideological functions:

[the divines] resolve to make the Anabaptists odious to the people, and nothing, they think, will sooner do it than by making the people believe that they are the harbourers of such an opinion as would dissolve all society, and bring into confusion the state. Now this they speak of the Anabaptists in general, knowing that the people will apply it to the Anabaptists in England . . .[9]

Indeed the appearance of pamphlets describing in salacious detail the blasphemous and licentious behaviour of the Ranters coincided with the efforts of the Rump Parliament to head off Presbyterian disaffection. In 1650 legislation was passed which appeared to herald a campaign to implement a Puritan reformation of manners—the so-called Blasphemy and Adultery Acts. The Ranters, as vivid examples of the irreligion and sexual immorality rife amongst the multitude, provided a convenient rationale for such legislation.[10] The Presbyterian cleric Richard Baxter lends contemporary support to the argument that scare campaigns against popular radicalism were organized to consolidate the authority of the new republic:

[Cromwell] made more use of the wild-headed sectaries than barely to *fight* for him; they now serve him as much by their Heresies, their Enmity to learning and the Ministry, their pernicious Demands which tended to Confusion, as they had done before by their Valour in the Field. He can conjure up at pleasure some terrible apparition, of Agitators, Levellers, or such like, who as they affrighted the King from *Hampden-Court*, shall affright the People to fly to *him* for refuge.

A few pages later in his memoirs Baxter states that 'the horrid Villianies' of the Ranters 'did as much as anything did, to disgrace all *Sectaries*, and to restore the credit of the Ministry and the sober unanimous Christians'.[11]

The analysis of the Ranters as a 'terrible apparition' conjured from a series of textual images of inversion and transgression has been of general value to early modern studies in drawing attention to the hostile construction of religious and political identities in print. However, Davis's focus on a discursive construction imposed from the outside takes insufficient account of how those who were accused of being Ranters shaped their own textual identity.[12] Consequently the most constructive

[9] Walwyn, *The Compassionate Samaritane* (1644), in *WWW*, 120.
[10] Blair Worden, *The Rump Parliament* (1974; 2nd edn., Cambridge, 1977), 232–4.
[11] *Relinquiae Baxterianae*, ed. Matthew Sylvester (1696), 70, 77.
[12] A point made by e.g. Smith, *Perfection Proclaimed*, 8 n. 27; Ann Hughes, 'Early Quakerism: A Historian's Afterword', in David Loewenstein and Thomas N. Corns (eds.),

response to Davis has come from literary critics, who have proceeded to get on with analysing the writings of those individuals called Ranters. For during the very period that the study of seventeenth-century radicalism became widely discredited amongst historians who privileged manuscript over printed sources historicist literary critics began to extend their boundaries of study to include the tracts and pamphlets published between 1640 and 1660. Consequently radical writing during the English revolution has become established as a legitimate category of early modern literary achievement.[13] At the same time developments in cultural theory, often grouped under the label of 'the linguistic turn', have tested the solidity of boundaries 'between the represented and the real', arguing that it is through language that human beings constitute and comprehend their world and their own identities within that world. This sensitivity to the linguistic inscription of reality has placed heuristic value on the literary analysis of printed sources, and in particular those forms of controversial writing previously excluded from the literary canon, such as the polemical pamphlet and the religious tract.[14] Questions of rhetoric, style, genre, allusion, and audience thus become as relevant to a reconstruction of the past as the traditional political, social, and economic concerns of the historian. The claim that the English revolution will not be properly understood until a cultural history of radicalism is written—rather than a social history concerned with how many people held radical beliefs, or a political history concerned with the concrete constitutional impact of radical ideas—testifies to the influence of literary scholarship on early modern historiography over the last decade.

Yet while literary work on radical writing has demonstrated the limitations of revisionist arguments about the inadequacy of printed sources, literary critics have mostly failed to engage with the revisionist demonstration of the power of projected images in early modern England, preferring to work within a 'basic Marxist framework' inherited from Christopher Hill.[15] Particularly influential in the literary sphere has been

The Emergence of Quaker Writing: Dissenting Literature in Seventeenth Century England (London, 1995), 142–8 (143).

[13] The interest in the literary qualities of radical writing in recent years has been bound up with more general claims for the 1640–60 period as a legitimate focus of literary, as well as historical, study. On the traditional neglect of the period by literary scholars see Susan Wiseman, *Drama and Politics in the English Civil War* (Cambridge, 1998), 7–18.

[14] Peter Lake and Kevin Sharpe, 'Introduction', in Lake and Sharpe (eds.), *Culture and Politics in Early Stuart England* (Stanford, Calif., 1994), 4–6; Lynn Hunt, 'History, Culture, and Text', in Hunt (ed.), *The New Cultural History* (Berkeley, Calif., 1989), 1–24.

[15] Nigel Smith, review of Hawes, *Mania and Literary Style*, in *Modern Philology*, 97 (1999), 278; Nicholas McDowell, review of David Loewenstein, *Representing Revolution in Milton*

Hill's contention in a lecture on radical prose style that radical texts brought 'the speech of ordinary people' into the previously elite sphere of printed opinion and were addressed to a popular rather than a 'Latin-educated or court audience'. They were designed to be read by 'craftsmen and yeoman' and 'read aloud to illiterate audiences'. Eloquent in its rough, natural simplicity, radical writing is consequently seen to have its roots in 'utilitarian artisans' prose' rather than the grammatical and rhetorical training of the early modern schoolroom. Indeed the schematic division of seventeenth-century prose style along political and religious lines has long been a feature of English literary history. In Joan Webber's still influential formulation, the prose of the 'conservative Anglican' is complex, learned, and humorous, producing stylistic shifts and 'an "I" that plays games with the audience', while that of the 'radical Puritan' is 'plain and rude, more direct, more popular'.[16] The writers discussed in the following chapters are a thorn in the side of all these generalizations. To further our appreciation of the discursive formation of radical identities, we first need to acknowledge the operation and measure the impact of polemical myths and stereotypes. In this chapter I trace the generation and application of the perdurable cultural stereotype of the heretic as ignoramus. As we have seen in Chapter 1, scholars of radicalism in the English revolution have tended to replicate this stereo-type in their representation of radical belief as by definition a manifesta-tion of unlearned lay culture. The accusation of ignorance was of course directed at the heterodox to invalidate their claims to be heard; the radicals themselves, including those with a considerable degree of formal education, responded by valorizing ignorance as apostolic holy simpli-city. Yet we shall discover that the university-educated radicals discussed in Chapters 3–5 work rhetorically at two levels in a manner which is almost self-contradictory: they authenticate the stereotype of the heretic as ignoramus while simultaneously undermining it through a display of their learning. Far from being the passive construction of polemical literature, then, these writers actively engage with the hostile images of themselves circulated in print and appropriate those images in the process of using the printed text to fashion their own heterodox identities, both

and His Contemporaries: Religion, Politics, and Polemics in Radical Puritanism (Cambridge, 2001), in *Notes and Queries*, NS, 49 (2002), 524–5.

[16] Hill, 'Radical Prose in Seventeenth Century England: From Marprelate to the Levellers', *Essays in Criticism*, 32 (1982), 95–118 (103–5, 116), repr. in *Collected Essays of Christopher Hill*, i. *Writing and Revolution in Seventeenth Century England* (Brighton, 1985), 75–95; Joan Webber, *The Eloquent 'I': Style and Self in Seventeenth Century Prose* (Madison, Wisc., 1968), 6–14.

individual and collective. Agency is asserted through the manipulation and subversion of the polemical categories of orthodoxy.

In warning of the terrible consequences of allowing 'illiterate Mechanick persons' to usurp the office of the university-trained clergy, Thomas Edwards urged Parliament to implement its own 1645 act against lay preaching. Yet despite his charge of illiteracy Edwards explicitly connects the issue of lay preaching with the failure of Parliament to enforce its Licensing Act of 1643: 'witnesse that Ordinance against mens preaching who are not ordained Ministers, witnesse that Ordinance about Printing'. Indeed as evidence for his claims about the explosion of blasphemy in England Edwards frequently cites and occasionally quotes from recent heretical books, blaming the production and circulation of these books on the impotence of the Licensing Act. Listing the offending texts which teach 'new Law and new Divinity', he calls for them to be publicly burnt at 'the close of the Fasting dayes'. That Edwards perceived the threat to come from the radicals' books as much as the radicals themselves is betrayed by the analogy that he employs to explain his method of differentiating between types of heretic, even though they 'all agree in Independencie and in forsaking the communion of the Reformed Churches': 'A scholar that makes a Catalogue of Books, writes down *Decimo Sextos* as well as *Folios* in it, because they all be Books, and yet puts a great deal of difference between the one and the other'.[17] Edwards conceives of his catalogue of heresies as a bibliography, and indeed by citing heterodox books on the market he provides a bibliography of radical belief for his readers. In this respect, the intended refutation was also a repository of heresy.

The displacement of heresy from individual to book is apparent from the converse perspective in the famous images of books as martyrs in *Areopagitica* (1644), Milton's printed oration to Parliament in which he both proclaims the godliness of 'the men cry'd against for schismaticks and sectaries' and urges the repeal of the 1643 Licensing Act:

We should be wary therefore what persecution we raise against the living labours of publick men, how we spill that season'd life of man preserv'd and stor'd up in

----

[17] Edwards, *Gangraena*, i. sig. A5ᵛ, 9, 34, 38, 58–9, 203.

Books; since we see a kind of homicide may thus be committed, sometimes a martyrdome, and if it extend to the whole impression, a kinde of massacre, whereof the execution ends not in the slaying of an elementall life, but strikes at that ethereall and fift essence, the breath of reason it selfe, slaies an immortality rather than a life.

Milton—in great part reacting to the hostile reception of *The Doctrine and Discipline of Divorce* (1643), one of the books that Edwards would have had included in his textual autos-da-fé—shifts the imagery of physical persecution from writer to book and from individual to abstract personification, referring to the 'torn body of our martyr'd Saint' and the 'cropping [of] the discovery that might bee yet further made in both religious and civill Wisdome'; although, in one of the work's many contradictions, he goes on to recommend that the 'most effectuall remedy' for those books found 'mischievous and libellous' after publication is 'the fire and the executioner'.[18] The increasing circulation of Lollard books in the vernacular in the fifteenth century led to 'written materials [becoming] the object of official destruction as well as, or even in preference to, the individual heretic'.[19] That Milton conceived of books as heretics and Edwards of heretics as books, and that the dispute over religious toleration was conducted in terms of the ethics and efficacy of the Licensing Act, indicates how the interaction between heresy and literacy had become a more pressing issue than ever during the 'first European civil war to be fought within a well-established culture of the vernacular printed word'. The press facilitated an expression of oppositional opinions in the 1640s that was 'unprecedented in [British] cultural history'.[20] In demanding the destruction of heretical books, Edwards sought to drive heresy back into illiteracy; for Milton, however, the encounter with heresy becomes virtually a duty of literacy.

The 'illiterate Mechanick persons' of *Gangraena* thus spread their heterodox ideas not only through illegal preaching, but through illegal writing. The threat to godly religion and morality posed by illiterate 'sectaries' is identified both with their use of the spoken word and with their use of the printed word, with their literacy. To the twenty-first-century reader, this argument appears inherently contradictory. The apparent contradiction is evident also in the radicals' polemical self-

18 *CPWM*, ii. 492–3, 550, 554, 569.
19 Anne Hudson, '*Laicus Litteratus*: The Paradox of Lollardy', in Peter Biller and Hudson (eds.), *Heresy and Literacy, 1000–1530* (Cambridge, 1994), 222–36 (231).
20 Glen Burgess, 'The Impact on Political Thought: Rhetorics for Troubled Times', in Morrill (ed.), *The Impact of the English Civil War*, 67–83 (67); 'Introduction', to N. H. Keeble (ed.), *The Cambridge Companion to Writing of the English Revolution* (Cambridge, 2001), 1.

representation. Writing in response to his clerical opponents, William Walwyn refers to himself as one of the 'unlearned and illitterate men' whom the clergy despise and exploit. In fact the contradiction is merely the effect of an anachronistic definition of terms. 'Literate' and 'illiterate' only gradually assumed their modern senses with the developing predominance of vernacular literacy. In the earlier seventeenth century they largely retained the medieval sense of their Latin roots, *litteratus* and *illitteratus*. These terms denoted 'two "education-worlds": "literate", the education-world of Latin and the cleric . . . "illiterate", the education-world of the vernacular and the lay person'.[21] Walwyn's comments on his education and reading illuminate the sense of these terms in the 1640s. Responding to the charge that he valued the pagan ethics of classical texts over the Christian doctrine of the Scriptures, Walwyn emphasized his lack of Latin and his status as *illitteratus*:

> I can read only such as are translated into English; such a wise Jesuite am I, that with all my skill, I cannot construe three lines of any Latin author, nor do I understand any, except common proverbs, as are more familiar in Latine then in English, which sometimes I use not to dignifie myself, but because of the pertinancy in them sometimes . . .

When Walwyn then refers in the same passage to his clerical critics as 'despisers of unlearned and illiterate men', he would seem to be using the term in its medieval sense of ignorance of Latin (as his spelling of 'illitterate' suggests) and to believe that opponents such as Edwards mean the same thing when they represent him as an 'illiterate Mechanick'.[22] So it is literacy in Latin, not in the vernacular, that Edwards erects as a boundary between clergy and laity, orthodox and radical. This is an important point to bear in mind when we read condemnations and defences of the 'unlearned' in seventeenth-century religious controversy.

The characterization of the radical as *illitteratus* is used as a mode of attack in *Gangraena* and of apology in *Walwyns Just Defence*. In employing the theme of illiteracy both to discredit and defend heterodox positions, Edwards and Walwyn were working within long-established polemical traditions. In her account of the trial of the Lollard Walter Brut in Hereford in 1393 Anne Hudson explains why he caused his interrogators such consternation:

---

[21] *Walwyns Just Defence*, in *WWW*, 397; Peter Biller, 'Heresy and Literacy: Earlier History of the Theme', in Biller and Hudson (eds.), *Heresy and Literacy, 1000–1530*, 1–18 (4).

[22] *Walwyns Just Defence*, 397. Edwards had accused Walwyn of being 'a man of an equivocating Jesuiticall spirit'; *Gangraena*, ii. 26–30.

Brut in particular challenged many of the assumptions of his accusers: *laicus* by definition should be *illitteratus*, but Brut was far from that, and could even be brought to defend himself in fluent Latin; a lay heretic should be incapable of defending his case before the bishop's officials, let alone of quoting the Bible at length, of citing canon law and the fathers. The taunts of [Bishop] Trefnant's helpers, whether present at the trial or not, show how they tried to push Brut back into the stereotype of the lay heretic: Brut's name was used by his opponents for predictable jokes, '*Walterus est brutus idest obrutus*' (Walter is stupid, over-whelmed). Yet at the same time Trefnant's use of a formidable team of experts . . . reveals his unwilling realisation that Brut could not be assimilated to that com-forting convention.[23]

As *laicus litteratus*, Brut (who may once have been a fellow of Merton College, Oxford, although Hudson finds the evidence unconvincing) made his interrogators uncomfortable by undermining the stereotype of the heretic as illiterate which was projected in a remarkably uniform manner by the religious authorities in a range of European countries in the Middle Ages.[24] Hudson points out that the Lollard heresy was itself 'in origin learned, indeed academic . . . its immediate source was the thought of John Wyclif', Oxford don.[25] Nonetheless Brut's accusers sought to press him into an image of the heretic as illiterate that had a 'repetitive and ubiquitous presence' in the Middle Ages: 'the theme is implicit in all of the [Catholic] Church's later action against vernacular texts' and is to be found 'universally in chronicles, canon law, inquisitor's treatises, polemics'. In representing the heretic as by definition *illitteratus*, the clerical authorities sought to demonstrate the 'heretic's unfittedness to preach'. By the end of the thirteenth century the topos had expanded from the simple counterpoising of the illiterates of the sect to the literate men of the Church into a theme which encompassed social status and gender. Heresy was depicted as flourishing amongst 'the poor, workmen, women and idiots' in polemics characterized by the 'repetitive listing of sects and [the] reproduction of the stereotype of heretical depravity'. Thomas Edwards was clearly invoking the established conventions of anti-heretical literature in listing the many 'errors and strange opinions scattered up and down' the country (271 in all) and dismissing the theo-logical arguments of the sectarians as 'both unsound and weak, fit to take women and weak people, but not to satisfie any scholar'. *Gangraena* has

23 Hudson, '*Laicus Litteratus*: The Paradox of Lollardy', 229.
24 Biller, 'Heresy and Literacy: Earlier History of the Theme', *passim*; see also Peter Biller, 'The *Topos* and Reality of the Heretic as *Illitteratus*', in D. Harmening (ed.), *Religiöse Laienbildung und Ketzerabwehr in Mittelalter* (Wurzburg, 1994), 1–27.
25 Hudson, '*Laicus Litteratus*: The Paradox of Lollardy', 228.

been described as a 'new form of popular journalism' but it also signalled the re-emergence of a genre and of generic polemical themes that had been established some three centuries earlier.[26]

Those radicals in revolutionary England who appealed to the scriptural example of the simplicity and meanness of the prophets and Apostles to justify their authority to pronounce on religious matters were also repeating the response of medieval heretics to the accusations of the Catholic clergy: 'the topos of the heretic: illiterate was appropriated by heretics and turned round, in their version of the unlettered early apostles'. The medieval heretic appealed to texts such as Acts 4: 13, in which John and Peter are described as '*sine litteris, et idiotae*', and to the Pauline tradition of holy simplicity. The Lollard Walter Brut, despite defending himself in fluent Latin and according to the traditional disputative modes of canon law, also appealed to the 'biblical tropes of humility and inadequacy with words', referring to Isaiah and Daniel as examples of how God reveals himself to '*peccatoribus et laycis ydiotis*'. Brut declared that '*non cognovi litteraturam*'—an assertion which is simultaneously contradicted by his use of Latin.[27] In the moment of seeking to confirm the stereotype Brut undermines it. Yet Brut and his inquisitors both appealed to cultural archetypes which had become established in the Middle Ages and which shaped both the polemical depiction of the heretic (lowly and unlearned and therefore unfit to preach) and the self-representation of the heretic (lowly and unlearned in the manner of God's chosen ones in the Scriptures). These themes were to continue to dominate the religious controversies of the Reformation and of the English revolution.

The disputes during the 1640s and 1650s between orthodox and radical Puritans over the relationship between education, ordination, and religious knowledge can be understood in terms of two different versions of Reformation history. The latter appealed to the Protestant tradition of confessional polemical history established in England by John Bale's *The Image of Both Churches* (1545) and, most influentially, John Foxe's *Acts and Monuments* or 'Book of Martyrs' (first edn. 1563). Bale offered a 'way of periodizing the history of the [Protestant] church and a reading of this history as a continuing struggle between the defenders of the Word of God who made up the true church and their persecutors, from those who

[26] Biller, 'Heresy and Literacy: Earlier History of the Theme', 1, 4, 5; R. N. Swanson, 'Literacy, Heresy, History, and Orthodoxy: Perspectives and Permutations for the Later Middle Ages', in Biller and Hudson (eds.), *Heresy and Literacy 1000–1530*, 279–93 (280); Edwards, *Gangraena*, i. 33; Tolmie, *The Triumph of the Saints*, 131.

[27] Biller, 'Heresy and Literacy: Earlier History of the Theme', 9; Hudson, '*Laicus Litteratus*: The Paradox of Lollardy', 225.

suffered under the Roman emperors to such recent martyrs as Thomas Bilney, John Frith, and William Tyndale'. Foxe represented the history of the true Church in the form of a series of episodes recounting the triumphant suffering of individual English martyrs, extending this history back to the Lollards, who were treated as proto-Protestants. Foxe's martyrs comprised the poor, the uneducated, and women as well as learned bishops such as Latimer, Ridley, and Cranmer. One of the distinguishing features of Foxe's narratives was their juxtaposition of styles. As John R. Knott puts it, the

plainness and simplicity of the Protestant martyrs [were opposed to] the formality and ceremonialism of the spokesmen of the church. The ideal was what Paul had called 'the simplicity that is in Christ' (2 Cor. 11. 3), its antithesis the worldliness and regard for the external manifestations of holiness and religious authority that Foxe associated with the rise of the Roman church . . .[28]

The pattern of persecution, suffering, and godly heroism established by Foxe exerted an enormous hold over the early modern English imagination: in 1571 it was ordered that a copy of *Acts and Monuments* be placed in every cathedral church, and some of the more notable individual accounts of martyrdom were recast into ballad form. Despite its initial embrace by the religious establishment, the subversive potential of Foxe's martyrology is evident in its influence on the textual self-representation of a range of dissenters, from the Elizabethan separatists Henry Barrow and John Greenwood to the Leveller John Lilburne, John Bunyan, and George Fox in the mid-seventeenth century.[29] The example of Foxe's simple martyrs was combined with the scriptural model of the prophets and Apostles as *sine litteris, et idiotae* to support anticlerical polemic. This representative argument is from John Fry's *The Clergy in their Colours* (1650), all copies of which Parliament ordered to be burnt:

It hath been the pleasure of God in all ages, to confound the wise and mighty by poor and despicable instruments in the eyes of the world. Witness many of the Prophets, Christs Apostles, and Disciples in their times. Let us come to latter times, and see if it hath not been so to this very age. Read Mr. Fox his *Acts and Monuments*, and there you will find both men, and women, little skilled in the Tongues, Disputing, yea, and Confuting the Doctors in matters of Religion, for which they lost their lives.[30]

[28] John R. Knott, *Discourses of Martyrdom in English Literature, 1563–1694* (Cambridge, 1993), 46, 69.
[29] Tessa Watt, *Cheap Print and Popular Piety, 1550–1640* (Cambridge, 1991; paperback edn. 1994), 90–1, 100–1; Knott, *Discourses of Martyrdom*, chs. 4, 6, 7.
[30] John Fry, *The Clergy in their Colours* (1650), sigs. A3^v–A4^r. Fry, an MP, was suspended from the Commons in 1649 over accusations of blasphemy.

In identifying themselves with 'the simple and the mean things of this earth' the radicals of the 1640s and 1650s were appealing to a powerfully evocative rhetoric of Protestant martyrdom, which had a wide currency in early modern England through the popularization of the genre of confessional polemical historiography.

The heresiographers appealed to a different version of Reformation history which cohabited rather uneasily with that outlined above. In this latter version the topos of the heretic as illiterate was applied to sectarians and radicals who were perceived as challenging the divine authority of the true Protestant church. Thomas Edwards repeatedly cites in *Gangraena* the writings of Luther, Calvin, Zwingli, and Bullinger against the Anabaptists and the 'Libertines' in support of his position. Luther represented the Anabaptist leaders as 'a simple but radically anti-intellectual people' who were incapable of disputing with him because of their lack of learning.[31] Calvin ridiculed the Anabaptists as 'giddy men [who] despise all reading' and associated the Libertines' location of supreme religious authority in the personal experience of the Holy Spirit with practical antinomianism and sexual promiscuity. For Bullinger, the Anabaptists had no right to preach and expound Scripture because they were 'an ignorant people . . . without the knowledge of tongues, without the gift of interpretation'. Their false claim to direct divine inspiration was merely a means of disguising their intellectual inadequacy to engage in scriptural debate.[32] Indeed the Peasants' Revolt of 1524–5 and the appearance of the various movements of the radical Reformation provoked the magisterial reformers to retreat from their initial demands for universal access to the vernacular Bible and to display an increasing ambivalence towards their earlier notion of the spiritual sufficiency of the simple lay person. Rather 'the ability to read and properly interpret the Bible became tied to professional exegetes, trained in the three biblical languages and most commonly in possession of a degree from a Protestant university'. Unsupervised access was replaced by 'a preliminary process of catechization which was considered sufficient access for the majority'. The claim of prophetic inspiration which the reformers associated with their radical opponents could be made by anyone. The reformers responded by restricting revelation to the text of Scripture, the sense of which, they now

[31] Edwards, *Gangraena*, i. sigs. B2ᵛ–B3ʳ, 182–3, 186–7, 210–11; John S. Oyer, *Lutheran Reformers Against Anabaptists* (The Hague, 1964), 133.

[32] R. W. Collins, *Calvin and the Libertines of Geneva*, ed. F. D. Blackley (Toronto, 1988), 153–4, 164–5; Robert Weimann, *Authority and Representation in Early Modern Discourse* (Baltimore, Md., 1996), 51. Michael Heyd, *'Be Sober and Reasonable': The Reaction to Enthusiasm in the Seventeenth and Early Eighteenth Centuries* (Leiden, 1995), 31.

maintained, could only be correctly interpreted and disseminated by those sufficiently educated and trained within the official structures of the reformed Church. In opposition to Anabaptist declarations of personal illumination, Zwingli, following Erasmus' interpretation of 1 Cor. 14, defined 'prophecy' as the exposition of scriptural passages and 'prophet' as a preacher sufficiently schooled in Hebrew, Greek, and Latin. In Zurich Zwingli instituted the daily exercise of 'prophesying' in which ministers, canons, and students engaged in public readings and exegesis of the Bible in the original languages. Calvin similarly ascribed the title of 'prophet' to a ministerial office in the Genevan Church government, although Calvin conceived of these trained clerics as voicing God's anger at human corruption and iniquity in the manner of the Old Testament prophets.[33] The magisterial reformers thus employed the stereotype of the heretic as illiterate for the same polemical purpose as the Catholic clergy in the pre-Reformation period—to disqualify those with beliefs deemed heterodox from challenging or assuming the role of the ordained minister and from engaging in religious debate. The heretic was characterized as representative of the ignorant and irreligious multitude, evoking the threat of popular disorder and the subversion of social, religious, and educational hierarchies. The ubiquity of the theme across northern Europe is evident in the English translation of a polemical history of the German Anabaptists by Freidrich Spanheim, Calvinist Professor of Theology at Leiden, that was published in 1646 as *Englands Warning by Germanies Woe* and quoted approvingly by Thomas Edwards:

From hence came it, that the authority of the Ecclesiastical order was weakened, by the licentiousnesse of *Enthusiasts*, venting their own dreams and inventions: and the choice of those, whose souls attend the holy things, committed to the rude multitude; the sacred keyes also, which ought to be born by the representative church, exposed to the pleasure of every one, and so a kind of Anarchy and intollerable disorder brought into the House of God.[34]

The polemical stereotype of the heretic circulated throughout the literate culture of early modern England and can be found not only in religious and controversial tracts but in various forms of both learned and 'popular' writing. In his discussion of the form of religious melancholy which afflicts 'pseudo-prophets' Robert Burton represents this form of

[33] Bob Scribner, 'Heterodoxy, Literacy and Print in the Early German Reformation', in Biller and Hudson (eds.), *Heresy and Literacy, 1000–1530*, 255–78 (275–6); Swanson, 'Literacy, Heresy, History, and Orthodoxy', 291; *Hudrich Zwingli*, ed. G. R. Potter (1978), 66; Heyd, '*Be Sober and Reasonable*', 29–30.

[34] *Englands Warning by Germanies Woe* (1646), 45; Edwards, *Gangraena*, i. sig. B3ʳ.

madness as a consequence of ignorance; it is the 'ruder sort . . . of mean conditions and very illiterate [who] turn prophets, have secret revelations, will be of privy council with God'. In the account by Nashe's Jack Wilton of the behaviour of the Anabaptist revolutionaries in Munster in the 1530s the unfortunate traveller witnesses 'base handicrafts, as cobblers and curriers and tinkers . . . expostulate with God' and claim 'inspiration was their ordinary familiar'.[35] William P. Holden has shown how a particular subversive belief or activity tends to be isolated and attached to a specific sect in hostile representations of radical religion in early modern literature: the Baptists were associated with the communism alleged of the German Anabaptists of the radical Reformation while the perfectionist beliefs of the Family of Love ('Familism') were linked, like those of the Libertine movement in Calvin's Geneva, with sexual promiscuity.[36] These images of popular revolt and lower-order libertinism were polemical projections with little basis in reality. Christopher Marsh has painstakingly shown how the images of the profane Familist circulated in sensational pamphlets and on the stage were remote indeed from the reality of prosperous individuals who were generally tolerated by their local communities and who outwardly conformed to the ceremonies of the established Church. The Family of Love in England were an elite rather than a popular religious movement: there were even Familists in the Elizabethan and Jacobean courts.[37] Although there is little evidence of the survival of English Familist 'communities' after the 1620s, a spate of pamphlets reporting the recent sexual antics of Familists appeared in the early 1640s. One typical pamphlet reported that a conventicle of Familists had replaced the Bible with Ovid's *Ars Amatoria* in their prayers and ceremonies and had set about seducing local women. At a more engaged and intellectual level, the Presbyterian cleric Samuel Rutherford argued at length that Familist antinomianism was at the root of all the heresies that had shot up in the 1640s, while in an account of his debates with Abiezer Coppe, the Berkshire cleric John Tickell simply assumed that 'Ranterisme' was a variety of Familism, attempting to make sense of Coppe's language with reference to a book entitled 'A Key to Familisme'

[35] Burton, *The Anatomy of Melancholy*, ed. Thomas C. Faulkner, Nichola J. Keissling, and Rhonda L. Blair, 3 vols. (Oxford, 1989–94), iii. 387–8; Nashe, *The Unfortunate Traveller and Other Works*, 278.

[36] W. P. Holden, *Anti-Puritan Satire 1572–1642* (New Haven, Conn., 1954), 42.

[37] Christopher Marsh, *The Family of Love in English Society, 1550–1630* (Cambridge, 1994), esp. 113–16, 124–7, 208. On the stereotypical image of the Familist see J. D. Moss, 'The Family of Love and its English Critics', *Sixteenth Century Journal*, 6 (1975), 35–52; Kristen Poole, *Radical Religion from Shakespeare to Milton: Figures of Nonconformity in Early Modern England* (Cambridge, 2000), ch. 3.

(which does not appear to be extant). Although the English translations of the prophetic writings of Hendrik Niclaes, the Dutch founder of Familism, were republished during the 1640s and 1650s, Nigel Smith has concluded that 'it is hard to show any recurrence of Niclaes's way of writing'.[38] Rather the term 'Familist' was applied indiscriminately to forms of belief deemed enthusiastic or antinomian or simply heretical, usefully invoking its commonplace equation with popular irreligion and immorality.

These polemical images of radical religion were mostly used before 1640 to tar Puritanism with a sectarian brush. In *The Unfortunate Traveller* Nashe had one eye on the religious controversies of the 1590s, using Jack Wilton's account of Munster to elide popular sectarianism and enthusiasm with Puritanism. After his gory account of the 'unpitied and well-performed slaughter' of the Anabaptists, Wilton explains the moral of the story: 'Hear what it is to be Anabaptists, to be Puritans, to be villains. You may be counted illuminate botchers for a while, but your end will be "Good people, pray for us"'. In his discussion of the attractions of Puritanism to 'the multitude', 'the vulgar sort', and to 'them whose judgements are commonly weakest by reason of their sex' Richard Hooker cited the claim of 'they of the family of love' that 'it is the special illumination of the holy Ghost, whereby they discern those things in the word, which others reading yet discern them not'. The appeal of such claims of revelation to 'the simple and ignorant' lay in their negation of the value of learning, reason, and experience.[39] Hooker evidently sought to discredit Puritanism as a socially subversive ideology through association with Familism and the chaotic behaviour of the 'many-headed monster' of the common people. In fact, as we shall see in the next section, orthodox Puritans placed particular emphasis on the high degree of formal education and book learning required of the preacher.

The history of the cultural construction of the heretic in England helps to explain an apparent irony of the pamphlet wars of the 1640s: the polemical strategy of Presbyterians such as Edwards against the sectarians and Independents is virtually identical to that employed by royalist writers who sought to discredit Puritanism by associating it with the spread of popular heresy. The prolific royalist poet and propagandist

---

[38] Anon., *A Description of the Sect called the Familie of Love* (1641); Samuel Rutherford, *A Survey of the Spiritual Antichrist, opening the secrets of Familisme and Antinomianisme*, 2 pts. (1648); John Tickell, *The Bottomless Pit Smoaking in Familisme* (Oxford, 1651; 2nd edn. 1652), 46; Smith, *Perfection Proclaimed*, 180–1.

[39] Nashe, *The Unfortunate Traveller*, 285–6; Richard Hooker, *Of the Lawes of Ecclesiastical Polity*, ed. Arthur Stephen MacGrade (Cambridge, 1989), 15–16.

John Taylor explicitly identified the expanding activity of separatist and sectarian Churches in the early 1640s with the challenge of Parliamentary Puritanism to the established religious order. The archetypal image projected by Taylor (who was himself a waterman with no university education) of the sectarian as an ignorant, hypocritical, and secretly licentious tub preacher clearly anticipates the rhetoric of Presbyterian heresiography of the mid-1640s:

> A preacher's work is not to geld a sow,
> Unseemly 'tis that a judge should milk a cow,
> A cobbler to a pulpit should not mount,
> Nor can an ass cast up a true account.

The preaching of 'cobblers, tinkers, pedlars, weavers, sow-gelders, and chimney-sweepers' turns the proper division of function in society upside down. Moreover, the outward devotion of these tub preachers conceals their desire to pervert sexual and domestic order: 'though they are superciliously rigid and censorious, yet they seem very charitable, for rather than their sisters shall want food, they will fill their bellies, and rather than they shall be naked, they will cover their bellies'.[40] Puritan heresiographers found a mode of attacking heretics and enthusiasts of impeccable Protestant authority in the writings of the original reformers but, like the waterman John Taylor, they were also invoking stereotypical images deeply embedded in English culture.

INFUSION OR ACQUISITION: PURITANISM AND EDUCATION

In a study of nonconformist literature of the later seventeenth century N. H. Keeble has argued in relation to the repudiation of learning by radicals and its defence by Presbyterian and Independent clerics that '[w]e are dealing, in fact, not with differences of kind but of degree, not with opposing contentions but with a shared position based upon a premise common to all nonconformists; that though man may be rational, he is not merely rational'. Although the radical and the more orthodox Puritan differed in 'the extent to which they admitted humane assistance', this was 'a difference which narrowed through [the post-Restoration] period'.[41] Certainly anti-intellectualism during the English

---

[40] John Taylor, *A Swarme of Schismatiques and Sectaries* (1641), 2, 7; [Taylor], *The Anatomy of Separatists, alias Brownists* (1642), 2.

[41] Keeble, *The Literary Culture of Nonconformity in Later Seventeenth Century England*, 170.

revolution lays bare the ambivalence in Puritan attitudes towards reason and learning. The Calvinist doctrine of the innate depravity of man can be seen in part as a reaction to the humanist conflation of the Christian and classical lives of moral virtue, which led humanists to espouse a philosophy of education based on the possibility of approaching earthly perfection through learning and which glorified the rational capabilities of man.[42] As the marginal glosses on Corinthians in the Geneva Bible illustrate, the hotter type of Protestants found in Scripture a condemnation of the notion that learning was a sufficient means to faith and comprehension of the divine: 'herein Paul reprocheth even the best learned, as thogh not one of them colde perceive by his owne wisdome this mysterie of Christ reveiled in the Gospel'. Paul, who had been converted by the irrational imposition of the Spirit upon his will, warned against the glorification of reason and learning, reproving the Corinthians (in the words of the Geneva marginalia) as 'curious teachers of human sciences, as they which lothing at the simplicitie of Gods worde, preache philosophical speculations' and esteem 'the outwarde shewe of wisdom and eloquence, [more] than true godliness'.[43]

Nevertheless, as John Morgan has shown, 'the Puritan road to Jerusalem did, in spite of questions raised during its construction, detour through Athens'. In practice 'orthodox' Puritans of the early modern period considered humanist learning to be 'immensely valuable because it could be blended with the enthusiasm of faith to produce a more logical interpretation of Scripture and an intellectual side of Protestantism more secure against the assaults of the Roman Antichrist'. Maintaining the orthodox Protestant position that direct revelation was no longer available, Puritans looked to education to develop their understanding of the Word of God as recorded in the scriptural texts. Writing in 1654 in response to radical attacks on the university curriculum, the Presbyterian cleric Thomas Hall made the cessation of prophecy the centrepiece of his apology for formal education as a necessary qualification of a preacher: 'True, in the Apostolicall times, God poured out an extraordinary measure of his spirit on many, who had Learning and Languages by immediate infusion, wee now by acquistion; they had it Given, we Gotten; they by Revelation and Inspiration, we now by Industry and Study'.[44] The Bible was regarded as sufficient for delivering

[42] Ernst Cassirer, Paul Oskar Kristeller, and John Herman Randell, jun. (eds.), *The Renaissance Philosophy of Man* (Chicago, Ill., 1965), 19.

[43] Marginal glosses on 1 Cor. 1: 20, 3: 15 and 2 Cor. 5: 12 in the 1560 edn. of the Geneva Bible.

[44] John Morgan, *Godly Learning: Puritan Attitudes towards Reason, Learning and Educa-*

God's message to humanity if read with the assistance or 'ordinary illumination' of the Spirit. As the Scriptures had suffered from the accretions
and deletions of the Roman Church, the purity of the original message
had to be recovered. The need for a purified text impelled study of the
ancient and oriental languages and of classical grammar and rhetoric. The
Geneva Bible was a landmark in English Protestant endeavours to free
scriptural knowledge from the Latinate culture of Catholicism embodied
by the Vulgate, but it was also the product of immense linguistic scholarship. Calvin himself had approved the classical curriculum as the basis of
his academy in Geneva and 'in puritan schools [in early seventeenth-
century England] the regimen was unreservedly classical in the humanist
mould'. In his influential work on the school curriculum, *Ludus
Literarius, or The Grammar Schoole* (1612), the Puritan cleric John
Brinsley's recommended authors include Cicero, Virgil, Horace, Terence,
Juvenal, Ovid, Aesop, and Homer as well the Scriptures in Latin, Greek,
and Hebrew. Brinsley also incorporated the revisions of Aristotelian
rhetorical theory by Petrus Ramus, reflecting the influence on English
Puritanism of William Perkins's Ramist-based preaching manual, issued
in Latin in 1592 and translated as *The Arte of Prophesying* (1607). As
regards higher education, the general approach of Puritans to the universities before 1640 was 'to accept the basic curriculum, though to
modify texts and subjects; to work within existing structures, though to
introduce activities which would in practice demonstrate the aphorism
that learning was but a handmaid to divinity . . . the structure of educational institutions, and the content as affected by Renaissance urgings,
seemed to satisfy their need for an academic base'.[45]

In an effort to realize their vision of a learned ministry which was
equipped to interpret Scripture in the original languages, dispel superstition amongst the laity, and inculcate godly virtue in succeeding
generations, pre-war Puritans recognized the value of the universities and
sought to develop a ministerial caste qualified to preach by educational
attainment. They led the demand for a more godly and a more learned
clergy. Yet there was a paradox in the Puritan conception of the relationship between education and ordination: while the licence to preach was

tion, *1560–1640* (Cambridge, 1986), 78, 306, 245, 179, 195; Thomas Hall, *Vindiciae Literarum:
The Schools Guarded: or, the excellency and usefulness of Arts, Sciences, History, and all Sorts of
humane Learning, in subordination to Divinity, and Preparation for the Ministry* (1654),
'To the Reader', sig. A4^{r-v}, 62. On the magisterial reformers' insistence that 'extraordinary
inspiration' had ceased, see Heyd, *'Be Sober and Reasonable'*, ch. 1.

[45] Morgan, *Godly Learning*, 302, 232, 306 and *passim*; W. S. Howell, *Logic and Rhetoric in
England, 1500–1700* (Princeton, NJ, 1956), 258–65.

only to be given to those who were called by God to that vocation, their learning was testament to their vocation. The minister's supra-rational moment of spiritual calling or conversion, at the heart of the Puritan version of religious experience, was evinced in his command of logic, rhetoric, and the ancient languages.[46] The paradox is echoed in William Perkins's concept of 'experimentall theology', whereby the regenerate man may be assured of his arbitrary, predestined salvation by applying syllogistic logic to his conscience. Thomas Hall provides an appropriately syllogistic summation of the Puritan conception of reason as subordinate but not opposed to faith and of learning as the 'needful qualification' of the minister:

Wee grant that the abuse of Philosophy, when it is preferred before Divinity, or puffs men up with pride, or is used to adulterate and corrupt the truth and simplicity of the Gospell, that then is odious and abominable . . . But the question between us and the Anabaptists, is, whether the right and sober use of Philosophy, and other humane Learning be requisite for a Divine. This we affirm, the Anabaptists deny. I shall therefore set down this Antithesis to their Thesis, and will confine it by Arguments, viz. That the knowledge of Arts, Sciences, History, Languages, &c. are very usefull and needfull qualifications for a Minister of the Gospell . . .
That which is necessary for a Divine may not be contemned, [whether the neccesity be absolute or onely of expediency.]
But humane Learning is necessary for a Divine, *Ergo*, it may not be contemned. The Major no sober man will deny: The Minor I will prove by its parts.[47]

This conjunction of vocation and education enabled the Puritan clergy to represent themselves as both a spiritual and an intellectual elite. Non-separating Puritans did not differ from less zealous Calvinists in pre-war England in their conception of a learned ministerial caste as a vital plank in the social and political hierarchy. They differed only in their notion of the vigour with which the minister should fulfil his vocation of instilling godly virtue in the laity and in certain points of emphasis on the means by which he should do so—such as the close, dynamic relationship between preacher and congregation. This relationship was challenged by the Laudian ascendancy of the 1630s. Yet between 1640 and 1660 the Presbyterian clergy and most Independent ministers, the vast majority of whom were graduates, supported the traditional role of the universities in

---

[46] William Perkins, 'A Treatise of the Vocations or Callings of Men', in *The Works of W. Perkins* (Cambridge, 1605), 915; see also Morgan, *Godly Learning*, 80.
[47] R. T. Kendall, *Calvin and English Calvinism to 1649* (Oxford, 1979), 8–9; Thomas Hall, *Vindiciae Literarum*, 'To the Reader', sigs. A5ᵛ, A6ᵛ.

training a stipendiary ministry. So Presbyterian ministers such as Thomas Edwards and Thomas Hall and Independents such as John Owen could agree with their episcopal opponents in rejecting the authority of uneducated lay people to preach, for they all agreed that 'extraordinary inspiration' of the kind experienced by the prophets and Apostles had ceased. Owen, Dean of Christ Church, Oxford, in the 1650s, chose to refute the Quaker doctrine of the 'inner light' in Latin in *Exercitationes adversus Fanaticos* (1658), drawing a furious response from Samuel Fisher. Owen's book, according to Fisher, was 'designed more to the *sporting* of thy own and thy dark *School-Fellowes lewd spiteful Spirits* by playing upon the Quakers in secret, in your dark Divinity among your selves [than] to confute the *Quakers plainly and openly*'.[48]

As 'supernatural Revelation' is not to be expected in the post-Apostolic age, insisted Richard Baxter, the use of 'reason, memory, study, books, methods, forms &c.', as guided by the 'ordinary' motions of the Spirit, can be the only means of truly 'know[ing] the Creator and his works'.[49] The flip side of Baxter's irenic notion of spiritual enlightenment as a gradual process of reading and learning was the fierce condemnation of claims to immediate intuition of divine knowledge in the manner of the prophets and the Apostles—claims which rendered irrelevant the notion of 'humane' learning as the handmaid of divinity and the 'needfull qualification' of a preacher. So while the radical and the orthodox Puritan may have begun with a common conception of man as not merely rational, they came to sharply opposed conclusions. The question of the relevance of learning to religious knowledge was central to arguments for or against an established Church government and a separate ministerial caste. In the absence of a disciplined national Church in the 1640s and 1650s, this was a matter of immense religious and political significance.

The centrality of the relationship between spiritual authority and education to debates about theological, soteriological, and ecclesiastical matters in the 1640s and 1650s is evident from public disputations between Presbyterian clerics and religious radicals. In a survey of printed versions of these disputations Ann Hughes has found that invariably the 'orthodox silence the radicals through their learning; the radicals are "sorry disputants", lacking educated oral skills and ignorant or scornful

---

[48] Owen maintained that '[i]n the continuation of his Work [God] ceaseth from putting forth those extraordinary effects of his Power which were needful for the laying of the Foundation of the Church in the World' (quoted in Nuttall, *The Holy Spirit in Puritan Faith and Experience*, 30). Samuel Fisher, *Rusticus ad Academicos* (1660), 'Second Exercitation', 11.

[49] Baxter quoted in Nuttall, *The Holy Spirit in Puritan Faith and Experience*, 50; see also 26–7.

of the rules of disputation'. The polemical identification of heresy and ignorance to ridicule the heretic's intellectual inability to discuss spiritual matters is exemplified by Daniel Featley's *The Dippers Dipt* (1645), one of the more eloquent and influential antisectarian pamphlets of the mid-1640s, going through five editions in under two years. Featley (an orthodox Calvinist and anti-Laudian royalist) laments the rise of 'Mechanick Enthusiasts', 'sublime Coachmen', and 'illuminated Trades-men' who turn 'Tubs into Pulpits, Aprons into Linnen Ephods' by claim-ing that direct divine inspiration, rather than a university education or clerical ordination, qualifies a person to preach and interpret Scripture. Just as royalists in the 1640s accused the vulgar followers of Parliament of blasphemously prying into the divine secrets of kingship, Featley argues that under the pretence or delusion of prophetic inspiration 'the trade of expounding Scripture is a mystery which every Artizan arrogateth to himself'. Such inspiration is a thing of the past—'those irradiations of the Spirit, together with the glistening of fiery tongues, have not been seen in any Christian church these many ages'—and so these unlettered tub preachers are necessarily ignorant of divine truths and unfit to preach: 'they understand not the Scripture in the Originall languages, they cannot expound without Grammar, nor persuade without Rhetorik, nor divide without Logick, nor sound the Depth of any Controversie without Philosophy and School-Divinity'.[50] *The Dippers Dipt* purports to be 'a true relation of the meeting in Southwark between Dr Daniel Featley and a company of Anabaptists'. The inclusion of his academic title points to Featley's polemical strategy, which is based on demonstrating the igno-rance of his sectarian interlocutors, their intellectual inability to engage in the formal terms of scriptural debate and, consequently, the folly of attempting to transform 'Mechanicks of the lowest rank into Priests of the highest places'. Such rupturing of the ecclesiastical and educational order is represented as unnatural and monstrous. The transformation of 'mechanick' into minister is 'a Metamorphoses after Ovid, not made by Poeticall license, but Propheticall Liberty'.[51]

Locating his theological authority in his university education and

---

[50] Ann Hughes, 'The Pulpit Guarded: Confrontations between Orthodox and Radicals in Revolutionary England', in Anne Laurence, W. R. Owens, and Stuart Sim (eds.), *John Bunyan and his England, 1628–88* (London, 1990), 31–50 (43); Featley, *The Dippers Dipt* sig. B3ʳ, 128–9, 185. Cf. Clement Walker, *Anarchia Anglicana: Or, The History Of Independency*, 2 pts. (1649; 2nd edn. 1661), i. 140: 'They have cast all the mysteries and secrets of government . . . before the vulgar (like pearls before swine) and have taught both the soldiery and people to look so far into them as to ravel back all governments to the first principles of nature'.

[51] Featley, *The Dippers Dipt*, sigs. B3ʳ, B4ᵛ, 209–10.

knowledge of Greek and Latin, Featley exposes the root of the Anabaptists' heresy to lie in their illogical argument, lack of linguistic training, and adherence to mistranslations of the Bible. He employs a
succession of syllogisms to deconstruct the Anabaptists' logic, and dismisses their responses as meaningless without the formal syllogistic
method taught in the universities:

> If you dispute by Reason, you must conclude syllogistically in mood and figure,
> which I take to be out of your element . . . This argument is so far from a demon-
> stration, that it is not so much as a topical syllogisme, but merely sophisticall,
> therin any who hath ever saluted the University, and hath been initiated in Logick,
> may observe a double fallacy.
>
> > The first is, *fallacia homonymie* in the premises.
> > The second is, *ignoratio elenchi* in the conclusion.

Consequently his sectarian interlocutor can be dismissed as 'an illiterate
artificer'. Featley peppers his prose with Latin tags which have the
rhetorical function of condescendingly emphasizing his intellectual
superiority—'Your question is, *Quid constituit visibilem Ecclesiam*? What
makes a visible Church?'—and uses his command of the 'Original' to
argue that Anabaptist belief is founded upon etymological error and
ambiguity:

> βάπτω, from whence Baptize is derived, signifieth as well to *Die*, as to *Dip*: and it
> may be, the Holy Ghost, in the word Baptize, hath some reference to that
> signification because by Baptisme *we change our view* . . . therefore admitting that
> in the word Baptize there were something of βάπτω, *tingo*, to *Dip* or *Die*, yet it will
> not follow, that it neccessarily signifieth *Dipping*, for it may as well imply this
> spiritual *Die*, to which no Dipping is neccesary.[52]

Featley's ploy of citing examples of his opponent's mistranslations of
Scripture was in fact a stock theme of anti-heresy polemic in the Middle
Ages.[53] His opponents defeated by superior scholarship, Featley's polemic
builds to a rousing climax which is worth quoting in full for its explicit
identification of illiteracy, enthusiasm, and social anarchy:

> And now Christian Reader, thou hast heard a Harmony, listen not to discords;
> thou hast heard a consort of silver Trumpets, hearken not to a single oaten-pipe,
> or the harsh sound of Rams hornes; thou hast heard the suffrages of all the learned
> Divines in the Reformed Churches; regard not the votes of a few illiterate
> Mechanicks, much lesse the fancie and dreames of fanaticall Enthusiasts; who
> because they are *Anomalaes* themselves, would have not by their good will there

---

52 Ibid. sig. B3ᵛ, 4, 18, 41, 70, 128.
53 Biller, 'Heresy and Literacy: Earlier History of the Theme', 4.

should bee any Rules; because they are wandering Starres, they would have none fixt; because they are dissolute, they would have no bonds of Lawes; because they are Schismaticks, and Non-conformists, they would have no Discipline in the Church; because they are dunces, and ignorant both of Tongues and Arts, they would have no learning, nor Universities: Lastly, because they walke inordinately, they would have no coercive power in the Magistrate to restraine them.[54]

FALLEN WISDOM AND NAKED TRUTH

Medieval representations of the relationship between heresy and illiteracy, religious knowledge and ignorance, whether employed negatively by the orthodox or positively by those accused of heterodoxy, continued to structure the religious polemic of seventeenth-century England. Scholars of the period have tended to repeat these polarized rhetorics without looking beyond the polemical representations to discover whether they are always accurate or applicable. In 1545 John Bale declared in *The Image of Both Churches* that after the seventh angel has blown his trumpet, 'the simple, poor weaklings, idiots and infants, shall utter the wisdom of God to the confusion of the great wise men and sage seniors of the world'. Yet Bale himself 'qualified as an impeccable Renaissance humanist'.[55] A century later the radical Independent and former Parliamentary army chaplain John Webster condemned the identification of formal education and ministerial office in a series of sermons published as *The Judgement Set* (1654), announcing that '[h]ere thou shalt not find Terms of Art, nor quirks of humane learning, Fallen Wisdome . . . but naked truth declaring itself through an earthern vessel in simplicity and plainesse of speech'. Yet on one page alone references are to be found to Lucian, Horace, and Cervantes. Webster claimed to have been educated at Cambridge; although there is no extant evidence to confirm this, his writings suggest he had a considerable degree of learning. In *Academiarum Examen* (1654), a tract much discussed by students of intellectual history, Webster decried the scholastic and humanist dominance of the university curriculum and urged that the conventional course in rhetoric, logic, and the ancient languages be replaced by schemes for the empirical investigation of nature based on a fusion of Baconian, Neoplatonic, and alchemical principles. Webster was dismissed as a 'credulous Fanatick' and one of the 'vulgar Levellers' by John Wilkins (Warden

---

[54] Featley, *The Dippers Dipt*, 175–6.
[55] Paul Christianson, *Reformers and Babylon: English Apocalyptic Visions from the Reformation to the Eve of the Civil War* (Toronto, 1978), 19, 14.

of Wadham College, Oxford, from 1648) and Seth Ward (Savilian Professor of Astronomy at Oxford from 1649) but he persistently (and much more ostentatiously than Wilkins or Ward) displays his learning. Webster's complaint is replete with references to classical and patristic texts and peppered with Latin quotations.[56]

As we have seen in Chapter 1, the representation of the religious radical as *illitteratus* in seventeenth-century England was by no means a purely polemical fabrication. However, we need to recognize that early modern commentators reflexively invoked this enduring cultural stereotype in seeking to condemn and discredit anyone who expressed views deemed heretical. The most celebrated writer who fell victim to this process of stigmatization was John Milton. *The Doctrine and Discipline of Divorce*, initially published anonymously in 1643, was received by the opponents of religious toleration as yet another instance of the heresy and libertinism abroad in England. Edwards demanded that Milton's tract be publicly burnt; Featley referred to it as 'a Tractate of Divorce, in which the bonds of matrimony are set loose to inordinate lust', naming it as one of the recent books 'tending to carnall liberty, Familisme' and disseminating 'most damnable doctrines'.[57] Milton, who had proudly declared in *The Reason of Church Government* (1642) that his poems had been received with rare acclaim in Italy during his grand tour, had been reinvented as a libertine tub orator, as sectarian *illitteratus*. His response seems to have been twofold. In *Areopagitica* he reversed the pejorative categories and imagery of the Presbyterian heresiographers:

There be who perpetually complain of schisms and sects, and make it such a calamity that any man dissents from their maxims. 'Tis their own pride and ignorance which causes the disturbing, who neither will hear with meekness, nor can convince, yet all must be supprest which is not found in their *Syntagma*. They are the troublers, they are the dividers of unity, who neglect and permit not others to unite those dissever'd peeces which are yet wanting to the body of Truth.

Milton turns the argument of schism back on the Presbyterians. This rhetorical strategy is further evident in the oft-quoted passage in which he develops a scriptural text previously used to justify religious conformity (1 Kings 6: 7) into a vision of 'the men cry'd against for schismaticks and

---

[56] John Webster, *Academiarum Examen* (1654), 55–6; [Seth Ward and John Wilkins], *Vindiciae Academiarum* (Oxford, 1654), 5–6, both repr. in A. G. Debus (ed.), *Science and Education in the Seventeenth Century: The Webster–Ward Debate* (New York, 1970). For a recent discussion of the intellectual and cultural significance of Webster's attack on the university curriculum see R. W. F. Kroll, *The Material Word: Literate Culture in the Restoration and Early Eighteenth Century* (Baltimore, Md., 1991), 194–201.

[57] Edwards, *Gangraena*, i. 34; Featley, *The Dippers Dipt*, sig. B2ᵛ.

sectaries' constructing Solomon's Temple of the Lord in revolutionary England. Such 'spirituall architecture' requires that 'there must be many schisms and many dissensions made in the quarry and in the timber, ere the house of God can be built'.[58]

In the midst of his powerful defence of those called sectaries, Milton elides images of the citizens of London as both manual workers and scholars. He envisages them 'sitting by their studious lamps, musing, searching, revolving new notions and ideas . . . fast reading, trying all things'. Yet they are also 'wise and faithful labourers' tilling 'a towardly and pregnant soile', 'fashion[ing] out the plates and instruments of arm'd Justice', 'squaring the marble', and 'hewing the cedars' of the Temple of the Lord. As Michael Wilding has put it, here 'the physical labours of the common people are . . . represented as dignified, noble, beautiful'. More than this, though, Milton represents the downwards dissemination of texts as the means of completing the English Reformation. The Ovidian image of books as 'those fabulous Dragons teeth [which] being sown up and down, may chance to spring up armed men' identifies the advancement of knowledge with the Protestant militancy of the earthy, labouring classes, wresting the image from its traditional pejorative associations with peasant revolt. We might also recall that Daniel Featley (after *Areopagitica* had been published) condemned the transformation of mechanics into ministers as a monstrous Ovidian metamorphosis.[59] In *Areopagitica* Milton appropriates the stereotype of the sectarian as 'illiterate mechanick' and turns it upside down to valorize the apocalyptic progress of artisanal scholarship.

On the other hand, it has been persuasively argued that Milton reacted to his designation as a 'sectarie' by vigorously asserting his respectability as a man of learning and sound Protestant principle. He added his name to the second edition of *The Doctrine and Discipline of Divorce* of 1644, addressing it to Parliament and distancing himself from accusations of libertinism by increasing the degree of imagery denigrating the

[58] *CPWM*, ii. 554–5, 555 n. 244. Milton's reversal of imagery associated with arguments for religious uniformity is indicated by the description of Thomas Edwards's objectives in William Walwyn's *A Parable or Consultation of Physitians Upon Master Edwards* (1646), in *WWW*, 249: 'the building of God's owne house, sweeping out of heretics and schismaticks, stopping the mouthes of illiterate mechanick preachers, and beautifying this holy building, with the glorious ornament of uniformity, the Mother of Peace and all blessed things'.

[59] *CPWM*, ii. 492; Michael Wilding, 'Milton's *Areopagitica*: Liberty for the Sects', in T. N. Corns (ed.), *The Literature of Controversy* (London, 1987), 7–38 (17). On royalist use of Ovid's story of Cadmus to depict the Parliamentarian cause as a peasant revolt, see Nigel Smith, *Literature and Revolution in England, 1640–1660* (New Haven, Conn., and London, 1994; paperback edn. 1997), 45, 101.

physicality of sex. In *Colasterion* (1645), a reply to a specific critique of his views on divorce, Milton transfers the characteristic anti-heretical themes of lowly birth, educational inadequacy, and sexual promiscuity on to his anonymous critic.[60] Milton had appealed to the tradition of confessional polemical history in *Areopagitica,* citing the examples of true witnesses persecuted for heresy such as Wyclif; in *The Judgement of Martin Bucer* (1644) he appeals to the alternative version of Reformation history, translating and quoting at length the opinions of the magisterial reformers as proof of the orthodoxy of his views. Above all, the publication of the *Poems* of 1645, including letters paying tribute to his scholarship and verses in Italian, Latin, Greek, and Hebrew, emphatically asserts his status as *litteratus* and, indeed, his membership of England's literati. The seemingly conflicting responses of Milton to his new-found public image as a sectarian tub preacher perhaps illustrate Christopher Hill's argument that Milton's attraction to the radical ideas of the 'third culture' was finally restricted by his 'middle-class and academic upbringing and outlook'. As an 'elitist Puritan scholar', he preferred to appeal 'to the conscience of the educated elite whom he knew and respected' and grew increasingly contemptuous of the capacities of the common people.[61]

Both Milton's sense of his unjust treatment at the hands of the heresiographers and his distaste for the popular misinterpretation of his ideas are apparent in his sonnets of 1646, 'On the Detraction Which Followed Upon My Writing Certain Treatises' and 'On the New Forcers of Conscience Under the Long Parliament'. In the former Milton laments having exposed his opinions on divorce to those who lack the intellectual refinement to understand them, anticipating his expression of regret in the *Defensio Secunda* (1654) that he had not published *The Doctrine and Discipline of Divorce* in Latin:

> I did but prompt the age to quit their clogs
> By the known rules of ancient liberty,
> When straight a barbarous noise environs me
> Of owls and cuckoos, asses, apes and dogs.
> As when those hinds that were transformed into frogs
> Railed at Latona's twin-born progeny
> Which after held the sun and moon in fee.
> But this is got by casting pearl to hogs;
> That bawl for freedom in their senseless mood,

---

[60] Thomas N. Corns, 'Milton's Quest for Respectability', *Modern Language Review,* 77 (1982), 769–79.

[61] Hill, *Milton and the English Revolution,* 160, 248–9.

> And still revolt when truth would set them free.
> License they mean when they cry liberty.

This time the Ovidian reference recalls Featley's invocation of the *Metamorphoses* in its negative class connotations. Milton refers to the episode in which a group of foul-mouthed peasants are transformed into frogs for muddying the pool at which the twins of Leto, Apollo and Diana, sought to drink. In the latter sonnet Milton ponders his reinvention as sectarian *illitteratus*:

> Men whose life, learning, faith and pure intent
> Would have been held high in esteem with Paul
> Must now be named and printed heretics
> By shallow Edwards and Scotch What-d'ye-call.[62]

Milton's association of the charge of heresy with the neglect of his learning reveals his anxiety to disassociate himself from the pervasive stereotype of the heretic as ignoramus. The following chapters will explore the intricacy with which radical writers of the 1640s and 1650s at once appropriate and undermine this stereotype as an aspect of their general subversion of the rhetoric of orthodoxy, demonstrating in the process how more extreme expressions of the radical imagination could transcend Milton's defensiveness.

---

[62] *CPWM*, iv. 610; Milton, *Complete Shorter Poems*, ed. John Carey (Harlow, 1971; 8th repr. 1992), 293 ll. 8–11, 295 ll. 9–12; Ovid, *Metamorphoses*, trans. Mary Innes (Harmondsworth, 1955), vi. 317–81.

3

Of Language and Flesh: Power, Pedagogy, and the Intellectual Origins of Leveller Ideas

LATIN DRAMA AND LEVELLER IDEAS: RICHARD OVERTON

Thomas Edwards has recently been awarded the title of 'first discoverer of the Levellers'. The 'prime targets' of the third part of *Gangraena* were 'the men who were later to be recognized as the leaders of the Leveller party'—John Lilburne, William Walwyn, and Richard Overton—and his summary of their constitutional radicalism anticipates fairly accurately the contents of the first *Agreement of the People* (3 November 1647). This document is 'the first proposal in history for a written constitution based on inalienable natural rights'.[1] By attacking the political theories of the future Leveller leaders within the genre of the heresiography, Edwards explicitly linked political radicalism with religious heterodoxy. Lilburne, Walwyn, and Overton had a history of religious activism and involvement in separatist congregations: the three men appear in the first and second parts of *Gangraena* as prominent heresiarchs as well as in the third part as political radicals or 'civil heretics'. Most scholars have concurred with Edwards's connection between radical religious belief and Leveller ideas, even if they cannot agree over the nature and importance of that connection.[2] The emergence of Leveller political principles was for Edwards a stark demonstration of his argument that the failure to suppress heresy and establish a Presbyterian Church government would inexorably lead to popular revolt, the abolition of private property, and the collapse of the legal, political, and social order: '[having] declared against monarchy and aristocracy, and for democracy: they have

---

[1] David Wootton, 'Leveller Democracy and the Puritan Revolution', 418–19.

[2] For a summary of scholarly positions see Wootton, 'Leveller Democracy', 435–8. The most detailed study of the links between the emergence of the Levellers and the sectarian activity of 1640s London remains Tolmie, *The Triumph of the Saints*. See also Keith Lindley, *Popular Politics and Religion in the English Civil War* (London, 1997).

expressed themselves in such a manner concerning that that they make it no other than an anarchy, making all alike, confounding of all ranks and orders, reducing all to Adam's time and condition and devolving all power upon the state universal and the promiscuous multitude'. The egalitarian politics of men such as Lilburne, Walwyn, and Overton were a terrible confirmation of the anarchic consequences of allowing 'illiterate Mechanick persons' to engage openly in religious speculation.[3] We have explored in the previous chapters the ironic convergence of opinion between the contemporary enemies of the radicals and their latter-day scholarly friends, and there has been a tendency amongst those who see the Levellers as the forbears of modern ideals of popular democracy to 'romanticize and sentimentalize' the lowly social and cultural backgrounds of their leaders. Yet Lilburne, son of a Durham gentleman, was from a wealthier background than that arch anti-democrat Thomas Hobbes, son of a Wiltshire parson.[4] In fact the interaction between elite and popular in the radical culture of the period is exemplified by the Leveller leadership, who were

on the lower fringes of the social and educational elite, with enough in common with the poorer classes and small businessmen to act as their spokesmen, but at the same time with the social and educational confidence which would make them potential leaders. These were men who had both worn leather or woollen aprons and sat at school desks. Perhaps half of them could read Latin and half could not, half were the sons of gentlemen and half were not. In this respect they straddled the major social and educational divides of the nation.[5]

Some of the ideologists of the Leveller movement thus had experience of and access to elite cultural traditions. In his recent argument for the neglected influence of classical republicanism on Leveller ideas, Samuel Glover foregrounds the availability of translations on the London book market. At the same time he observes that the Leveller theorists and spokesmen were 'comparatively highly educated men in an era when being well-educated was synonymous with having an understanding of classical rhetoric and republican history'.[6]

Richard Overton's pre-Leveller text *Mans Mortalitie* (1643/4) exemplifies this point.[7] Overton argues in *Mans Mortalitie* for the indivisibility of

---

[3] Edwards, *Gangraena*, i. sig. A5ᵛ, 33–4; iii. preface.

[4] Thomas N. Corns, *Uncloistered Virtue: English Political Literature, 1640–1660* (Oxford, 1992), 132; Richard Tuck, *Philosophy and Government 1572–1651* (Cambridge, 1993), 2–3.

[5] Wootton, 'Leveller Democracy', 413.

[6] S. D. Glover, 'The Putney Debates: Popular Versus Elitist Republicanism', *Past and Present*, 164 (1999), 47–80 (59).

[7] The first edition of *Mans Mortalitie* is dated 1643 on the title page; however, Thomason

flesh and spirit and rejects the orthodox Christian belief in the existence of a soul that survives the death of the body. He seeks to prove, as his title page succinctly puts, 'both Theologically and Philosophically, that whole Man (as a *rationall Creature*) is a Compound wholly mortall, contrary to that common distinction of *Soule* and *Body*'.[8] In the course of his argument Overton makes more than two dozen references to classical sources and supplies a sophisticated account of how Platonic dualism has been grafted on to Judaeo-Christian doctrine to produce the pernicious fiction of the immortal soul, which he argues has no basis in either Scripture or natural reason. It was long thought that Overton was a 'self-educated printer' with a sectarian past stretching back to the Jacobean period: his confession of faith for admission to a Mennonite congregation in Amsterdam was presumed to have been submitted around 1615 because it was discovered with other documents of that date.[9] While our knowledge of Overton's origins remains sketchy, it now seems clear that he was in fact the Richard Overton who matriculated at Queens' College, Cambridge, in 1631 (as a sizar, indicating he was not from a wealthy background). He was probably about fifteen or sixteen at the time. Marie Gimelfarb-Brack has persuasively argued that his Baptist confession of faith—which is in Latin—actually dates from 1639–43; the lack of anti-Presbyterian sentiment or heterodox religious belief in Overton's writings before *Mans Mortalitie* points to the later date of 1643.[10] So, despite his frequent appearances in *Gangraena* and other heresiographical writing of the 1640s, Overton does not in fact fit the polemical stereotype of the heretic as *illitteratus*.

Reading the rhetorical strategies of *Mans Mortalitie* through Overton's intellectual biography will allow us to draw some conclusions about the relationship between Levellerism and humanist pedagogy which will complement and complicate Glover's claims about the influence of

dates his copy 19 January 1643/4, so the date of publication (new style) could be January 1644. Thomason crossed out 'Amsterdam' as the place of publication and wrote in 'London'. Overton controlled, with his fellow General Baptist Nicholas Tew, a secret press in Coleman Street in London around this period and most likely printed the first edition himself; see Perez Zagorin, 'The Authorship of *Mans Mortalitie*', *The Library*, 5th ser., 5 (1950), 179–83; Tolmie, *The Triumph of the Saints*, 151–3.

    [8] *Mans Mortalitie* (1643), ed. Harold Fisch (Liverpool, 1968), 3. All references hereafter are to this edition.

    [9] Norman T. Burns, *Christian Mortalism from Tyndale to Milton* (Camb., Mass., 1972), 1; Champlin Burrage, *The Early English Dissenters*, 2 vols. (Cambridge, 1912), i. 250, ii. 216–18.

    [10] Marie Gimelfarb-Brack, *Liberté, egalité, fraternité, justice! La vie et l'oeuvre de Richard Overton, niveleur* (Berne, 1979), 4–6, 86–90; B. J. Gibbons, 'Richard Overton and the Secularism of the Interregnum Radicals', *The Seventeenth Century*, 10 (1995), 63–75 (64–5).

humanism on Leveller thought. Ann Hughes has recently argued that it is less fruitful to read Leveller literature for 'coherent abstract policies' on issues such as the parliamentary franchise than to reconstruct the 'identity and agency offered to its readers'. Leveller texts can thus be treated as 'a means by which a new political movement was imagined or called into being, rather than as a straightforward reflection or presentation of pre-existing demands or interests'.[11] The pre-Leveller text *Mans Mortalitie* develops an intellectual framework in which Leveller ideology itself could be 'imagined or called into being': Overton's rejection of the humanist educational system in which he had himself been trained combines with his heretical conception of the body to offer 'identity and agency' to readers excluded from the structures of knowledge and power in seventeenth-century England.

Overton's career as an oppositional political writer and advocate of deregulated religion spans the 1640s. In the early years of the decade he issued a string of satirical pamphlets against Laud and the bishops composed in dramatic or semi-dramatic form. In the mid-1640s he resurrected the indecorous satirical style of the Elizabethan Marprelate tracts, under the pseudonym of 'Martin Marpriest', to attack the intolerance of the Presbyterian clergy. In the later 1640s he was involved in the composition of most of the Leveller manifestos and in issuing defiant protests against his persecution and that of other Leveller leaders by Parliament and later Cromwell. While a less directly polemical and more theologically speculative text than Overton's other writings, *Mans Mortalitie* is, as we shall see, a deeply political work in an age when religious speculation was always politically significant.[12] The radical implications of Overton's abolition of the soul are measured by the reaction of authority and orthodoxy: *Mans Mortalitie* provoked several lengthy printed rebuttals and was named by heresiographers, both Presbyterian and Anglican, as an extreme example of the irreligion rife in England in the absence of a national Church discipline. It was cited, alongside Milton's writings on divorce, when in August 1644 Parliament made moves to suppress recent heretical books under the Licensing Act of the previous year.[13] Indeed *Mans Mortalitie* has been most often discussed

[11] Ann Hughes, 'Gender and Politics in Leveller Literature', in Susan D. Amussen and Mark A. Kishlansky (eds.), *Political Culture and Cultural Politics in Early Modern England* (Manchester, 1995), 165.

[12] Harold Fisch states in the introduction to his edition of the text that it 'lacks any political aim or context' and bears a 'somewhat eccentric relation to the rest of [Overton's] literary output'; *Mans Mortalitie*, p. xvi.

[13] Burns, *Christian Mortalism from Tyndale to Milton*, 159–69; *Commons Journal*, 26 August 1644.

in terms of its possible influence on the development of Milton's monism and mortalism as imaginatively represented in *Paradise Lost* and bluntly stated in the *De Doctrina Christiana*. It has even been suggested that Milton might have had a hand in the revised version of Overton's text published under the title *Man Wholly Mortal* in 1655.[14] While there is no firm evidence to support such a claim, it seems reasonable to suppose that Milton would have looked at *Mans Mortalitie* when it first appeared, given both his angry incredulity at the similarly hostile reception of his divorce tracts and the incipient monism evident in those tracts.[15] However, the more immediate relationship between the philosophical and theological principles espoused by Overton in *Mans Mortalitie* and the formation of Leveller ideology in the mid-1640s, in which Overton played a leading role, has received comparatively little attention.[16]

The dramatic form of many of Overton's polemical pamphlets combined with their frequent references to the theatre and echoes of specific plays (in particular Shakespeare) led Margot Heinemann in her essay on 'Popular Drama and Leveller Style' to argue that Overton had been an actor or playwright, or both, in London in the 1630s.[17] One piece of evidence in her persuasive case for Overton's theatrical career is his

[14] See Dennis Saurat, *Milton: Man and Thinker* (1925; 2nd edn. 1946), 279; Saurat's claims for Milton's involvement in *Man Wholly Mortal* were refuted by George Williamson in 'Milton and the Mortalist Heresy', *Studies in Philology*, 32 (1935), 553–79, repr. in his *Seventeenth Century Contexts* (London, 1963). The most detailed discussion to date of the mortalist heresy in early modern England, which compares the positions held by Overton, Milton, and Hobbes, is Burns, *Christian Mortalism from Tyndale to Milton*. Burns, following the now discredited biography of Overton as formally uneducated printer, tends to underestimate Overton's intellectual range.

[15] On the monistic elements in the divorce tracts see Stephen Fallon, 'The Metaphysics of Milton's Divorce Tracts' in David Loewenstein and James Grantham Turner (eds.), *Politics, Poetics and Hermeneutics in Milton's Prose* (Cambridge, 1990), 69–83.

[16] There has been no concerted development of William Haller's brief discussion of this relationship in *Liberty and Reformation in the Puritan Revolution* (New York, 1955), 176–8. The comments of Howard Shaw are representative: 'What is important about [*Mans Mortalitie*] is not so much its content as the adventurous rationalism of its thought' (*The Levellers* (1968; 2nd edn. 1971), 32). See now, however, Erica Fudge's highly original discussion of the relationship between Overton's conceptions of the human and the animal in *Mans Mortalitie* and Leveller ideas about the individual and society (*Perceiving Animals: Humans and Beasts in Early Modern English Culture* (Hampshire, 2000), 143–70).

[17] Margot Heinemann, 'Popular Drama and Leveller Style—Richard Overton and John Harris', in Maurice Cornforth (ed.), *Rebels and Their Causes: Essays in Honour of A. L. Morton* (London, 1978), 69–92. Her argument here is largely repeated in the epilogue to *Puritanism and Theatre: Thomas Middleton and Oppositional Drama under the Early Stuarts* (Cambridge, 1980). For further discussion of the dramatic style of Overton's political satire see Nigel Smith, 'Richard Overton's Marpriest Tracts: Towards a History of Leveller Style', in T. N. Corns (ed.), *The Literature of Controversy: Polemical Strategy from Milton to Junius* (London, 1987), 39–66.

presence in the list of actors for the lost Latin play *Versipellis*, first staged at Queens' College, Cambridge, in 1631–2 and written by Thomas Pestell, chaplain to the Earl of Essex. Despite the sharp decline in the production of university drama in the 1630s, Queens' was 'especially active' at this time and a comedy house was constructed at the college in the opening years of the decade.[18] Developing Heinemann's speculation about Overton's involvement in dramatic circles in Caroline Cambridge, we might see a hint of his future religious politics in his choice of college production. While Overton appears in the cast list for *Versipellis* by Pestell, who moved in Puritan gentry circles and was fined by Laud's High Commission in 1633, he is missing from the cast of another play performed at Queens' that academic year, *The Rival Friends*, composed by Peter Hausted for a visit by Charles and Henrietta Maria. While most of the players in *Versipellis* also appeared in *The Rival Friends*, Overton seems to have chosen not to act in a play that was written by a prominent Laudian and contains a good deal of anti-Puritan and anti-sectarian satire. Hausted was to be attacked by an angry mob at the university church in 1634 for preaching too vigorously against nonconformity; he is probably best known for his alleged collaboration with the King in writing *Ad populum: Or, a Lecture to the People* (1644), a vituperative anti-Parliamentarian poem.[19]

Further evidence of Overton's involvement in Cambridge drama is to be found in *Mans Mortalitie*, where there is a reference (missed by Heinemann) to the Latin comedy *Pedantius*, first performed at Trinity College, Cambridge, in 1581. Probably written by Edward Forset, a Fellow of Trinity, it was enduringly popular at Cambridge and was finally published in 1631, the year in which Overton matriculated. The character of Pedantius is a humanist tutor, described as *paedagogus*, whose mastery of rhetorical *copia* within the gendered boundaries of the classroom is comically revealed to be useless when faced with the concrete external realities of debt and failure with women (the character is a caricature of Gabriel Harvey, and consequently the play was a particular favourite of Harvey's *bête noire* Thomas Nashe).[20] The other main comic character in the play is Dromodotus, a scholastic logician who is described as *philosophus* but who constantly inserts meaningless or absurd grammatical

[18] G. C. Moore-Smith, *College Plays Performed in the University of Cambridge* (Cambridge, 1923), 10.

[19] Moore-Smith, *College Plays Performed in the University of Cambridge*, 7, 9, 85, 109–10; F. S. Boas, 'University Plays', in Sir A. Ward and A. R. Waller (eds.), *The Cambridge History of English Literature, vi. The Drama to 1642, Part Two* (Cambridge, 1910; repr. 1969), 324.

[20] Boas, 'University Plays', 306.

and logical tags into his speech. In its caricature of academic types and parody of the university curriculum, *Pedantius* is a fairly typical example of Renaissance academic drama. Yet, as with many Elizabethan Latin plays, *Pedantius* seems to have been designed to educate its audience in humanist techniques as well as entertain them with parody of those techniques. According to the Oxford dramatist William Gager, plays were staged in the universities not only to 'recreate our selves' but 'to practyse owre owne style either in prose or verse . . . to embowlden owre yuthe; to trye their voyces, and confirme their memoryes'.[21] The published text of *Pedantius* draws attention to this fusion of parody and pedagogy by prefacing the play with a list of rhetorical tropes that the reader is presumably supposed to look out for in the dialogue.

Overton's reference to *Pedantius* comes after one of the most remarkable passages in *Mans Mortalitie*. While Overton believed in an ultimate resurrection at which all human beings would be raised bodily to face divine judgement, one of the consequences of his denial of the immortal soul is the abolition of heaven and hell as geographical locations where the soul is sent for punishment or reward after the death of the body: 'the present going of the *Soule* into *Heaven* or *Hell* is a meer *Fiction* . . . the *Resurrection* is the beginning of our *immortality,* and then Actuall *Condemnation* and *Salvation,* and not before' (3).[22] The provocatively festive vision of destruction and liberation projected in the prefatory poem, probably written by Overton himself, leaves us in no doubt as to why *Mans Mortalitie* elicited such outrage from orthodox Calvinists such as Thomas Edwards:

> The Hell-hatch'd Doctrine of th' Immortall Soule
> Discovered, makes the hungry Furies houle,
> And teare their snakey haire with grief appal'd,
> To see their Errour-leading Doctrine quail'd,
> *Hell* undermin'd, and *Purgatory* blowne
> Up in the aire, and all the spirits flowne,
> *Pluto* undone, thus forced for to yeeld
> The frightned *Soules* from the *Elizian Field.*

[21] Quoted in J. W. Binns, *Intellectual Culture in Elizabethan and Jacobean England: The Latin Writings of the Age* (Leeds, 1990), 121.

[22] Overton, like Milton, held the form of mortalism known as 'thnetopsychism'. In *Christian Mortalism from Tyndale to Milton* Burns rightly warns against the anachronistic identification of Overton's monism with either deism or secular materialism: see esp. 157–61. See also the forceful repudiation of the historiographical tendency to regard Overton's mortalism as really secular ideology wrapped up in religious terms in Gibbons, 'Richard Overton and the Secularism of the Interregnum Radicals', *passim.*

> And squallid *Charron* now may leave his Trade,
> To see *all Soules* made subject to the *spade*,
> And *Cerberus* his dismall fate deplore,
> To thinke that he shall scare the *Soules* no more.[23]

This poem is in fact derived from a speech in Marlowe's *Doctor Faustus* (first published 1604) in which Faustus defiantly responds to Mephastophilis' initial warning that his renunciation of Christ and the Scriptures has put his soul in danger of damnation:

> This word damnation terrifies not him,
> For he confounds hell with Elysium:
> His ghost be with the old philosophers.
> But leaving these vain trifles of men's souls,
> Tell me, what is that Lucifer thy lord?[24]

If Overton is indeed the author, the poem provides more evidence of his familiarity with the commercial theatre. The 'hungry Furies' who 'houle' at Overton's discovery of their '*Errour-leading Doctrine*' are presumably those Puritan ministers who obtain their authority and power from terrifying the people with hellfire sermons on the torments of damned souls. In his satirical pamphlets of the mid-1640s Overton repeatedly attacks the Presbyterian clergy for their false claims to superior spiritual knowledge and their self-aggrandizing manipulation of the fears of the ordinary people; in *The Araignement of Mr. Persecution* (1645) he mocks his 'Presbyterian Adversaries' for being 'so invective against [*Mans Mortalitie*] in their pulpits' in a desperate effort to 'maintaine their repute with the people' (20). Yet while the poem emphasizes Overton's destruction of hell, it also celebrates, if less triumphantly, his abolition of heaven ('the *Elizian Field*'). Overton insists that both heaven and hell will not come into being until the dissolution of creation at the general resurrection: 'they are but in *posse*, not in *esse* till the Resurrection' (36). References to the existence of heaven and hell in Scripture should thus be interpreted figuratively as descriptions of spiritual states or conditions in the created world, as 'expressions after the manner of men, to shew the gradation of condition betwixt the wicked and the righteous, the one the extreamest debasement, the other the extreamest exaltation, which could not be better figurated to sence, then by Heaven and Earth' (40).

---

[23] N. C., 'To his worthy friend the Author upon his Booke', in *Mans Mortalitie*, 5, ll. 1–12. Overton is fond of inserting poems in his texts that are clearly his own work but signed with different initials: see e.g. 'To his Friend the Author upon his Booke' by A. B. in *The Araignement of Mr. Persecution* (1645), sig. A3ᵛ, which has some stylistic similarities with the poem before *Mans Mortalitie*.

[24] *Dr Faustus: The A-Text*, ed. Roma Gill (2nd edn., London, 1989), iv. 58–62.

One of the questions that then arises from this denial of the literal existence of heaven is the location of the resurrected Christ. Overton's monistic understanding of the human body leads him to maintain that Christ's 'whole humanity (soul and body as 'tis called) suffered death' and then 'totall Resurrection'; consequently he must now inhabit a material location: 'Reason tels us that [Christ] must be within the compasse of the Creation, for there is no *beyond*, without it *place* or *being* is impossible . . . every place must be materiall, for *non datur vacuum*, and every matter must imply creation, else it could not be: therefore he is within the Creation' (41, 47, 48). Overton concludes that Christ must have ascended to the sun, which he describes in a long and eloquent passage as 'the Epitome of God's power, conveyour of life, growth, strength, and being to every Creature' (49). Overton's conception of the sun as the material headquarters of Christ derives from his definition of God as 'the true light which lighteneth the world, and every one that commeth therein, and this glory chiefly in the Sun, the Moderatour and upholder of the whole Creation. Therefore, there must Christ be, or else he sitteth not at the *right hand of God* in all things' (53). The sun is 'now the Author of motion, generation, and subsistence' on earth, but it is merely a reflection of the light which is God's '*face*, or true light, which by mortality cannot be seen' and will not be revealed until the apocalypse, when it will dissolve creation in a 'consuming fire' (51, 53). Christ thus resides in the sun awaiting the '*restitution of all things, Act. 3. 21*' (48). The punning identification of the risen Son of God with the rising sun is of course a common one in early modern English literature. It is rather more startling to claim that the Son is actually in the sun. Having earlier ridiculed those who waste their time speculating about whether hell is located in the earth, the sea, or the sky ('some have feigned it in *Mount Ætna*'), Overton concludes his meditation on Christ's ascension to the sun by comparing those theologians who pointlessly seek to locate the precise astronomical position of heaven to Dromodotus, the foolish and arrogant academic in *Pedantius* who tries to order all experience into the categories of syllogistic logic: 'I know no better ground they have for it, then such as *Dromodotus* the Philosopher in *Pedantius* had to prove there was Divels: *Sunt Antipodes*: Ergo *Dæmones. Sunt Cæli*: Ergo *Cælum Empyreum*' (39, 54). Overton adds his own parody but the quotation is accurate, indicating either that he possessed the 1631 edition of *Pedantius* or that he had acted in a performance of the play, perhaps in the role of Dromodotus, while at Cambridge.[25]

<hr>

[25] See [Edward Forset], *Pedantius* (1631), 11–12.

To expand on this unexpected allusion to *Pedantius* with which Overton concludes his discussion of Christ's habitation of the sun we first need to consider both the theological principles that had attracted him to sectarian religion earlier in 1643 and the philosophical and political implications of his monistic view of the body. According to General Baptist doctrine, Christ's sacrifice has made redemption available to all human beings and damnation is the result of individual choice and action in this life. This doctrine of general redemption placed 'heavy emphasis upon individual responsibility in the matter of salvation, [and] appealed to those who were appalled by the extreme antinomian consequences of the Calvinist doctrine of double predestination'.[26] Overton is quite clear on this: 'None can be condemned into Hell, but such as are actually guilty of refusing of *Christ* because immortality or the *Resurrection* cannot be by Propagation or succession, as mortallity from Adam to his Issue, and so the Child, though temporally, yet shall it not eternally be punished for his Father's sinne, but his Condemnation shall be of himself (5)'. David Wootton has argued that the Levellers' egalitarian, democratic principles did not derive from the theological doctrine of free grace, because this doctrine did not necessarily involve a belief in either universal salvation or free will; but clearly Overton takes the position in *Mans Mortalitie* that all are potentially saved and that every individual has been granted the freedom to determine their own fate.[27]

Overton's insistence on the spiritualization of flesh also provides the philosophical grounds for a radically activist and egalitarian politics. Stephen Fallon and John Rogers have recently shown how the attribution of spiritual energy to bodily matter could validate the natural integrity, agency, and self-determining capacity of the individual. A monistic representation of the body could thus provide an ontological justification of the exercise of free will against the arbitrary determinism of both Calvinist theology and Hobbesian mechanist philosophy, which stripped human beings of agency and made them the helpless subjects of irresistible external forces. By extension to the spheres of political and religious organization, monistic materialism, or 'vitalism', offered an alternative to traditional theories of hierarchy and absolutism as the natural, divinely ordained way of things and could thus function as a philosophical analogue for ideas of popular sovereignty and liberty of conscience: 'Vitalism, in short, banishing the centralizing logics of Calvinism and mechanism alike, secured into the fabric of the physical

---

[26] Tolmie, *The Triumph of the Saints*, 73.
[27] 'Leveller Democracy and the Puritan Revolution', 437–8.

world a general scheme of individual agency and decentralized organization that we can identify as protoliberalism'.[28] We cannot be sure, as
Norman Burns points out, that Overton anticipated Milton's vitalist
cosmology in *Paradise Lost* and 'extended his monistic view [of man] to
the rest of the universe'; however, Overton's insistence that '*place* or *being*
is impossible' outside matter suggests that he does not conceive of a
separate spiritual realm anywhere in the creation, and perhaps indicates
an emergent notion of the corporeality of God.[29] Fallon makes no
reference to Overton, and Rogers only mentions *Mans Mortalitie* in passing in a footnote, referring to Overton as 'one of the century's earliest
monistic radicals'. However, their arguments about the radical political
and religious ramifications of monistic materialism are exemplified by
Overton's leading role in the development of Leveller ideology. 'For the
vitalist radical', writes Rogers, 'the flesh is heir to its own source of power
and agency'; and his point is illustrated by Overton's declaration of
natural rights in *An Arrow Against All Tyrants and Tyranny* (1646): 'To
every Individuall in nature is given an individuall property by nature, not
to be invaded or usurped by any . . . [f]or by naturall birth all men are
equally and alike borne to like propriety, liberty and freedome' (3).[30]

Overton's monistic philosophy and sectarian theology thus complement each other: the former redeems flesh from Calvinist notions of
depravity and impotence, while the latter stresses the universal availability of salvation and the importance of individual agency. We can now
place Overton's speculation about the divinity of sunlight in *Mans
Mortalitie* in the wider context of his anti-Calvinist theology and heterodox ideas about the relationship between man, nature, and the divine.
Just as the sun shines over all of the world and all creatures can see (and
feel) the power of God in the light of the sun, which rises daily to dispel
darkness and sustain life, so all have been granted the opportunity to
escape hell and receive salvation through the death and rising of the Son
of God. Academic efforts to work out the exact location of Christ and
heaven in the stars are laughably futile because Christ is in the sun and the
light of the sun is everywhere and visible to everyone. The reference to
Pedantius emphasizes Overton's universalism—or rather potential universalism, given the capacity of the individual to bring about their own
'condemnation'. We can compare the comments of the horticultural

---

[28] Stephen Fallon, *Milton among the Philosophers: Poetry and Materialism in Seventeenth
Century England* (Ithaca, NY, 1991), 96–9; John Rogers, *The Matter of Revolution: Science,
Poetry, and Politics in the Age of Milton* (Ithaca, NY, 1996; paperback edn. 1998), 1–16 (12).

[29] *Christian Mortalism from Tyndale to Milton*, 160 n. 16.

[30] Rogers, *The Matter of Revolution*, 37–8 n. 73.

reformer John Beale, who despite being an Anglican cleric held distinctly heretical ideas about the nature of the universe and the presence of Spirit in creation. In a letter to Samuel Hartlib in 1660 in which he questions the premisses of Cartesian mechanism Beale asserts that 'to the humble & obedient children of God' divine truths are 'more cleare . . . than the light of the Sun can bee, & hath as little neede of demonstration'.[31] For Beale, sunlight provides a fitting natural analogy for the clarity and universality of divine truth, which needs no academic or scientific explication. For Overton, sunlight is more than an analogy for the divine—it is the reflected face of God.

The learned search for the location of the Son in a celestial '*Cœlum Empyreum*' is just as futile for Overton as the obsessive Calvinist scrutinizing of the soul to locate evidence of salvation—of the presence of Christ within—given that every individual has been freely granted grace. The Puritan imperative to anatomize the soul in its relation to the corrupt external world of matter and the body is rendered irrelevant by both Overton's monism and his General Baptist theology, and he literalizes the process of spiritual self-dissection to expose the bizarre logic of orthodox dualistic metaphysics:

Now seeing all this while we have had to do with this immortall Soul, we cannot find, or the *Soularies* tell us what it is, such likewise is its residence; for if we ask, where it is? They *flap us i'th mouth* with a *Ridle, tota in toto,* & *tota in qualibet parte,* the whole in the whole, and the whole in every part: that is, the whole immortall Soul in the whole body, and the whole Soul wholly in every part of the body . . . and so, were a man minced into *Atomes,* cut into innumerable bits, then would be so many innumerable whole Souls, else could it not be wholly in every part.

> *Monstrum horrendum, ingens; cui quot sunt*
> *Corpore crines,*
> *Tot vigiles* Animæ *supter, mirabile dictu!*
> And thus the *Ridle* is unfolded. (72)

As with the allusion to Dromodotus, the foolish philosopher who can only perceive the world within the formal limits of the syllogism, Overton here uses the language of scholastic logic to ridicule academic speculation about the nature of the soul. Just as he parodies the academic play *Pedantius* to mock the theologians in their own institutional language of learning, on this occasion he comically rewrites Virgil's description of Fame in the *Aeneid*—hinting, perhaps, that the real objective of these

---

[31] Quoted in Michael Leslie, 'The Spiritual Husbandry of John Beale', in Leslie and Timothy Raylor (eds.), *Culture and Cultivation in Early Modern England: Writing and the Land* (Leicester, 1992), 151–72 (159–60).

'Soularies' in their debates about man and the divine is not truth but reputation.[32]

The claim that Overton is using the reference to *Pedantius* to equate academic pretension with the dangerous errors of Calvinist theology may seem strained, but in fact he frequently employs the register of the academic curriculum to attack the Puritan clergy for their arrogance, intolerance, and corrupt elitism. In the best of his satirical play pamphlets, *The Araignement of Mr. Persecution* (1645), he describes how the spirit of Persecution has passed through the bodies of characters such as Mr Spanish Inquisition and Mr High Commission into 'the godly shape of a Presbyter'

and then Scholer like, as if it had been for a goodly fat Benefice, in the twinkling of an eye jumpt out of *Scotland* into *England*, and turn'd a reverend *Synodian*, disguis'd with a Sylogisticall pair of Britches (saving your presence) in *Bocardo*, and snatching a Rhetoricall Cassok he girt up his loynes with a Sophisticall Girdle, and ran into the wildernesse of *Tropes* and *Figures*, and there they had lost them, had it not been for the *Spirits Teaching*, by whose direction they trac'd him through the various windings, subtile by-Pathes, secret tracts, and cunning Meanders the evening wolves, wild Boares and Beasts of the Forrest in the briery thickets of Rhetoricall Glosses, Sophistications and scholastick Interpretations had made . . . (1–2)

The anti-Platonist Overton here puts the concept of metempsychosis to satirical use. 'Bocardo' was both the name of a prison in the old North Gate of Oxford and a term for a tricky stage (the third mood in the third figure) of a syllogism. Punning on 'bocasin', a form of lining cloth, Overton associates the Presbyterians' concealment of their true motives under the disguise of sophistical logic and rhetoric with their deceitful arguments for the persecution of formally uneducated lay preachers.[33] The image of the Presbyterian clergy as 'wild Boares and Beasts of the Forest' alludes to Psalm 80: 13, where the wild boar devours the vineyard of Israel. Milton applies this image to the prelates in *Of Reformation* (1641): 'these wild Boares that have broke into thy Vineyard, and left the print of their polluting hoofs on the Soules of thy Servants'.[34] However, Overton's allusion is more complex in that he reverses expectation by having the wildly destructive Presbyterian boar belong to the carefully

[32] See the *Aeneid*, 4.181: 'Monstrum horrendum, ingens, cui quot sunt corpore plumae, | Tot vigiles oculi subter, mirabile dictu'. In Overton's parody this becomes: 'Ominous, awful, vast; for every hair on the body is a waking soul beneath, wonderful to tell'.

[33] On 'Bocardo' see the *OED*.

[34] *CPWM*, i. 614. I am most grateful to Karen Edwards for showing me the draft entry on the boar for her forthcoming Milton bestiary.

ordered area of the sophistical thicket. In other words, it is the clerical imposition of 'Rhetoricall Glosses, Sophistications and scholastick Inter-pretations' on spiritual knowledge that has laid waste the garden planted by God. The voracious appetite of the boar is the greed of the clergy, satisfied by maintaining the false identification of spiritual authority with formal learning and ordination: in the same pamphlet a minister is 'newly *Metamorphosed* by a figure which we Rhetoricians call METONOMIA BENEFICII from *Episcopallity* to *Presbytery*' (16). The characters of Mr Persecution, Sir John Presbiter, and Mr Assembly-of-Divines are always appealing to their education and learning as evidence of their superior spiritual knowledge and authority. Sir John Presbyter's defence of Mr Persecution is conducted in the language of syllogistic logic and peppered with Latin tags, while it is on the grounds of both his educational attain-ments and clerical status that Mr Persecution pleads for mercy from Lord Parliament: 'My Lord, I am a Clergie Man, and beseech your Honour for the benefits of my Clergie: I have been of all the Universities of Christendom, taken all their Degrees, proceeded through all Ecclesiastical Orders and Functions, and my Lord, at present am under the Holy Order of Presbyterie' (19–21, 40).

Overton is ridiculing the Presbyterians in terms of the formal learning which they, like the bishops before them, invoked to distinguish a clerical elite from the laity. As we saw in Chapter 2, orthodox Calvinist clerics such as Thomas Edwards and Daniel Featley demanded the persecution and imprisonment of lay preachers on the grounds of their inability to expound Scripture in Latin and Greek. Formal education in logic, rhetoric, and the classical languages became a polemical tool in the clerical propaganda campaign against the sects. The emphasis of the Puritan clergy during the 1640s on Latin literacy as the qualification that excluded the laity from involvement in theological matters points towards the elitism of the humanist pedagogical system as it was struc-tured into a set of social relations. Walter J. Ong writes in his classic essay on 'Latin Language Study as a Renaissance Puberty Rite':

when Latin passed out of vernacular usage, a sharp distinction was set up in society between those who knew it and those who did not. The conditions for a 'marginal environment' were present . . . in helping to maintain the closed male environment the psychological role of Latin should not be underestimated. It was the language of those on the 'inside', and thus learning Latin at even an infra-university level was the first step toward initiation into the closed world . . .[35]

---

[35] Ong, 'Latin Language Study', in *Rhetoric, Romance and Technology: Studies in the Interaction of Expression and Culture* (Ithaca, NY, 1971), 113–41 (119, 121). On the fundamental

Thomas Edwards and other orthodox Puritans sought to maintain the 'closed male environment' of a clerical caste by erecting Latin education as a boundary; religious radicals such as Overton sought to break down the boundaries between clergy and laity and reconstitute what Overton describes as the 'arbitrary power' of Church authority according to a decentralized vision of religious self-determination and self-organization. The university play *Pedantius* is a product of the exclusive world of Latin education that Ong describes, performed by and for those who have been initiated into that closed male environment. At a rhetorical level, Overton's display of his knowledge of Latin and of the Latin-speaking world of academia undermines the accusation of the Puritan clergy that the radical must be, by definition, *illitteratus*. Moreover, Overton takes a Latin joke about the absurd application of syllogistic logic out of its original academic environment and relocates it in a heretical vernacular pamphlet that rejects the exclusive right of a university-educated clergy to pass authoritative judgement on religious matters. The effect of this relocation is to collapse hierarchies: it is no longer an *in-joke amongst* the academic community; rather it becomes a *satire on* the pride and pretension of that community and its claims to absolute knowledge.

Overton's reference to Cambridge drama in *Mans Mortalitie* begs comparison with Milton's bilious recollection in *An Apology against a Pamphlet* (1642) of witnessing ministers and future ministers disport themselves in student productions:

in the Colleges so many of the young divines, and those in next aptitude to Divinity have beene so oft upon the Stage writhing and unbuttoning their Clergie limmes to all the antick and dishonest gestures of Trinculo's, Buffons, and Bawds; prostituting the shame of that ministry which either they had, or were nigh having, to the eyes of Courtiers and Court-Ladies, with their Groomes and Madamoiselles. There while they acted, and overacted, among other younger scholars, I was a spectator; they thought themselves gallant men, and I thought them fools.[36]

Milton, who was still at Christ's College when Overton came up to Queens', combines his contempt for both the Anglican emphasis on ceremonial religion and the effeminate luxury of the Caroline court with an expression of Puritan distaste for the immorality of theatrical display.

conservatism of humanist pedagogy as it was manifest in institutional and social relationships see more recently Anthony Grafton and Lisa Jardine, *From Humanism to the Humanities: Education and the Liberal Arts in Fifteenth and Sixteenth Century Europe* (Cambridge, Mass., 1986), pp. xiii–xiv.

36 *CPWM*, i. 887.

The suggestion of grotesque sexual as well as dramatic performance in the image of the (cross-dressed?) student actors 'writhing and unbuttoning their Clergie limmes' associates Milton's attack on the closed male environment of Cambridge with the accusations of sodomy aimed at the monasteries by early English reformers such as John Bale.[37] While the passage emphasizes Milton's university background, he separates himself as disgusted spectator from the degenerate actions of his fellow students. Milton maintains that these dramatic activities demean both the intellectual pursuits of the scholar and the religious office of the cleric, and he wants his readers to be convinced in this passage that he himself would never have set foot on such an unreformed stage. Overton, on the other hand, flaunts his specific knowledge of university drama and quotes a line from one of the more popular Cambridge plays. The ex-actor Overton is not driven by any anti-theatrical prejudice or concern for the solemnity of clerical status but, like Milton, he invokes his educational experience to satirize the institutional connection between the universities and the clergy. Yet, while Milton is appalled by the lack of moral seriousness and intellectual application displayed by future ministers, Overton rejects the very notion of a separate clerical caste distinguished from the laity by the extent of their institutional education. Overton agrees, as we shall see, with his fellow future Leveller William Walwyn, who argued in 1644 that the clergy locate their spiritual authority in a training of 'seven yeares at least' in logic, rhetoric, and languages to 'keep all in a mystery, that they only may be the Oracles to dispense what, and how they please'.[38]

Overton's use of *Pedantius* allows us to make wider claims about the relationship between humanism and Leveller political theory. Overton's General Baptist faith placed, as we have seen, immense importance on the role of the individual in their own salvation. Immortality becomes wholly conditional upon the choices made in this life, a soteriological position that, as we have also seen, is in line with his monistic ascription of spiritual agency to flesh in the realm of natural philosophy. Consequently the role of education becomes central to salvation, for the individual makes the right and the rational choices through the accumulation of knowledge. As Erica Fudge has recently pointed out, Overton's abolition of the soul leads him to argue that the differences between humans and animals 'are not innate but created, are potential rather than actual . . . they have to be augmented by an external addition like

---

[37] On Bale see Alan Stewart, *Close Readers: Humanism and Sodomy in Early Modern England* (Princeton, NJ, 1997), 38–83.

[38] Walwyn, *The Compassionate Samaritane*, in *WWW*, 110.

education'.[39] For Overton, 'Humanity though glorifyed is but a Creature', just as angels are 'creatures as glorious as glorified humanity' (48). He believes that redemption and immortality are potential rewards that God has given human beings the freedom to lose, but he also considers 'full' humanity to be a potential state that depends upon nurture rather than nature: 'all mans Faculties, yea those of Reason, Consideration, Science &c. all that distinguish Man from a Beast, are augmented by Learning, Education &c. lessened by Negligence, Idlenesse &c.' (20).

We might draw a comparison of Overton's notion of a sliding scale of 'Creatureship', according to which the individual can both ascend to the level of fully human and descend to the level of beast, with the monist scale of matter outlined by Raphael in *Paradise Lost*, according to which substance is more or less spiritually refined depending on its distance from God.[40] It has recently been suggested that Raphael's scale of matter is a metaphysical expression of Milton's post-Restoration disillusion- ment with popular sovereignty. The stratification of nature according to spiritual purity thus measures Milton's movement during the 1650s away from 'a Leveller-influenced theory of the body politic whereby a commonwealth of rational men organize themselves' to an aristocratic republican vision of 'the political state as a rude multitude governed from above by a "rational" elite'.[41] At the same time, however, Raphael's hier- archical stratification is not solidified but flexible according to merit: matter in Milton's vitalist universe is possessed of the agency to move closer to God '[i]f not deprav'd from good' (v. 471). In his Leveller writings Overton goes beyond Milton in synthesizing an egalitarian and revolutionary politics with a monistic metaphysics. The people of England are denied their natural right and liberty to organize themselves by the tyrannical rule of political and clerical elites; they are 'deprav'd of good' not by their own actions or merit but by the oppressive apparatus of Church and State. Persecutory and elitist structures of power prevent the people from augmenting the faculties of 'Reason, Consideration, Science' that constitute humanness, so making impossible the achieve- ment of difference between man and beast. As Overton writes in *A Defiance Against All Arbitrary Usurpations* (1646):

The poore deceived people are even (in a manner) bestiallized in their under- standings, become so stupid, and grosly ignorant of themselves, and of their own

[39] Fudge, *Perceiving Animals*, 153.
[40] Milton, *Paradise Lost*, ed. Alastair Fowler (Harlow, 1971; 14th repr. 1991), v. 404–505.
[41] Rogers, *The Matter of Revolution*, 107, 111; see also Fallon, *Milton Among the Philosophers*, 109.

natural immunities, that they are even degenerated from being men, and (as it were) unman'd, not able to define themselves by birth or nature, more than what they have by wealth, stature or shape, and as bruits they'll live and die for want of knowledge, being void of the use of Reason for want of capacitie to discern, whereof, and how far God by nature hath made them free . . . (2)

Overton claims that the common people of England are prevented by the monopoly over knowledge maintained by ruling elites from exercising the rational capacity and freedom of will that God has granted to human nature. Denied the liberty to become properly human, they have become 'bestiallized in their understandings'. Overton's argument has some of its roots in traditional Reformation polemic. The Calvinist Francis Rous in 1622 described popery as 'generally a Religion very neere fitted for brute beasts, for it teacheth them to be saved in ignorance, and by beleeving as the Church beleeves. Which is upon the matter of beleeving that which they know not, and by not knowing what they beleeve'.[42] Overton ironically turns familiar anti-Catholic arguments against the Presbyterians. However, the language which he uses—'grosly ignorant', 'degenerated', 'not able to define themselves'—derives from his monist conviction that matter can become either progressively more spiritual and pure or progressively more material and gross.[43]

The terms of Overton's polemic are also a specific response to those such as Thomas Edwards who would deny the common people the freedom to learn for themselves about their relationship with the divine on the grounds that they are 'illiterate Mechanick persons'. 'Mechanick' was a term not only synonymous with the mean, the vulgar, and the unlettered in early modern discourse, but also associated with 'the material or *materia* as the formless to be shaped', 'something placed at the bottom of a hierarchy to be governed or ruled'.[44] Explaining his method in *Gangraena*, Edwards maintains that 'to have given [the heresies to] the Reader as I found them, would have been to have brought the Reader into a wilderness, and to have presented to publike view a rude and undigested Chaos' (i. 4). Like 'mechanical', 'rude' was a derogatory term of class distinction. In its meaning from Latin of 'rough' and 'unwrought', 'rude' denoted not only the uncultured and ignorant but that 'which needs to be formed, ordered, or "digested" in the sense of being

---

[42] Francis Rous, *The Diseases of the Time Attended by their Remedies* (1622), 189–90.

[43] As with Milton, an aspect of Lady Anne Conway's monistic materialism was the notion that 'sin makes the spirit (i.e. mind and body) grosser, coarser, more corporeal' (D. P. Walker, *The Decline of Hell: Seventeenth Century Discussions of Eternal Torment* (London, 1964), 138–9).

[44] Parker, ' "Rude Mechanicals" ', 46, 48.

submitted to a ruling disposition or ordering'—as in the command of Shakespeare's King John to 'Set a form upon that indigest | Which he hath left so shapeless and so rude' (V. vii. 26–7).[45] Edwards goes on to explain how the 'undigested Chaos' of sectarian errors has been 'carefully declined in this following discourse, by joyning in one things scattered and divided'. As Jonathan Scott notes, Edwards's interest in *Gangraena* was 'in giving radicalism form'. More than this, though, Edwards's use of the term 'declined' indicates that he conceives of his method according to a grammatical model. His grammar of heresy allows him to 'digest' or impose linguistic order upon the 'Chaos', the formless *materia*, of popular sectarianism.[46] Similarly his claim to be 'joining in one things scattered and divided' illustrates how the material craft of fitting together parts was employed in this period as a figure for the proper joining of words and sentences. By metaphorical extension the joining of parts was used to signify 'the construction of order not only in grammar, rhetoric, and logic but also in the social and political hierarchy their ordering reflected'.[47] Edwards tells his readers that he has joined 'two or three . . . more branches' to 'one and the same errour' to avoid 'a heap of Tautologies'. The linguistic education that Edwards uses to mark the hierarchical boundary between clergy and laity also provides the ideological as well as the practical structure of his organizational method: the declining and joining of errors allows him to exert control over popular heterodoxy and incorporate it into the 'proper' social, political, and religious order. There may seem to be a contradiction between Edwards's use of the artisanal craft of joining as a metaphor for his method and his argument that the 'illiterate Mechanicks' who actually engage in such trades need to be governed by a university-educated elite. In fact the discursive appropriation of mechanical crafts in the context of re-enforcing the existing social order was a common humanist trope. Sir Thomas Smith, Cambridge Professor of Civil Law and 'grammatical humanist', who was concerned to establish classical standards of refinement in English learning and literature, compares in *De republica Anglorum* (*c*.1562–5) the ruler or government of a commonwealth to the carpenter's 'rule' as the instrument 'to which all workes be to be conformed'. In his subsequent discussion of the various strata of the social hierarchy, Smith nonetheless declares that 'all artificers, as Taylors, Shoomakers,

---

[45] Parker, ' "Rude Mechanicals" ', 44.

[46] Scott, *England's Troubles*, 238. Kristen Poole also sees Edwards as creating 'a grammar for the language of Babel' (*Radical Religion from Shakespeare to Milton*, 120).

[47] Parker, ' "Rude Mechanicals" ', 49–50.

Carpenters, Brickmakers, Bricklayers, Masons, &c.' have 'no voice or authoritie in our common wealth, and no account is made of them but onlie to be ruled, not to rule'.[48]

Overton directly engages with the underlying ideological basis of the argument for clerical religion in a text such as *Gangraena* by accusing the clergy of excluding the people from learning and knowledge in order to rule over them as undefined matter. Robbed of their humanity, the people are reduced, to borrow a phrase from Donne, to 'a lump, where all beasts kneaded be'.[49] Ultimately, this violation of the individual's 'selfe propriety' is not only an 'affront to the very principles of nature': it has the terrible consequence of preventing people from understanding 'how far God hath made them free' in making salvation dependent upon their actions. Overton defiantly declared from his cell in Newgate in 1647 that 'so long as I know the Lord liveth, who will once judge every man according to his deeds, whether good or evil . . . then I am sure I shall have righteous judgement, without respect of persons'.[50] The 'poor deceived people', however, have been made ignorant of their own spiritual agency by the clerical usurpation of their natural rights as rational, self-determining creatures. Overton cuts to the elitist core of the humanist pedagogical system as it was structured into a whole series of social institutions in Renaissance England, and in particular clerical religion, whether Anglican or Presbyterian. The notion of *humanitas* as a potential state, dependent on the cultivation of intellectual and verbal skills, is central to Ciceronian educational theory. The bestial imagery 'endemic in humane discourse from Cicero to the Elizabethans and beyond' served to distinguish the fuller humanity of the classically trained orator from the barbarous condition of the ignorant and inarticulate (we might recall Milton's depiction of those unlettered sectarians whom he believed to have misinterpreted his learned arguments on divorce as 'owls and cuckoos, asses, apes and dogs').[51] As Erica Fudge observes, 'if humanist pursuits fulfil human potential, make, in fact, the human truly human, then those who could not join in, who were not literate, would seem to be not human'.[52] Overton argues that humanism is in fact used to support

---

[48] Quoted in ibid. 51. On Smith as 'grammatical humanist' see Mike Pincombe, *Elizabethan Humanism: Literature and Learning in the Later Sixteenth Century* (Harlow, 2001), 59–65.

[49] John Donne, 'To Sir Edward Herbert, at Juliers', l. 1 (*The Complete English Poems*, ed. A. J. Smith (Harmondsworth, 1971; repr. 1986), 218).

[50] Overton, *An Arrow Against All Tyrants*, 3; Overton, *The Commoners Complaint* (1647), 23.

[51] Pincombe, *Elizabethan Humanism*, 20.

[52] *Perceiving Animals*, 70.

hierarchies of 'arbitrary power' by organizing the categories of literate and illiterate, clergy and laity, orthodox and heretic, human and beast. Those excluded from knowledge and power by the boundaries of Latin literacy—boundaries which are drawn along the lines of class and gender—lose their identity and agency and exist only as the shapeless, coarsened matter of the governed, 'void of the use of Reason'. Overton had himself been initiated into this elite, closed society of humanist pedagogy and was familiar with the conventions of that society, such as the comic performance of the curriculum in in-house entertainments like *Pedantius*. In his Leveller vision of an egalitarian society where all humans were free to become truly human and so more divine, Overton was able to put that familiarity to satirical use.

The specific reference in *Mans Mortaltie* to *Pedantius* may gesture further at the association in Overton's thought between the humanist pedagogical system and the oppression of the laity by clerical power. If Overton did own the 1631 edition of *Pedantius*, he would have been familiar with the striking frontispiece, which shows the characters of Dromodotus and Pedantius facing each other, the latter prominently holding in his right hand a birch for flogging his pupils. The birch and the ferula became symbolic in early modern England of the rigid disciplining of body as well as mind in the humanist system. Beating was a means of forcing the boy to understand that learning Latin grammar was both a physical ordeal in itself and an initiation into the harsh public world of male power. This 'causal relationship between grammatical training and the punishment of boys' became axiomatic in the sixteenth and seventeenth centuries: physical pain was required both to correct the faults inculcated in the vernacular world of the commonalty and to regulate pedagogical orthodoxy.[53] The endemic violence of humanist education is evident in countless school statutes of the period and in pedagogical texts such as the *Shorte Dictionarie for younge begynners* (1553), in which John Withals lists the following as essential vocabulary for the scholar: 'A rod to doe correction with; to beate; to be beated; A Palmer to beate or strike scholers in the hande; A rebuke; A stripe; to beate or strike; A Blowe or clappe with the open hand; A buffet with the fist; to buffet . . . the marke or print of a hurt in the body'. The 'fetishized rod' wielded by Pedantius thus became 'an emblem of order and knowledge' in early modern England, with the pedagogue assuming in the classroom the sovereign authority of monarch or magistrate to discipline

---

[53] Stewart, *Close Readers*, 88; Ong, 'Latin Language Study as a Renaissance Puberty Rite', 115.

the bodies of his disobedient subjects.[54] Beating was also encouraged by Calvinist ideas about the inherent depravity of the flesh in general and of the wilful child in particular. John Brinsley describes in some detail the range of punishments to be administered to boys in an effort to 'beate the Latine into their heads'; Brinsley thought the birch sanctified by God as an earthly instrument of correction.[55]

Overton himself would certainly have experienced the institutional relationship between bodily disciplining and authorized knowledge fostered by the humanist system. In his Leveller tracts he argues that it is this same relationship between violence and the imposition of conformity which underpins and maintains the 'arbitrary power' of institutional religion and of the ordained, university-educated clergy, whether Anglican or Presbyterian, over the common people. The repetition of violent acts performed by authority on the body of the heretic in *The Araignement of Mr. Persecution* recalls the list of various methods of beating the disobedient schoolboy in Withals's *Short Dictionarie*:

But this fellow PERSECUTION ... *Hangeth, Burneth, Stoneth, Tortureth, Saweth a sunder, Casteth into the fiery* Fornace, *into the Lions Denne, Teareth in peeces with* Wild Horses, *Plucketh out the eyes, Roasteth quicke, Bureth alive, Plucketh out the* Tongues, *Imprisoneth, Scourgeth, Revileth, Curseth, yea, with* Bell, Book and Candle, *Belyeth, Cutteth the* Eares, *Slitteth the* Nose, *Manacles the Hands, Gaggeth the* Mouthes, *Whippeth, Pilloreth, Banisheth into Remote Islands* ... (10)

Overton argues that the violent imposition of uniform belief supports tyranny and divides nations, families, and friends, ensuring that there can never be 'Peace and Friendship Nationall and Domestike' (11). Above all, State persecution violates the natural right and freedom of human beings as individual 'rationall creatures' to determine their own beliefs (24). Milton uses the imagery of pedagogical correction to make a similar point about the free circulation of knowledge in *Areopagitica*: 'What advantage is it to be a man over it is to be a boy at school, if we have only scrapt the ferular, to come under the fescu of an Imprimateur? If serious and elaborate writings, as if they were no more than the theam of a Grammar lad

---

[54] Withals quoted in Stewart, *Close Readers*, 93; Wendy Wall, ' "Household Stuff": The Sexual Politics of Domesticity and the Advent of English Comedy', *English Literary History*, 65 (1998), 1–45 (19). Wall reproduces the frontispiece of *Pedantius* to illustrate her argument about the symbolic status of the birch. On pedagogical violence in early modern England see also Richard Halpern, *The Poetics of Primitive Accumulation: English Renaissance Culture and the Genealogy of Capital* (New York, 1991), 21–45.

[55] Morgan, *Godly Learning*, 149; John Brinsley, *The posing of the parts; or, A most plaine and easie way of examining the accidence and grammar* (1611; 7th edn. 1630), 87; Brinsley, *Ludus Literarius, or the Grammar Schoole* (1612), ed. E. T. Campagnac (Liverpool, 1917), 290.

under the Pedagogue must not be utter'd without the cursory eyes of a
... licenser?'.⁵⁶ Overton calls, like Milton, for liberty of conscience and a
pedagogical method based not upon violence and coercion but conversation and persuasion (though Overton's method, unlike Milton's,
excludes neither Catholic nor unbeliever):

> But if the Papist knew the Protestant, the Protestant the Papist to love another: &
> would not molest or in the least injure one another for their *Conscience*, but live
> peaceably and quietly one by another; bearing one with another, and so of all
> Religions: What man would lift up his hand against his Neighbour? ... shall the
> more knowing trample the ignorant under his feet? we should carry our selves
> loving and meeke one towards another, *with Patience perswading and exhorting*
> *the contrary minded* ... (11, 12)

Richard Halpern has drawn attention to the apparently contradictory fact
that physical punishment intensified in the English educational system
with the adoption of a humanist programme that was predicated on the
efficacy of the 'gentler method' of rhetorical persuasion.⁵⁷ The contradiction may be explained by the co-option of the humanist curriculum
to define the ruling elites of Church and State against a class-based
commonalty. If the corrective beatings that became included in the institutional application of the humanist programme functioned as an 'internalization of symbolic violence designed to replace the openly violent
codes of feudalism', then the learning of Latin grammar initiated boys
into a set of hierarchical social relations that were founded on power as
well as knowledge.⁵⁸ In his emphasis on the pedagogical efficacy of persuasion and argument and on the democratizing role of education in
enabling human beings to understand themselves and their God-given
freedoms, the Leveller Overton was the true heir of the humanist ideal.

SCEPTICAL HUMANISM AND LEVELLER IDEAS:
WILLIAM WALWYN

The opponents of William Walwyn accused him of 'work[ing] upon the
indigent and poorer sort of people', 'men of low and mean birth, breeding and quality', with the aim of 'rais[ing] up their spirits in discontents
and clamours'.⁵⁹ Certainly Walwyn's repeated rejection of the relevance

---

⁵⁶ *CPWM*, ii. 531.
⁵⁷ Halpern, *The Poetics of Primitive Accumulation*, 35.
⁵⁸ Mary Thomas Crane, *Framing Authority: Sayings, Self, and Society in Sixteenth Century
England* (Princeton, NJ, 1993), 55–6; see also Stewart, *Close Readers*, 85–6.
⁵⁹ John Price, *Walwins Wiles* (1649), in *LT*, 297, 303, 307.

of education to religious knowledge exemplifies the anticlerical and anti-intellectual rhetoric associated with popular lay radicalism. In line with the Protestant tradition of confessional polemical history, he opposed the holy simplicity of the prophets and Apostles to the grand but spiritually empty learning of the clergy and the university professors. In direct response to Thomas Edwards's condemnation of the preaching of 'illiterate Mechanick persons', Walwyn declared that God 'made not choise of the great, or learned men of the world, to be his Prophets and publishers of the Gospell; but Heards-men, Fisher-men, Tent-makers, Toll-gatherers, etc.'.[60] Indeed the clerical emphasis on learning as a necessary qualification to preach and interpret the Bible is exposed as a vehicle for antichristian values of greed and exploitation. Earlier, in *The Compassionate Samaritane* (1644), an apology for universal liberty of conscience and one of the books that Edwards demanded be publicly burnt, Walwyn asked his readers to

examine what [learning] is; what good the world receives from it; whether the most learned or unlearned men have been the troublers of the world; how presumptuous and confident the learned scribes, priests and doctors of the law were, that they best understood the Scriptures; how the poor and unlearned fishermen and tent-makers were made choice of for Christ's disciples and apostles, before any of them; how in process of time they took upon them to be ministers, when they had acquired to themselves the mysteries of art and learning, and confounded thereby the clear streams of the Scripture, and perverted the true Gospel of Jesus Christ, and by politic glosses and comments introduced another Gospel, suitable to the covetous, ambitious and persecuting spirit of the clergy (which their esteem with the people made authentic), they began then to scorn the simplicity and meanness of the apostles. (*WWW*, 111)

The keystone of the ideological structure of clerical religion is seen here as the false identification of spiritual authority with educational attainment. Just as Overton's wild Presbyterian boars destroy the simple garden of the Scriptures with their sophistical rhetoric, the rapacious ministers in Walwyn's brief history of the clergy seek to monopolize scriptural interpretation, employing 'politic glosses' to distort the clear message of the gospel for their own gain. Ordination on the grounds of a humanist training in literature and languages is demystified as an exploitative confidence trick played upon the ordinary people: 'by reason of his continual exercise in preaching, and discoursing, by his daily study and reading, by

---

[60] Walwyn, *A Prediction of Mr. Edwards his Recantation and Conversion* (1646), in *WWW*, 233.

his skill in arts and languages', the minister 'presume[s] it easy to possess us, that [he is] more divine than other men' (108–9).

Several pages later, however, Walwyn develops his plea for liberty of conscience by arguing 'that to force men, against their mind and judgement, to believe what other men conclude to be true would prove such tyranny as the wicked Procrustes (mentioned by Plutarch) practised, who would fit all men into one bed by stretching them out that were too short, and by cutting them shorter that were too long' (113). We might assume that the use of this classical exemplum is to be interpreted ironically given the earlier diatribe against the humanist curriculum. Yet in *Walwyns Just Defence* (1649) he cites Plutarch, Seneca, Lucian, Thucydides, Montaigne, and Pierre Charron, amongst others, as his favourite 'humane authors' whom he 'had been accustomed to the reading of . . . for twenty yeers' (*WWW*, 397–8, 410). He provocatively directs his clerical opponents amongst the Independents to one of the most celebrated passages in Montaigne's *Essaies* (1580–8; trans. John Florio, 1603) to ridicule their lack of Christian charity:

And in his twentieth Chapter, pag: 102. he saies, speaking of the Cannibals, the very words that import lying, falsehood, treason, dissimulation, covetousnesse, envy, detraction, and pardon, were never heard of amongst them. These and like flowers, I think it lawfull to gather out of his Wildernesse, and to give them room in my Garden; yet this worthy Montaign was but a Roman Catholique; yet to observe with what contentment and swoln joy he recites these cogitations, is wonderful to consider: And now what shall I say? Go to this honest Papist, or to these innocent Cannibals, ye Independent Churches, to learn civility, humanity, simplicity of heart; yea, charity and Christianity . . . (399–400)

In 'On the Cannibals' Montaigne argues that while the cannibals of Brazil may lack any sort of intellectual accomplishment and live without law, trade, and property, they exist in a state of natural innocence and equality which recalls man's original estate in Eden. While they may roast people for food, Europeans roast people for heresy; a point which evidently appealed to Walwyn in his condemnation of the immorality and irrationality of religious persecution. Quoting Montaigne at some length, he reveals that he has been 'long accustomed' to reading the *Essaies* and although he does not 'approve of [them] in all things', they 'have made so deep an impression in me' that 'I recite these passages because I am in love with them' (401). Indeed Walwyn not only quotes from the *Essaies*; his defence of his reading and of his plain and open-hearted character is largely an unacknowledged paraphrase of Montaigne's 'On the Useful and the Honourable'. Walwyn was fond of this essay and evidently felt it particularly applicable to the situation in England in the 1640s, for Montaigne deals with the clash between public and private virtue in the state of civil war and strongly asserts the claims of charity and friendship.[61]

God may prefer to reveal spiritual knowledge to the poor and unlearned but this did not prevent Walwyn from using his financial means to engage with the classical and late humanist intellectual traditions in the process of forming his radical beliefs during the 1630s. Walwyn was the grandson of the Bishop of Hereford and the son of a prosperous Worcestershire landowner. His brother went to Oxford, while William was privately tutored before being apprenticed to a London silk merchant in 1619, becoming a member of the Merchant Adventurers—one of the economic monopolies that would be most strongly condemned by the Levellers—by 1632. According to Humphrey Brooke, who went into print to defend his father-in-law's respectability, Walwyn had 'from the profits of his Trade, maintained his Family in a middle and moderate but contentful condition'.[62] It was this economic independence that allowed Walwyn to peruse the bookshops of Caroline London and expand his library. His desire to read about different cultures and values appears to have been kindled after he was converted to the doctrine of universal redemption. As we saw in Chapter 1, adherents of 'free grace' such as William Dell and John Saltmarsh, who were called 'antinomians' by their opponents, 'did not proclaim the spiritual equality of all mankind but only the spiritual equality of the Saints . . . despite the attacks of their critics that they had interpreted Calvinist theology to mean universal redemption'. Walwyn is unique amongst the radicals of the period in accepting the polemical title of antinomian to signify his belief that 'all [are] justified freely by his grace through the redemption that is in Jesus Christ'.[63] He writes in *Walwyns Just Defence* that after he had become 'establisht in that part of doctrine (called then, Antinomian) of free justification by Christ alone' he found himself liberated from the anxieties provoked by either the notion that salvation

---

[61] Walwyn quotes Montaigne's representation of Epaminondas as the model of virtue and charity in times of war just after he has appealed to his many friends to testify 'whether they ever saw more plainnesse and open-heartednesse in man'; *Walwyns Just Defence*, in *WWW*, 402; cf. Michel de Montaigne, *The Complete Essays*, trans. M. A. Screech (Harmondsworth, 1993), 891–906. Montaigne writes of himself: 'I have an open manner, readily striking up acquaintance and being trusted from the first encounter' (893).

[62] For Walwyn's biography see *BDBR* and 'Introduction', in *WWW*, 1–51; Humphrey Brooke, *The Charity of Church-Men* (1649), in *LT*, 344.

[63] Solt, 'Anti-intellectualism in the Puritan Revolution', 307; Walwyn, *The Power of Love* (1643), in *WWW*, 89.

is dependent on repentance and good works or the Calvinist threat of pre-destined damnation (*WWW*, 395–6). Free from 'those yokes of bondage, unto which Sermons and Doctrines mixt of Law and Gospel, do frequently subject distressed consciences', Walwyn came to believe him-self 'master of what I had heard, or read, in divinity: and this doctrine working by love, I became also, much more master of my affections, and of what ever I read in humane authors' (396, 398). Interest in 'humane' or 'carnal' literature tends to be one of the stumbling blocks to salvation that is overcome in the Puritan conversion narrative. Richard Norwood recounts how he

fell to reading of Virgils Eneade with much affection, but had no love nor delight nor faith in the word of God . . . acting a part in a play, the reading of play-books and other such books as aforementioned, and the vayne conceipts which they begat in me was the principal thing that alienated my heart from the word of God . . .[64]

However, Walwyn's assurance of his salvation and deliverance from external religious law seems to have released his intellectual curiosity and confidence.

Walwyn's reading became a matter of controversy as his radical beliefs and writing made him a public figure in the mid-1640s. In denying the charge of the Independent minister John Price that he believed there to be more wit in Lucian than in the Bible, he professed admiration for the lessons 'against ambition, pride and covetousnesse' in Lucian's dialogue 'Megapenthes' while admitting it to be a 'discourse . . . possibly not in all things justifiable'. Nonetheless Walwyn refused to back down: 'I count him a very weak man, that takes harm by reading it or such like things' (398). Indeed Walwyn became increasingly daring and provocative in his insistence that the so-called Christian nation of England could learn about moral values and behaviour from non-Christian peoples and texts. Thomas Edwards had declared that 'if *Mahomet* were living among us, hee would be a gallant fellow in these times, and be in great request for his revelations and new light'. Walwyn responded by recommending the implementation in England of the law against lying established by 'Almanzar the first (or third) of the Sarazens Emperors . . . as you may read in a little book called the *Life of Mahomet*, and are we not in a low forme for Christians, when we are not so wise as such Schoole-masters?'

64 Richard Norwood, 'Confessions' (written 1639–40), *in Grace Abounding with Other Spiritual Autobiographies*, ed. John Stachniewski with Anita Pacheo (Oxford, 1998), 130.

(422–3).[65] Walwyn puts into practice Milton's argument in *Areopagitica* that 'truth lies in the choices made available to the individual in the course of acquiring knowledge, that is reading'. Indeed his attitude towards books brings out the antinomian implications of Milton's assertion that '[t]o the pure all things are pure [Titus 1: 15], not only meats and drinks, but all kinde of knowledge whether of good or evill; the knowledge cannot defile, nor consequently the books, if the will and conscience be not defiled'.[66] Walwyn's willingness to draw ethical lessons from Muslim and Catholic also reflects the moral, historical, and religious relativism that is central to his arguments for liberty of conscience and was influenced in particular by his reading of Montaigne and Charron. Walwyn's adaptation of French scepticism has previously been noted by William Haller and Nigel Smith, but receives more detailed attention here as an instance of how a Continental intellectual tradition shaped one form of radical expression during the English revolution.[67]

Montaigne, following the arguments of the ancient Greek philosopher Pyrrho of Elis as recorded by his disciple Sextus Empiricus, maintained the fundamental uncertainty of all human knowledge, including that based on sense perception, and the subjectivity and relativity of rational method. For Montaigne, experience, history, and the example of non-Christian cultures demonstrate that in response to any statement that might be made—whether scientific, philosophic, or theological—the contrary can be advanced with equal reason. We must thus suspend all judgement until God chooses to enlighten us. The irony, of course, is that Montaigne developed his scepticism of the efficacy of reason through reasoning. Consequently if all opinions are equally justifiable, any attempt to impose a 'right' judgement on another is inherently irrational. As Montaigne puts it in 'On the Lame', in which he questions the rational basis of the persecution of witches, 'any man who supports his opinion with challenges and commands demonstrates that his reasons for it are

---

[65] *Gangraena*, i. 177. The *Life and Death of Mahomet*, attributed to Sir Walter Raleigh, was published in 1637.

[66] Nigel Smith, '*Areopagitica*: Voicing Contexts, 1643–5', in Loewenstein and Turner (eds.), *Politics, Poetics and Hermeneutics in Milton's Prose*, 103–22 (106); *CPWM*, ii. 512. Walwyn quotes Titus 2: 11–12 on the title page of *The Power of Love* (1643), in which he defends the antinomian beliefs of the Family of Love; Laurence Clarkson cites Titus 1: 15 in his Ranter pamphlet *A Single Eye All Light, no Darkness* (1650) as scripture proof that 'what Act soever I do, is acted by that Majesty within me'; *CRW*, 164.

[67] Haller, *Liberty and Reformation in the Puritan Revolution*, 170–2; Nigel Smith, 'The Charge of Atheism and the Language of Radical Speculation, 1640–1660', in Michael Hunter and David Wootton (eds.), *Atheism from the Reformation to the Enlightenment* (Oxford, 1992), 131–58 (143–56).

weak'.[68] For Walwyn, religious belief can never be imposed by the edict of Church or State, for two main reasons:

First reason: Because of what judgement soever a man is, he cannot choose but be of that judgement . . . Whatsoever a man's reason does conclude to be true or false, to be agreeable or disagreeable to God's Word, that same to that man is his opinion or judgement, and so man is by his own reason necessitated to be of that mind he is. Now where there is necessity there ought to be no punishment, for punishment is the recompense of voluntary actions.

Second reason: The uncertainty of knowledge in this life. No man, nor no sort of men, can presume of an unerring spirit . . . since there remains the possibility of error, notwithstanding never so great presumptions to the contrary, one sort of men are not to compel another, since this hazard is run thereby, that he who is in error may be the constrainer of him who is in the truth.[69]

Belief becomes rather a personal matter for each individual to derive from an ongoing process of rational investigation: "'tis excellency in any man or woman, not to be pertinacious, or obstinate, in any opinion, but to have an open eare for reason and argument, against whatsoever he holds'. Even the unbeliever must be reasoned with rather than persecuted: 'a man . . . whose mind is so far mis-informed as to deny a Deity, or the Scriptures . . . can Bedlam or the Fleet reduce such a one?'. Just as Montaigne provocatively located natural goodness in the society of cannibals to expose the hypocrisy and complacency of European Christian society, in his early writings Walwyn daringly (if anonymously) assumed the persona of those considered to personify blasphemy and irreligion in seventeenth-century England—the Catholic in *A New Petition of the Papists* (1641) and the Familist in *The Power of Love* (1643)—in an attempt to engage with and subvert the stereotypical depictions of their depravity used to bolster arguments against toleration:

Come, you are mightily afraid of opinions, is there no other that you feare? not the Anabaptists, Brownists or Antinomians? Why doe you start man? . . . free your-selves from common mistakes concerning those your brethren, then acquaint your selves with them, observe their wayes and enquire into their doctrines your selfe . . . your mindes are tainted therewith, because our publicke catechismes, bookes and Sermons are for the most part corrupted therewith.[70]

---

[68] For a full discussion of Montaigne's Pyrrhonian scepticism see R. H. Popkin, *The History of Scepticism from Erasmus to Spinoza* (Berkeley, Calif., 1979), ch. 3; Montaigne, *The Complete Essays*, 1167.

[69] Walwyn, *The Compassionate Samaritane*, in *WWW*, 103–4.

[70] Walwyn, *The Power of Love* and *Toleration Justified and Persecution Condemned* (1645), in *WWW*, 81, 159, 164.

Walwyn recommends here that each individual perform a kind of anthropological study of diverse religious beliefs. He also finds the official, institutional categories of religious knowledge and behaviour— what Montaigne would define as 'custom'—to be 'corrupted' precisely because they are presented as eternally given truths rather than historically and culturally contingent.[71]

Throughout his writings Walwyn maintained the position that no person possesses an 'infallible spirit to discern between truth and error' and that 'thousands are as liable to be mistaken as one single person'. He described himself as one 'that hateth no man for his opinion'. For Montaigne, witness to the bloody religious conflicts of sixteenth-century France, the uncertainty of knowledge in this life demanded the individual live undogmatically. The absence of any certain external moral standards did not, however, lead to the negation of all principles of behaviour: 'it is his soul a wise man should withdraw from the crowd, maintaining its power and freedom freely to make judgements, whilst externally accepting all received forms and fashions'.[72] Walwyn refused to align himself with any particular sect or radical religious group and continued to worship in his local parish church of St James Garlickhythe in London. This seemingly perverse conformism was the cause of his falling out with his former Baptist and Independent allies of the mid-1640s, as much as his antinomianism or political egalitarianism. Yet, while adopting Montaigne's sceptical arguments about knowledge and certainty, Walwyn's scepticism does not lead to fideism in the sense of 'a simple reliance upon a non-rational act of faith'. Walwyn maintains the natural capacity of every person to approach the truth through the exercise of his or her innate reason: 'every man must examine for himselfe . . . or else he must be conscious to himselfe, that he sees with other mens eyes, and has taken up an opinion, not because it consents with his understanding, but for that it is the safest and least troublesome as the world goes'.[73] The contrast is illuminated by what seems to be Walwyn's rewriting of this passage from the 'Apology for Raymond Sebond', Montaigne's most radical critique of the efficacy of reason:

And since I am not capable of choosing, I accept other people's choice and stay in

---

[71] I borrow here some of the terms used by Jonathan Dollimore in his discussion of Montaigne and custom in *Radical Tragedy: Religion, Ideology, and Power in the Drama of Shakespeare and his Contemporaries* (Hemel Hempstead, 1984; 2nd edn. 1989), 15 -18.

[72] Walwyn, *A Prediction of Mr. Edwards his Conversion and Recantation* and *The Power of Love*, in *WWW*, 81, 229, 234; Montaigne, 'On Habit', in *The Complete Essays*, 133.

[73] The definition of fideism is taken from Tuck, *Philosophy and Government*, 85; Walwyn, *Toleration Justified and Persecution Condemned*, in *WWW*, 158.

the position where God put me. Otherwise I could not keep myself from rolling about incessantly. Thus I have, by the grace of God, kept myself intact, without agitation or disturbance of conscience, in the ancient beliefs of our religion, in the midst of so many sects and divisions that our century has produced.

Where Montaigne looks to other people to make his mind up for him, Walwyn displays the experiential and introspective bias of his radical Puritan milieu by looking within to find the centred self: 'I carry with me in all places a touch-stone that tryeth all things, and labours to hold nothing but what upon plain grounds appeareth good and usefull . . . there are plain usefull doctrines sufficient to give peace to my mind: direction and comfort to my life'.[74]

At the same time there may be indications here of the influence of Pierre Charron's adaptation of Montaigne's scepticism in *De la sagesse*, which Walwyn read in Samson Lennard's translation of 1606. For Charron, moral virtue—which precedes religious belief, so raising the possibility of a 'moral' atheism—involves, in a world where nothing is certain and everything is rationally justifiable, giving every opinion its due. In the absence of supernatural revelation, all we may do is acknowledge our ignorance and live according to nature, which God has disposed to tend to the good. Yet the wise man will naturally arrive at his belief in a Christian (and, in Charron's case, a Catholic) God through a process of experience, self-education, and rational choice. This attitude involves a negation of the promise of reward in heaven and the threat of punishment in hell as a basis for behaviour in this life which is consonant with Walwyn's notion of universal grace and his repudiation of Calvinist doctrine:

These men will that a man be an honest man, because there is a Paradise and a hell: so that if they did not feare God, or feare to be damned (for that is so often their language) they would make a godly piece of worke . . . I will that thou be an honest man, not because thou wouldest go to paradise, but because nature, reason, God willeth it, because the law, and the generall policy of the world, whereof thou art a part, requireth it; so as thou canst not consent to be any other, except thou goe against thy selfe, thy essence, thy end.[75]

Convinced that 'the work of redemption and reconciliation with God was perfected when Christ died', Walwyn presents a more positive vision than

---

[74] I use the translation of this passage in Popkin, *The History of Scepticism*, 49; Walwyn, *A Whisper in the eare of Mr. Thomas Edwards* (1646), in *WWW*, 180. On experience and the self in Puritan forms of faith see e.g. Watkins, *The Puritan Experience*, 9–36.

[75] Pierre Charron, *Of Wisdome*, trans. Samson Lennard (1606), 299; see also Popkin, *The History of Scepticism*, 61; Tuck, *Philosophy and Government*, 84–8.

the French sceptics of man's natural virtue and rationality; even though he also maintains that all human knowledge is ultimately uncertain, negating the possibility of a correct or orthodox set of beliefs. As Montaigne himself puts it, 'we are born to go in quest of truth: to take possession of it is the property of a greater Power'. This is the essence of Walwyn's rejection of the superior spiritual authority of a university-educated clerical caste. If 'the people . . . would examine all that was said, and not take things upon trust from the ministers, as if whatsoever they spake, God spake in them . . . [t]hey would then try all things, and whatever they found to be truth they would embrace as from God'.[76]

As the extract above from Charron's *De la sagesse* suggests, both Montaigne and Charron, much influenced by Stoic philosophy, were concerned with the psychological well-being of the individual and with the restraint of those passions which might bring the individual into conflict with others or with 'the law, and the generall policy of the world'; even though, as the comparative study of different civilizations demonstrates, there is no rational or moral justification for these particular laws. By reducing all human knowledge to opinion, Pyrrhonian scepticism could be wielded as a weapon against heresy and sectarianism. Walwyn certainly sought to cultivate a rhetorical voice of dispassionate common sense, undermining the stereotype of the crazed, fanatical sectarian projected by the heresiographers. Excess of passion is comically relocated within the opponents of toleration in *A Parable or Consultation of Physitians Upon Master Edwards* (1646). In an updating of the Jonsonian comedy of humours, Walwyn acts as a spiritual physician performing an emergency operation on Edwards's brain to relieve him of life-threatening melancholic vapours. Walwyn also agreed with Montaigne and Charron in his conviction that 'the practice of States, though Christian, is variable we see: different from one another, and changing according to the prevalency of particular partees, and therefore a most uncertain rule of what is reasonable'. Yet he transformed the political conclusions of French sceptical thought in applying it to the context of seventeenth-century England. For Walwyn, the religious conflicts of the 1640s illustrated not that outward conformity to custom was necessary but that enforced religious uniformity was 'contrary to God, to reason, to the well-being of the State'. Rather active diversity will encourage moral virtue and social harmony: 'a Toleration being allowed, and every Sect labouring to make it appear that they are in truth, whereof a good life, or the power of

---

[76] Walwyn, *The Power of Love*, 90; *The Compassionate Samaritane*, 108; Montaigne, 'On the Art of Conversation', in *The Complete Essays*, 1051.

godliness being the best badge or symptome; hence will necessarily follow a noble contestation in all sorts of men to exceed in godlinesse'.[77]

While the French sceptics argued that the self-preservation of the individual entailed the outward acceptance of the current laws and customs of the State, Walwyn transferred to the State the obligation of preserving the individual's natural rights of religious self-determination. As David Wootton has shown, the Levellers 'saw the state as a purely secular institution, required to conform only to the principles of natural reason, and obliged to leave to the individual questions of private conscience which depended on belief, not certain knowledge'. Wootton emphasizes the theological basis of this argument in the doctrine of free grace: the abrogation of the legal dispensation of the Old Testament by the spiritual dispensation of the New meant that the Church was transformed from 'a holy commonwealth sustained by legal compulsion' to 'a purely voluntary assembly sustained by faith'.[78] Nonetheless Walwyn's engagement with *la crise pyrrhonienne* also shaped the development of Leveller ideas about the necessity of toleration and the negative liberty that should be facilitated by the State. At the same time, the conviction that all men had been released from the yoke of the Mosaic law by Christ's atonement led Walwyn to espouse a concept of the individual's innate freedom, rationality, and virtue that is consistent with the appeal to natural freedom and natural law of Leveller political theory, and which explains his attraction to Montaigne's images of cannibals living in a beneficent state of nature.[79] Lotte Mulligan has argued that Walwyn's belief in universal redemption resolved the uncertainties provoked by his reading of Montaigne and Charron.[80] It would seem rather that Walwyn found in

[77] Peter Burke, 'Tacitism, Scepticism and Reason of State', in J. H. Burns (ed.), *The Cambridge History of Political Thought, 1450–1700* (Cambridge, 1991; paperback edn. 1996), 479–98 (495–7); Walwyn, *Toleration Justified and Persecution Condemned*, 161–2, 164. For the depiction of separatists and sectarians as 'rational examiners' and 'mild discoursers' rather than the libertine enthusiasts projected in polemical literature see Walwyn, *The Compassionate Samaritane*, 103.

[78] Wootton, 'Leveller Democracy', 439.

[79] On the Levellers and natural law see G. E. Aylmer, *The Levellers in the English Revolution* (London, 1975), esp. 12; Richard Tuck, *Natural Rights Theories* (Cambridge, 1979), 149–50; Smith, 'The Charge of Atheism', 152.

[80] Lotte Mulligan, 'The Religious Roots of William Walwyn's Radicalism', *Journal of Religious History*, 12 (1982), 162–79. In arguing against the influence of a theology of universal grace on Leveller notions of natural freedom, David Wootton maintains that by 1649 Walwyn had retreated from his position that all men are saved and had adopted a position entailing redemption only for the elect, as outlined in John Saltmarsh's *Free Grace* (1645). Wootton does not make it clear that his evidence for this retreat comes not from Walwyn's own words, but from a defence of Walwyn against the charge of atheism by Humphrey Brooke, who states that after some discussion he and Walwyn had concluded that hell exists

the philosophy of doubt outlined in sceptical humanist literature an intellectual support for his arguments for complete liberty of conscience; arguments that were initially derived from his conviction that, whatever their opinions, all men have been redeemed by Christ's sacrifice. Far from breeding resignation and despair, Walwyn derived from his novel fusion of antinomianism and Pyrrhonism an optimistic conception of the moral dynamism of uncertainty and the self-sufficiency of grace vouchsafed as reason.

The charge that Walwyn was an atheist has been repeated by a modern commentator.[81] It seems difficult to substantiate considering the central role Walwyn assigns to free grace in his conception of self and society, although it would appear that Walwyn was willing to tolerate rather than persecute unbelievers and, like Charron, to consider the possibility of a form of 'moral' unbelief ('I have no quarrell to any man, either for beleefe or unbeleefe, because I judge no man beleeveth any thing but what he cannot choose but beleeve'). Yet the term 'atheism' in early modern Europe denoted in any case not unbelief but 'irreligion in the sense of a more or less extreme attack on orthodox Christianity', in particular the internalization of heaven and hell as earthly states and sceptical attitudes towards the Bible as a sufficient means of understanding man, the universe, and the divine—beliefs often found expressed in the radical writing of the English revolution.[82] Walwyn is, as Edwards charged, equivocal when it comes to the status of the Bible as a rule of faith. In response to the accusation that he had declared the Scriptures to be 'so plainly and directly contradictory to it self, that it makes me believe it is not the Word of God', Walwyn insisted that he had always used his other books 'in their due place; being very studious all that time in the Scriptures'; at one point he does refer to the Bible as 'the infallible Word of God'.[83] At the same time, his rule that '[n]o man, nor no sort of men, can presume of an unerring spirit' would seem to preclude the infallibility of any human interpretation of the Bible. In his impersonation of Edwards he has the

both within and without man, the latter 'succeeding judgement'. Brooke adds that they nevertheless found the idea that 'a man should be punished everlastingly for a little sinning in this world . . . contrary to reason'; Wootton, 'Leveller Democracy', 436–8; Brooke, *The Charity of Church-Men*, in *LT*, 335.

[81] David Wootton (ed.), *Divine Right and Democracy: An Anthology of Political Writings in Stuart England* (Harmondsworth, 1986), 272.

[82] Walwyn, *A Still and Soft Voice* (1647), in *WWW*, 274; Michael Hunter, 'The Problem of "Atheism" in Early Modern Europe', *Transactions of the Royal Historical Society*, 35 (1985), 135–57 (136); R. H. Popkin and Arjo Vanderjagt (eds.), *Scepticism and Irreligion in the Seventeenth and Eighteenth Centuries* (Leiden, 1993), 3.

[83] Price, *Walwins Wiles*, in *LT*, 297–8; *Walwyns Just Defence*, 397.

Presbyterian cleric admit that 'our preachings are like any other mens discourses, liable to errours, and mistakings, and are not the very Word of
God, but our apprehensions drawn from the Word'. The clergy can only
ever deliver 'uncertain and fallible Sermons'; to claim otherwise is to
make men 'digg to themselves broken Cisterns, that can hold no water'.
Walwyn of course rejected the superior authority of clerical exegesis on
the grounds of either learning in the ancient languages or '*jure divino* . . .
succession from the apostles'. Yet he also maintained that direct revelation was a phenomenon of the past: 'in these times . . . there are no true
Apostles, Evangelists, Prophets, Pastors, or Teachers, endowed with
power from on high, as all true ones are; by which, they are enabled to
divide the word of God aright'. Those who 'boast to have the Spirit of
God' speak 'according to the spirit of their own Imaginations'.[84]

In this latter point Walwyn was, as we have seen, in line with Protestant
and Puritan orthodoxy. Richard Baxter distinguished between 'two sorts
of the Spirit's motions'. The 'one is by extraordinary inspiration or
impulse, as he moved the prophets and apostles, to reveal new laws . . .
or to do some actions without respect to any other command than the
inspiration itself. This Christians are not now to expect'. The other sort 'is
not to make new laws or duties, but to guide and quicken us in the doing
of that which is our duty before by the laws already made. And these are
the motions that all true Christians must now expect'.[85] In other words,
Baxter is at pains to emphasize that the radical, even revolutionary, movement of the Spirit that reveals 'new laws' is finished, and has been replaced
by a conspicuously conformist and static type of 'ordinary illumination'.
In Baxter's writings this 'ordinary illumination' is complementary to, and
can seem indistinguishable from, reason; hence his emphasis on the
benefits of reading, education, and secular knowledge for expounding the
word of God as laid down in the Scriptures:

Grace presupposeth Nature: We are *men* in order of Nature at least before we are
Saints, and Reason is before Supernatural Revelation. Common knowledge therefore is subservient unto faith: We must know the Creator and his works . . .
Humane learning in the sense in question is also Divine: God is the Author of the
light of nature, as well as of grace . . .

Baxter repeatedly insists that the 'Spirit [which] assisteth us in our hearing, reading, and studying the Scriptures . . . worketh not on the will but
the reason'. Richard Hooker had made the same point in distinguishing

---

[84] *The Compassionate Samaritane*, 104; *A Prediction of Mr. Edwards His Conversion*, 232;
Vanitie of the Present Churches (1649), in *LT*, 261, 263, 269–70.
[85] Baxter quoted in Nuttall, *The Holy Spirit in Puritan Faith and Experience*, 50.

between the 'extraordinary' and 'common' ways 'whereby the spirit leadeth men into all truth', between '*Revelation*' and '*Reason*'. Hooker's immediate point is that since revelation has ceased, Puritan arguments from Scripture must rest not upon 'the fervent earnestness of their persuasion, but the soundness of those reasons whereupon the same is built, which must declare their opinion in these things to have been wrought by the holy Ghost, and not by the fraud of that evil Spirit which is even in his illusions strong'. It is hardly surprising that Baxter sounds like Hooker, as he proceeds to cite the *Laws* on the necessity of testimony and method: 'and even of the Mysteries of the Gospel, I must needs say with Mr. *Richard Hooker, Eccl. Polity.* That whatever men may pretend, the subjective Certainty cannot go beyond the objective Evidence . . . I am not so foolish as to pretend my certainty to be greater than it is, meerly because it is a dishonour to be less certain'.[86]

However, Baxter also sounds like Walwyn. The irony may in part be explained by their common intellectual resources. Walwyn cites 'peeces annexed to Mr. Hookers *Ecclesiastical Pollicy*' amongst his favourite books and in *A New Petition of the Papist* summons Hooker to defend the toleration of Catholics: 'Master Hooker in his five bookes of *Ecclesiasticall Polity*, page 138 affirmes, the Church of Rome to be a part of the house of God, a limbe of the visible Church of Christ, and page 130. He saith, we gladly acknowledge them to bee of the family of Jesus Christ'.[87] After the Restoration, in particular, *Of the Laws of Ecclesiastical Polity* (bks. i–iv, 1593; bk. v, 1597; bks. vi and vii, 1648; bk. viii, 1661) became 'a kind of touchstone of Anglicanism'. In the *Eikon Basilike* (1649) Hooker's *Laws* are Charles I's recommended reading for his daughter Elizabeth.[88] The attraction of the thought of Richard Hooker, immensely learned defender of the traditions and authority of the Elizabethan Church of England and one of the most influential critics of separatism and sectarianism in the early modern period, to Walwyn, Leveller leader, tolerationist, and opponent of any form of compulsory national Church, might seem unexpected. Yet the appeal no doubt lay in Hooker's sense of man and the universe as governed by reason, reflected in a prose style in which 'the complex sentence is the reflection of rational thought'; in Hooker's Aristotelian emphasis on the natural rationality of men against

---

[86] Baxter quoted in Keeble, *The Literary Culture of Nonconformity in Later Seventeenth Century England*, 161–2; see also Nuttall, *The Holy Spirit*, 171; Hooker, *Of the Laws of Ecclesiastical Polity*, ed. MacGrade, 16–17.

[87] *Walwyns Just Defence*, 397; William Walwyn, *A New Petition of the Papists* (1641), in *WWW*, 59.

[88] Roger Pooley, *English Prose of the Seventeenth Century, 1590–1700* (Harlow, 1992) 139.

the Calvinist emphasis on their innate depravity; in his rejection of Puritan biblical fundamentalism in favour of arguments from natural reason and natural law which would complement those from Scripture, and in his notion of an inclusive (though State) Church in which opposing parties can live together in good conscience.[89] Moreover, Hooker located original political authority in the people, who rationally consent to obedience to law (although this did not make the monarch contractually subject to popular control). In the eighth book of the *Laws*, not published until 1648, Hooker suggested, if ambiguously, that monarchy and episcopacy were not the only forms of State and Church government ordained by God.[90] One critic has found in Hooker's *Laws* the 'emergence of a modern hermeneutic with its appeal to reason, evidence, historical context and linguistic change'. However, these 'methods and premises can only partially sustain their predetermined conclusions', for 'the argument for tradition rests precisely on the *failure* of reason to deliver certainty'.[91] In demystifying the origins and role of the Church, and in appealing to reason and probability in his efforts to place the argument for religious unity on sturdier foundations than appeals to Scripture, Hooker actually exposed fault-lines which a radical sensibility such as Walwyn's could exploit to argue precisely the opposite case.

Walwyn's use of Hooker sheds further light on the analogies which have been drawn between Leveller and Lockean political theory. In *Two Treatises of Government* (1690) Locke found inspiration in Hooker's *Laws* for his notion of the state of nature as a state of equality and freedom, which he opposed to the monarchical origins of government outlined in Sir Robert Filmer's *Patriarcha* (1680). In *The Reasonableness of Christianity* (1695) Locke developed the Levellers anticlerical arguments that 'every person must decide for himself what the fundamental tenets of Christianity are'; consequently no group can arrogate to itself 'the authority to instruct mankind in religious matters for which they have neither the authority nor the knowledge to do so'.[92] In Walwyn's writings we can identify the beginnings of an English radical tradition which argued for religious toleration on the basis of sceptical and rational

---

[89] George Edelen, 'Hooker's Style', in W. Speed Hill (ed.), *Studies in Richard Hooker* (Cleveland, Ohio, 1972), 244; Wootton (ed.), *Divine Right and Democracy*, 214; Hooker, *Of the Laws of Ecclesiastical Polity*, p. xxx.

[90] Tuck, *Philosophy and Government*, 151–3.

[91] Debra Shuger, *Habits of Thought in the English Renaissance: Religion, Politics and the Dominant Culture* (Berkeley, Calif., 1990), 26, 34.

[92] On Locke and Hooker see Pooley, *English Prose of the Seventeenth Century*, 258; on Locke and the Levellers see Richard Ashcroft, 'Anticlericalism and Authority in Lockean Political Thought', in Lund (ed.), *The Margins of Orthodoxy*, 73–96 (81–2).

principles. It would seem that in his selective interpretation of Hooker, as in his reading of Montaigne and Charron, Walwyn found an intellectual resource which was consistent with—or, considering that he had been reading these books in the 1630s, which helped shape—the political and religious beliefs which he publicly espoused in the 1640s. Through the act of unprejudiced reading that Milton represents as the exercise of spiritual virtue in *Areopagitica*, Walwyn put into practice his arguments for religious toleration. Indeed Walwyn takes the Miltonic argument for the free exchange of knowledge to the logical conclusions that Milton was unprepared to accept by finding truth in texts written in support of both Catholicism and episcopacy.

For Walwyn, scepticism and enthusiasm were incompatible. In Chapter 5 we shall see that some Quakers who explicitly rejected the Bible as a sufficient rule of faith in favour of the continuous revelation granted by the 'inner light' also read Montaigne and Charron. For the moment it will suffice to point out that Walwyn's identification of grace with the exercise of natural reason and his orthodox stance on prophecy led him to a position similar to that from which Richard Baxter defended the necessity of learning for a minister of God. Yet Walwyn repeatedly rejected as fraudulent this connection between book learning and authoritative judgement on spiritual matters: 'though now you have [the Scriptures] in your owne language you are taught not to trust your owne understanding (have a care of your purses) you must have an University man to interpret the English'. As Joseph Frank puts it, Walwyn 'equates natural man with simple man, and subversive aristocrat with the product of higher education'—although perhaps subversive minister rather than aristocrat.[93] Yet in the light of the role of his reading in shaping his religious beliefs there is an irony in Walwyn's exhortation to his readers to ask themselves 'what good the world receives from [learning]' and in his identification of spiritual virtue with the 'simplicity and meanness of the apostles'. The irony is crystallized in Walwyn's defence of his reading against the charge of atheism. He cites the familiarity of Moses with the learning of the Egyptians and St Paul's quotation of Euripides—the very same examples that were summoned by the Presbyterian cleric Thomas Hall against radical criticism of the role of formal education in the training of ministers.[94]

Nonetheless Walwyn's use of a variety of texts, in particular the

---

[93] Walwyn, *The Power of Love*, 95; Joseph Frank, *The Levellers* (Cambridge, Mass., 1955), 21.

[94] *Walwyns Just Defence*, 398; Hall, *Vindiciae Literarum*, 11.

writings of the French sceptics, questions the validity of the argument that there was a great contrast between the uses made of print by English radicals of the mid-seventeenth century and those of the 1790s: 'the Levellers and others during the English Revolution drew very heavily on the Bible, Foxe['s *Acts and Monuments*] and a limited range of other authoritative texts, while the later radicals, though still powerfully drawn to the languages, imagery and ideas of these texts, also had a much wider range of genres available'.[95] Walwyn's reading is a warning against under-estimating the intellectual resources of 'popular' radicalism in the English revolution. Montaigne was as important an influence on Walwyn as on John Donne or Robert Burton, both of whom also sought (though less successfully) to negotiate the religious despair and psychological crisis provoked by Calvinist doctrine.[96] It must be emphasized, however, that Walwyn bought and read these classical and humanist texts in trans-lation. Despite proudly asserting his status as *laicus illitteratus* in defend-ing his reading of classical and Continental texts, he then confides that 'I wish I had the Latin' and blames not his deprived upbringing ('for my parents, I thank them, were not wanting') but the poor quality of his tutors. However, he immediately pulls himself away from this personal regret and back to his polemical purpose, insisting that he does not think 'any man the wiser for having many languages, or for having more than one', and that he has little to do with men 'skillful in languages, and arts and sciences'. Rather he declares with an appropriately Montaignian flourish that 'my care is rightly to understand myself in my native language, being troubled with no other; and of all chiefly I thank these that employ their charity in translation of well meaning authors, which I hope I may read without asking leave of those that through scrupulosity dare not'.[97]

[95] Barry, 'Literacy and Literature in Popular Culture', 83–4.

[96] On Donne and Montaigne see John Carey, *John Donne: Life, Mind and Art* (London, 1981), 234, 237–8; on Burton and Montaigne see Martin Elsky, *Authorizing Words: Speech, Writing and Print in the English Renaissance* (Ithaca, NY, 1989), 211–13; on Donne, Burton, and Calvinism, see Stachniewski, *The Persecutory Imagination*, chs. 5 and 6.

[97] *Walwyns Just Defence*, 397–8.

4

'In a Lunatick Moode': Humanism, Puritanism, and the Rhetorical Strategies of Ranter Writing

THE EDUCATION OF A RANTER

It was acknowledged by all sides in the historiographical debate over the existence of the Ranters that the figure of Abiezer Coppe was of central importance.[1] In terms of his representation in the media, Coppe was the most sensational and notorious heretic of the English revolution. He was salaciously portrayed as a debauched heresiarch and whoremonger, who would 'preach stark naked many blasphemies and unheard of villainies in the day-time, and in the night [get] drunk and lye with a wench, that had also been his hearer, stark naked'; or, more threateningly, as a demonic figure who roamed the streets of post-regicide London, enticing its weak-minded citizens down into 'that deep abyss, from whence he vomits out in print to the world, those horrid Blasphemies and impieties, then which the world never saw more desperate, maintaining swearing, uncleanesse *in terminus* to be lawful'.[2] The unsettling mixture of prophecy, sexuality, and social radicalism in Coppe's writing that so horrified contemporaries has become increasingly fascinating to literary critics, to the point where extracts are now included in the *Norton Anthology of English Literature*. Christopher Hill called attention to the literary merits of Coppe's writing in *The World Turned Upside Down* and his later lecture on radical style, believing it 'unlike anything else in the seventeenth century' and a form of 'experimental prose'. Such judgements echo the less benevolent

---

[1] See e.g. Davis, 'Fear, Myth and Furore: Reappraising the Ranters', 84; McGregor et al., 'Debate. Fear, Myth and Furore', 168.

[2] Anthony Wood, *Athenae Oxonienses*, ed. Philip Bliss, 4 vols. (1813–20), iii. 959; *An Answer to Doctor Chamberlaines Scandalous and False Papers* (1650), 6. This pamphlet is signed 'Philalethes'.

commentaries of Coppe's contemporary opponents, who referred to his 'strange and fearful *straine*' and 'phantastick' style.[3] Indeed despite Coppe's admission into the literary canon, critics often seem to be as confused about his intentions as John Tickell, who in 1651 accused Coppe of manipulating 'all expressions, ways and windings, to keep himself from being known'. One critic finds himself 'ultimately puzzled and uncertain about [Coppe's] status and seriousness'; another simply concludes Coppe has no intention other than 'play, parody and prankishness in themselves'.[4] Such declarations of defeat do not further our understanding of a complex writer and his response to his historical situation; nor does the inadequate conclusion that Coppe's prose is eventually only a recycling of biblical imagery, a 'display of Old Testament metaphorics' and 'a cento of biblical texts'.[5] Scriptural language is central to Coppe's prose, but he calls upon other cultural resources. A different approach to Coppe as a writer is required to revise some of the misguided notions that have persisted about the sophistication of his writing and which provides fuller answers to the questions posed by Ann Hughes: 'Why and how did [those called Ranters] turn to print as a means of communication? What audience did they envisage for their works? What is the significance of the stylistic devices which they adopted?'.[6] This chapter considers aspects of these questions in relation to Abiezer Coppe.

One way to evade the polemical stereotypes which revisionist historians have argued contaminate the evidence for the nature of radicalism in this period is to turn to individual biography, and to explore biographical sources which have been hitherto ignored or the significance of which has not been fully realized. The outline of Coppe's life, as described disapprovingly by Anthony Wood, is well known. Born in Warwick in 1619, Coppe was educated at Warwick School, before arriving at All Souls College, Oxford, in 1636, transferring to Merton College as a postmaster or scholar the following year. Upon the outbreak of civil war he left Oxford without completing his degree, returning to Warwick

[3] Hill, *The World Turned Upside Down*, 210; Hill, 'Radical Prose in Seventeenth Century England', 110. The contemporary observations are from anon., *A Blow at the Root* (1650), repr. in Davis, *Fear, Myth and History*, 197; John Tickell, *The Bottomless Pit Smoking in Familisme*, 39. An extract from *A Fiery Flying Roll* is included in the *Norton Anthology of English Literature*, ed. M. H. Abrams et al., 6th edn., 2 vols. (New York, 1993), i. 1744–8.

[4] Tickell, *The Bottomless Pit Smoking in Familisme*, 39; Corns, *Uncloistered Virtue*, 193; Byron Nelson, 'The Ranters and the Limits of Language', in Holstun (ed.), *Pamphlet Wars: Rhetoric in the English Revolution*, 61–76 (66).

[5] James Grantham Turner, *One Flesh: Paradisal Marriage and Sexual Relations in the Age of Milton* (Oxford, 1987), 89; Pooley, *English Prose of the Seventeenth Century*, 163–4.

[6] Hughes, 'Early Quakerism: A Historian's Afterword', 143.

before becoming a roaming Anabaptist preacher. According to Richard Baxter, '[Coppe] continued a most zealous re-baptizer God's many years, and re-baptized more than any one man that ever I heard of in the countrey, witnesse *Warwickeshire.*, *Oxfordshire*, part of *Worcestershire* &c'.[7] As with many of those who became prominent radicals, he served as chaplain to a provincial Parliamentary Army garrison, at Compton House in Warwickshire in 1646, apparently after a brief imprisonment for his Anabaptist activities. Around 1647–8 he seems to have had an association with the itinerant lay preacher Richard Coppin and with conventicles in Oxfordshire and Berkshire, before achieving notoriety with his ventures into print in 1649. These publications provoked his imprisonment under the Blasphemy Act of 1650, although he was actually imprisoned before the Act was on the statutes. The Rump Parliament ordered all copies of *A Fiery Flying Roll* (1649) to be publicly burnt.[8] After two recantations, he was released in 1651. Little is known of his later life. The Berkshire minister Tickell denied the authenticity of one of Coppe's recantation sermons in Burford in *The Bottomless Pit Smoaking in Familisme* (1651); later Tickell used an admission of association with Coppe by John Pordage, rector of Bradfield and advocate of the spiritualist theology of Jacob Boehme, in an attempt to have Pordage tried for blasphemy. In his journal George Fox records a meeting with 'a great company of Ranters' while he was in prison in 1655, the leader being one 'Cobbe', probably a mistranscription for 'Coppe'.[9] An anonymous broadsheet of 1657 entitled *Divine Fire-Works* is evidently Coppe's work, written in the style of his publications of 1649. After the Restoration Coppe became a doctor in Surrey, having changed his name to Higham; he died in 1672.[10]

Some new biographical evidence has come to light which, though minor in itself, emphasizes how assumptions that radical belief originated in a popular heretical underground have distorted critical perceptions of

---

[7] Richard Baxter, *Plain Scripture Proof of Infants Church Membership* (1651), 148.

[8] On details of Coppe's position at Compton House see Anne Laurence, 'Parliamentary Army Chaplains, 1642–1651', D.Phil. thesis, 2 vols. (Oxford University, 1981), ii. 310–11; on Coppe's imprisonment see Baxter, *Plain Scripture Proof*, 148.

[9] Christopher Fowler, *Daemonium Meridianum*, 2 pts. (1655, 1656), i. 60; Fox, *Journal*, ed. J. L. Nickalls (Cambridge, 1952), 195. In his 1998 edition of the *Journal* Nigel Smith changes 'Cobbe' to 'Coppe' (149).

[10] *Divine Fire-Works* bears the motto 'INABHIAM', presumably representing the Spirit dwelling in 'AB[IEZER] HI[GH]AM', with a pun on the divine self-defining declarations of 'I am' in Isaiah, Ezekiel, and Revelation. In the account of his conversion experience in *A Fiery Flying Roll* Coppe refers to the 'rotting of my old name, which is damned, and cast out (as a toad to the dunghill) that I might have a new name, with me, upon me, within me, which is, I am' (*CRW*, 83).

Coppe's prose. Thomas Dugard became Master of Warwick School in 1633 after graduating from the generally Puritan Cambridge college, Sidney Sussex, and taught Coppe for three years. Dugard's diary for the period 1632–42 leaves an account of the Puritan circle in which Dugard mixed in this period, revolving around Lord Brooke's hospitality at Warwick Castle. The diary makes several references to Coppe, and it is evident that Dugard regarded him as something of a protégé, using his influence to secure patronage for Coppe on his return from Oxford: in 1641, Coppe preached two Sunday sermons and five lectures in Warwick.[11] Such preaching was strictly speaking illegal, for Charles I's 'Instructions to Laud' decreed that market-day lectures were to be given only by 'grave and orthodox divines', whereas Coppe had not even completed his degree. The diary also records Coppe's excellence in Greek and Latin, describing his after-dinner visits to Dugard in 1634, at the age of fifteen, to read Homer and the *Epigrammata Sacra* of Richard Crashaw, published in Cambridge that year.[12] The record of Coppe's preaching at the age of twenty-two without any formal sanction or qualification points to the nature of the Puritan environment in which he grew up. The most striking feature of Dugard's account of his life in the 1630s in Warwickshire is the sheer amount of preaching which could be heard; Dugard often attended up to three sermons a day, took notes, and discussed them with his clerical and lay friends.[13] Little distinction seems to have been made between the preaching of beneficed clerics, schoolmasters like Dugard, and the merely eager such as Coppe. Dugard's own activities mirror those of the beneficed clergy, conducting baptisms, burials, and marriages, and he had preached on twelve occasions, including sermons at Warwick Castle, before he was even ordained as a deacon in 1634. Another young, unqualified pupil of Dugard's, John Roe, was encouraged to preach while on vacation from Emmanuel College, Cambridge, in December 1638 and 1639. This is possibly the same John Roe who later became chaplain to the Parliamentary garrison at Tynemouth Castle.[14] It becomes evident that Coppe was raised in an environment in Warwick in the 1630s and early 1640s in which formal religion had no distinct position

---

[11] British Library, Add. MSS 23146; the diary is in Latin. On Coppe's preaching see fos. 93[r], 97[r].

[12] 'Instructions to Laud, 1633', in *Documentary Annals of the Reformed Church of England*, ed. Edward Cardwell, 2 vols. (1844), ii. 230; BL Add. MSS 23146, fos. 31[v], 33[v].

[13] BL Add. MSS 23146, fo. 39[r] for an instance of a busy but not unusual day.

[14] For Dugard's preaching, see e.g. BL Add. MSS 23146, fos. 22[v], 30[r]; for his baptizing see fo. 51[r]; on Roe see fos. 31[v], 81[v], 87[r]; Anne Laurence, *Parliamentary Army Chaplains 1642–1651* (Suffolk, 1990), 169.

of authority over lay preaching or ad hoc services amongst a gathering of the godly, and the extreme anti-formalism (or what might rather be termed supraformalism) of Coppe's radical writing becomes comprehensible as an evolution from his adolescent experience.

Ann Hughes has discussed this diary and argued that it reveals Dugard to be 'part of a "parliamentary–Puritan connection", a broad circle of the godly that comprised minor provincial figures and prominent national politicians, and which helped create the challenge to Charles I's personal rule'.[15] Although Dugard himself was to remain a moderate Presbyterian throughout his career who willingly conformed at the Restoration, his diary records his frequent lunching with the anti-Laudian peer Brooke during the ten-year period, with such guests as Peter Sterry, Cambridge Platonist, Brooke's chaplain from 1638, and later chaplain to Cromwell. Sterry's involvement with the Dugard circle that provided patronage for Coppe is of interest not only in terms of Sterry's future political prominence: he was associated throughout his career with more extreme religious radicals, although the exact nature of the association remains uncertain. Sterry attached a refutation of practical antinomianism, before the term 'Ranter' was common currency, to the published version of his sermon on 1 November 1649 celebrating Cromwell's return from Ireland. This has been described as 'the first intellectually structured presentation of Ranter doctrine not based on gossip and hearsay', in which Sterry uses 'Ranter terminology and allegorical imagery'.[16] Opinion is divided over whether Sterry was trying to 'disengage' himself from such radicals, or whether he was their life-long opponent: he could be the owner of 'Mr. *Sterrys* place' in London where Laurence Clarkson recorded preaching 'some while' around 1647 in his autobiography.[17] Dugard's diary raises the possibility that after Coppe returned from Oxford he knew Sterry through Dugard when both Sterry and Coppe were preaching in Warwick in 1640–1. Combined with Clarkson's reference, this suggests that Sterry may have been involved in the 1640s with figures later called Ranters, whom he was quick to denounce as he became more closely linked with Cromwell (or as their beliefs became increasingly extreme). Richard

[15] Ann Hughes, 'Thomas Dugard and his Circle in the 1630s: A "Parliamentary–Puritan" Connexion?', *Historical Journal*, 29 (1986), 771–93 (784); see also Hughes, *Politics, Society and Civil War in Warwickshire, 1620–1660* (Cambridge, 1987), 71–80.

[16] On Dugard's meeting with Sterry see BL Add. MSS 23146, fos. 77^{r-v}, 81^v, 95^v; Peter Sterry, 'The Epistle Dedicatory' to *The Comings Forth of Christ* (1650); N. I. Matar, 'Peter Sterry and the Ranters', *Notes and Queries*, NS, 29 (1982), 504–6.

[17] Matar, 'Peter Sterry and the Ranters'; Christopher Hill, *A Nation of Change and Novelty*, 189–90; Laurence Clarkson, *The Lost Sheep Found* (1660), in *CRW*, 23.

Baxter begins his taxonomy of English enthusiasts with Sterry before going on to discuss the Ranters, claiming that their doctrines were 'almost the same'; in a posthumously published work, Sterry accepted that his theology may 'seem to confirm the *Ranters* in their *licentious Principles* and Practices'. D. P. Walker has shown the antinomian implications of Sterry's understanding of sin and universal grace, implications that Sterry himself evidently recognized. If Sterry knew both Clarkson and Coppe, Walker's speculation about the proximity of the beliefs of Sterry and Richard Coppin, for whom Coppe wrote a preface in 1649, assumes greater significance.[18]

While biographical detail about Coppe is so scant, such linking of sources closely connected with him is a valuable exercise in moving towards a fuller understanding of the social and cultural context from which the radical emerged. Anthony Wood's depiction of Coppe's days at Merton College, including the colourful anecdote that he took extra food from dinner, claiming it was 'a bit for his cat' when it was actually intended for a 'wanton housewife' whom he would 'several times entertain, for one night or more' in his rooms, is obviously to be viewed with some scepticism. However, Wood offers more reliable information concerning Coppe's tutor at Merton, Ralph Button, whom Wood calls 'a noted tutor' and 'good scholar' but 'puritannically affected'; he is described as one of the 'snivelling Presbyterians' then at Merton, and of his pupils Wood confides that 'some of them became famous, and some infamous'.[19] It seems Thomas Dugard was impressed with Coppe's progress under Button, for another of his prize pupils, John Murcot, was 'in Easter Term 1642 ... committed to the tuition of Mr. Ralph Button' at Merton. As with Coppe, Button left Oxford 'when the rebellion began' (although presumably not before 1642), for Gresham College, but returned in 1648 to be installed as university orator and Canon of Christ Church. He was ejected from these posts after the Restoration. It is evident that Button was a well-known Puritan and a respected scholar, who 'played an active role in attempting to radicalize Oxford theologically'.[20] The auction catalogue of his library hints at this radicalism, revealing he possessed over a thousand books and pamphlets, including some of the works that Nigel Smith has discussed as theological and linguistic influences upon radical religious writing, such as the *Theologia*

---

[18] Baxter, *Relinquiae Baxterianae*, 74–8; Peter Sterry, *Discourse of the Freedom of the Will* (1675), 156; Walker, *The Decline of Hell*, ch. 7, esp. 104–5, 119.

[19] For Wood on Coppe see *Athenae Oxonienses*, iii. 959–62, on Button, iii. 54, 307, 381, 476, 959; iv. 194, 442.

[20] Ibid. iii. 381; J. A. Berlatsky, 'Ralph Button', in *BDBR*.

Germanica (in the Latin edition of 1632, which was translated in 1646 by Giles Randall) and Nicholas of Cusa's *De Docta Ignorantia* (in the translation by John Everard, completed in the 1620s and published in 1650).[21] While interest in these spiritualist texts does not in itself imply heterodoxy, his association with Button suggests the theologically speculative milieu in which Coppe circulated in pre-war Oxford. Certainly the catalogue of Button's library demonstrates Coppe's access to most subjects that he might have wished to read about at Oxford through his tutor's library alone. Button's library contained many works by the celebrated Hebraist Johannes Buxtorf, and in *Musarum Oxoniensium* (1654), a volume of verse by Oxford scholars celebrating Cromwell's victory over the Dutch, Button contributes the only poem in Hebrew, suggesting he was a noted Hebraist. As we shall see, Coppe's use of Hebrew is an important aspect of the printed representation of his prophetic voice.[22]

These biographical insights serve to emphasize Coppe's humanist education, and provide a picture, if blurred, of his privileged Calvinist training. They confirm the claims of one contemporary that 'Mr. *Cops* . . . for a long time pretended both to learning, reason, and Religion, and for some time, as I am from very good hands informed, walked very strictly, til he first fell from submitting to Church Government'. The anecdotal fragment depicting Coppe reading Crashaw's Latin epigrams to Dugard is suggestive. It reveals that Puritans such as Dugard and Coppe were happily reading Crashaw in the 1630s and using his epigrams as a study in eloquence, despite Crashaw's 'Lectori' to the *Epigrammata Sacra* praising the Jesuit influences on his poetry, and the intense liturgical imagery of the epigrams.[23] Dugard's anecdote is a useful reminder of Coppe's linguistic ability and training, and gives an indication of his reading. It illustrates how the image of Coppe as a tub preacher, a caricature persisting from the anti-Ranter pamphlets documented by J. C. Davis through Christopher Hill's retrieval of radical culture to the notes of the *Norton Anthology*, needs to be revised.[24]

---

[21] *Catalogus Liborum Bibliothecis Selectissimus Doctorissimorum Virorium* (1681), 30, 36. Smith, *Perfection Proclaimed*, 107–43.

[22] *Musarum Oxoniensium* (Oxford, 1654), 6. See also *Momus Elenctius* (1654), a satirical poem on well-known figures in 1650s Oxford, 4: 'Next Button and Say, and G. O. did meet | In Hebrew well English'd and Latin shod feet'.

[23] Richard Crashaw, *Poetical Works*, ed. L.C. Martin (2nd edn., Oxford, 1957), 14.

[24] *An Answer to Doctor Chamberlaines Scandalous and False Papers*, 6. In the notes on Coppe in the 1993 edition of the *Norton Anthology* the editor comments on Coppe's use of 'corpse' to refer to his body: 'Though Coppe had a year or two at Oxford, he seems to believe that the English corpse can be equated with Latin *corpus* i.e. a body' (i. 1746). A glance at the *OED* would have shown this to be a not uncommon usage in the period, with one of the examples cited taken from *Paradise Lost*.

THE SCHOOLS OF ANTICHRIST

After leaving his position as chaplain to Major George Purefoy's regiment at Compton House, Coppe had an association with Richard Coppin in 1648, producing Coppe's long preface to Coppin's *Divine Teachings*. Historians have been unsure how closely the writings of Coppin, variously defined as a universalist and 'perfectionist Arminian', can be related to those of Coppe. The latter definition of Coppin's religious identity is suggested by J. C. Davis, who argues that the central theme of Coppin's teaching is the 'delegitimation of all authority except that of the indwelling God'.[25] This is a useful approach to Coppin, although it should be pointed out that while he believes every individual can achieve salvation, he maintains a hierarchy of God's chosen saints on earth: 'in the same fulnes as [Christ] is in one, he is in every one: But there is a difference, every one hath not a like manifestation of him . . . not the same knowledge of Christ'. Hill misleadingly quotes only half of this line to present the 'extreme democratic' conclusions of Coppin's religion; the missing half discloses Coppin's accompanying belief that God's saints are an elect few, perfected by revelation, not self-recognition. This is surely what Coppe means when he warns of 'the danger of arising into the Notion of Spirituals afore the Lord awaken a soul, and saies, come up hither'.[26] Coppin's religious beliefs seem to be a novel (and not entirely coherent) fusion of Calvinism, Arminianism, and universalism. In a debate with Coppin in 1651 John Osborn accused him of holding the same blasphemous doctrines as Coppe, an accusation that Davis dismisses, warning that historians should be 'cautious about guilt by association'.[27] Yet the fact that the two appeared in print together surely indicates shared concerns or a degree of shared belief. They may have met through Giles Calvert, who published both *Divine Teachings* and Coppe's first single-authored book, *Some Sweet Sips, of Some Spiritual Wine* (1649), and who, according to Laurence Clarkson, moved in the Ranter milieu.[28] Coppin's pamphlet is important as a comparative text to Coppe's writing, demonstrating how Coppe expresses similar ideas in a more complex and parodic style, drawing upon his advanced formal education.

[25] For various approaches to Coppin's religious identity see A. L. Morton, 'Richard Coppin', in *BDBR*; Hill, *The World Turned Upside Down*, 177–9; *CRW*, 11; Davis's definition is to be found in *Fear, Myth and History*, 39.

[26] Coppin, *Divine Teachings*, 9; Hill, *The World Turned Upside Down*, 177; Abiezer Coppe, *Some Sweet Sips, of Some Spiritual Wine* (1649), in *CRW*, 43.

[27] John Osborn, *The World to Come* (1651), sig. A2ʳ; Davis, *Fear, Myth and History*, 38.

[28] Laurence Clarkson, *The Lost Sheep Found*, in *CRW* 180–1.

In his autobiographical pamphlet *Truths Testimony* (1655), Coppin describes how in 1648, after his conversion experience in London, he came to Berkshire and Oxfordshire to preach, but was prevented from doing so by accusations of blasphemy. This led Coppin to turn to print to spread his message: 'And I having not my freedom to speak, fell a writing; which things were printed, and brought forth to publique view, in a book entitled *Divine Teachings*' (18). It was evidently in the Midlands area that Coppin came to know Coppe, whose writing of the preface to *Divine Teachings* suggests he was a figure of greater authority than Coppin, despite the latter being the older man. Coppe had only previously published a very brief preface to *John the Divines Divinity* by 'I. F.' in 1648. It seems that Coppe's success as a preacher in the Midlands, noted by Baxter and by a letter from Coventry to Parliament following Coppe's arrest in 1650, referring to him preaching 'formerly . . . admirable good oratory', ensured his position as a referee for Coppin. Coppe's reputation as a preacher in the 1640s is further suggested by the comments of Samuel Fisher (in the midst of an attack on Richard Baxter) in a collection of Fisher's Baptist writings issued in 1655:

when *Copp* was in his standing in the *Church of England*, I remember him very well, for I knew him better then than ever since, he had some bounds from conscience to his corruption, but having been inlightened higher than Mr. *Baxter* ever was yet in the will and way of God, and tasted of the heavenly gift, he did degenerate into wayes of wickedness . . . the higher the rise into reformation, the more desperate the fall into deformation . . .[29]

The first edition of *Divine Teachings* appeared with Coppe's preface in 1649, the same year as Coppe's *Some Sweet Sips, of Some Spiritual Wine*, which is dedicated to 'all the Saints . . . especially [in] *Hook-Norton*, and thereabouts in *Oxfordshire* . . . and for the Saints at *Abingdon*' (51); Coppe's pamphlet may have been distributed in the Midlands, since Thomason does not record acquiring a copy.[30] The theme of both *Divine Teachings* and *Some Sweet Sips, of Some Spiritual Wine* is the sufficiency of the knowledge revealed by the indwelling Spirit, contrasted with the empty pretensions of the formal or 'humane' learning valued by the Anglican and Puritan clergy. Coppin defiantly asserted, as we have seen, that his commission to preach came directly from the Holy Spirit and 'not from *Oxford* and *Cambridge*, or the schools of Anti-Christ' (*Truths Testimony*, 16), and there are some clear similarities between Coppin's anti-intellectual rhetoric in *Divine Teachings* and Coppe's long address

[29] *Several Proceedings in Parliament*, xvi (January 1650), 213; Samuel Fisher, *Christianismus Redivivus* (1655), 413–14. [30] 'Introduction' to *CRW*, 12.

to the 'Scholars of Oxford' in 'Epistle III' of *Some Sweet Sips*. Coppin's invocation of Galatians 1: 12 is repeated by Coppe at the beginning of his address: 'For I neither received it of men, neither was I taught it by men, but by the revelation of Jesus Christ'. For Coppin, the inner illumination of the Spirit dims all others: the enlightened 'shall have no need of the light of the sun, or of the Moon; as the light of all holy Worship, Ordinances, Prayers, Duties, Preaching, Teaching, hearing and Reading and the like which are vanishing lights, and like the Shadowes must away, when the Substance, which is the Sun of Righteousness appears'. Coppin describes how the resurrection of Christ—the sun/Son of righteous-ness—within the saint allows him to see that man's pretensions to wisdom are 'but the vail or covering, which is cast over all Nations, in which hath been hid the glory of God' (19). He alludes to the Song of Songs, used as a refrain by Coppe in *Some Sweet Sips* to convey the ecstatic experience of union with the Spirit of Christ, though in an erotic tone and incantatory style absent from Coppin's prose: 'The day *star* is up, rise up my *love*, my *dove*, my faire one, and *come away* . . . It is the voice my beloved that saith open to me—I am *risen indeed*, rise up my love, open to my faire one. I would faine *shine more* gloriously in you, than I did at a *distance* from you, at Jerusalem without you' (52; compare the Song of Songs 2: 10, 5: 2). Coppe describes how the Israelites were guided out of Egypt not by 'Sunne and Moone' but by '*This New Light*, This *Strange Light*' of the indwelling Spirit, that calls to the saints to 'Arise out of *Flesh*, into Spirit, out of Form, into Power, Out of *Type* into Truth, out of the *Shadow*, into the *Substance* . . . not hug appearances, or *Formes* in our bosome any longer' (60, 47–8). Coppin records how 'the in dwelling of God in us confounds and puts out lights we have formerly walked by, and taketh away formal, outward, shadowy and imperfect things which (formerly) we hugg'd in our bosomes' ('Contents'). Coppin closes *Divine Teachings* by contrasting the fallen, carnal methods of interpreting Scripture taught at the universities with the pure fountain of wisdom infused by the Spirit: '*Oxford* and *Cambridge*, which have been looked upon as a Well yeelding cleer and pure water, that is, cleer and pure learn-ing for the studying of the letter . . . yet in the use of it hath proved muddy, full of corruption' (22–3). In *Some Sweet Sips* Coppe similarly contrasts 'the cleere *pure God*', the '*Fountaine of Life*', with the corruptions of the ministry and the universities, which are 'the *Rivers of Babylon*'; the priests and professors are 'muddy men, profound men are Muddy, *Diviners, mad*, and *muddy*' (71). Rather God speaks through 'Fishers, Publicans, Tanners, Tent-Makers, Leathern Aprons as well as through University men—Long gowns, Cloakes or Cassocks' (60). Coppe adopts here the familiar anticlerical rhetoric of holy simplicity, the traditional response of those accused of heterodoxy to the hostile application of the topos of the heretic as illiterate. Yet Coppe had undergone the linguistic and rhetorical training that the orthodox clergy invoked to disqualify their radical opponents from preaching and scriptural interpretation. Whereas the unlettered Coppin emphasizes his absolute separation from the corruptions of elite cultural life—a purity reflected in the plainness of his prose style—the polemical and satirical focus of Coppe's address to the 'Scholars of Oxford' is precisely the educational experience that separated *litteratus* from *illitteratus* in early modern England: the learning of Latin grammar.

THE GRAMMAR OF THINGS

The full title of 'Epistle III' in *Some Sweet Sips* is an 'Apologeticall, and additionall word to the Reader, especially to my Cronies, the Scholars of Oxford'. By using the specific varsity slang of 'cronies', Coppe immediately signals his own familiarity with collegiate life but he does so only to expose the laughable pretensions of Oxford scholarship beside the true teachings of the Spirit. The division of the text into epistles identifies Coppe with St Paul, who after his conversion condemned, in the words of the Genevan marginalia, those who value 'the outwarde shewe of wisdom and eloquence, [more] than true godliness'. Coppe's initial inclusion of himself in the institution serves ironically to emphasize his remoteness from his former fellow students after his conversion. Oxford's Christ Church—where Coppe's former tutor Button was now a canon—is belittled beside '*Christ's* Church (the Church of the first born, which are written in heaven)', as is the university before 'the universal Assembly' (61). Coppe issues an ironic response to the type of panegyric delivered to Christ Church by Robert Burton in the *Anatomy of Melancholy*, who declared it 'the most flourishing Colledge in Europe'. *The Anatomy of Melancholy* may have been in Coppe's mind, as it was a favourite text of the clerical critics of the radicals for its diagnosis of sectarianism and enthusiasm as forms of madness and demonic possession; John Tickell refers his reader to Burton to discover the species of devil to which Coppe belongs.[31] The second section of 'Epistle III' is entitled 'a Christmas Caroll

---

[31] For the varsity origins of the term 'cronies' see the *OED*; Burton, *Anatomy of Melancholy*, i. 3. Tickell, *The Bottomless Pit Smoking in Familisme*, 42.

at the famous University of—the melody whereof was made in the heart, and heard in the corner of a late converted Jew'. What follows is one of the most striking pieces of writing, both linguistically and typographically, in any printed text of this period, in which Coppe at once displays and ridicules classical learning through parodic mimicry of the voice of educational authority in early modern England—Lily's Grammar. Also known as the *Regia grammatica* and the Authorized Grammar, it was designed in the early years of the sixteenth century by William Lily and John Colet (on the advice of Erasmus) to be the keystone of the humanist educational programme in England. This text was decreed the standard Latin grammar by Henry VIII in 1540 and technically, despite the appearance of other grammars in the seventeenth century (particularly after 1660), it remained exclusively sanctioned by the State until the mid-eighteenth century. During the mid-seventeenth century its use was ensured by the visitations of the bishops to grammar schools, and Lily's Grammar would certainly have been the text used at Warwick School in the 1630s.[32] In *Ludus Literarius* John Brinsley simply assumes that the schoolmaster will teach Latin grammar by 'Lillies Rules'. Milton's ideal college in *Of Education* (1644) would encompass 'those general studies which take up all our time from Lilly to the commencing, as they term it, Master of Arts'; although when he advises that boys should 'begin with the chief and necessary rules of some good Grammar, either that now us'd, or any better' his final qualification is more educationally (and perhaps politically, as we shall see) radical than it might appear to the modern reader.[33]

As boys spent their first four years at school learning intensively Latin language, Lily's Grammar can be described as the foundation text of the intellectual culture of early modern England. The textual apparatus, linguistic exercises, and typographical design of the Grammar would have been imprinted on the mind of any formally educated man in this period. The text as authorized by royal injunction consisted of two parts, *A Short Introduction of Grammar*, covering (in the vernacular) the eight 'parts of speech' and the rules of concord, and *Brevissima institutio seu ratio grammatices*, which dealt with (in Latin) the gender of nouns, the conjugation of verbs, and the rules of versification. In his address to the 'Scholars of Oxford' Coppe parodies the language and typographical

---

[32] Foster Watson, *The English Grammar Schools to 1660* (London, 1908), 257–79; Donald Leman Clark, *John Milton at St Paul's School: A Study of Ancient Rhetoric in English Renaissance Education* (New York, 1948), 132–42; G. A. Padley, *Grammatical Theory in Western Europe 1500–1700: The Latin Tradition* (Cambridge, 1976), 24–7.

[33] Brinsley, *Ludus Literarius, or the Grammar Schoole*, 22–3; *CPWM*, ii. 380, 383.

design of *A Short Introduction of Grammar* to bathetic effect, exposing the spiritual emptiness of 'humane' learning by defacing an icon of institutional education. As Foster Watson puts it: 'To the orthodox schoolmaster the Authorized Grammar was, as it were, a sacred book, and once known, all the facts of classical literature could find explanation or justification in it'.[34]

In describing 'Epistle III' as a 'Christmas Caroll' and dating it 'December 25th 1648', Coppe celebrates the redemption of the saints in whose heart Christ is reborn or, in Coppin's phrase, in whom Christ is 'manifest'. The regenerate Coppe has recovered Adam's ability to read the *signatura rerum*, the divine signatures present in all things: he hears the spirit of God preach 'Sermons through clouds and fire, fire and water, heaven and earth, through light and darkness, day and night . . . through bed and board, through food and raiment . . . Mine ear hast thou opened indeed' (60).[35] The redeemed are effortlessly fluent in this universal grammar, and *Some Sweet Sips* is represented as a primer for the language of the Spirit, a language that denies the conventions of syntax and linear progression:

Brave Schollars—that can meet him in this Paper, that can meet him here, and rejoyce in him; that can reade their lesson in this primer; that can read him within Book; but better Schollars they, that have their lessons without book, and can reade God (not by roate) but plainly and perfectly, on the backside, and outside of the Book, as well as the inside: that can take this Primer in their hands; and hold it heel upwards, and then reade him there . . . that can reade him downwards and upwards, upwards and downwards, from left to right, right to left: that can reade him in the Sun, in the Clouds, as well in the Clouds as in the Sun. (61)

The address 'To the Reader' of the Authorized Grammar by which Coppe and the 'Scholars of Oxford' were taught Latin uses similar language to Coppe's 'additionall word to the Reader'. The schoolmaster should:

in countenance and diligence of teaching make [the scholar] to rehearse so that he hath perfectly that what is behinde, he suffer him not to go forward . . . Wherin it is profitable not only that he can orderly decline his Noune and Verbe, but every way, forward, backward, by cases, by persons: that he can without stop or studie tell. And unto this I count not the Scholar perfect nor readie to go any further, till

---

[34] Watson, *The English Grammar Schools*, 284.
[35] The phrase *signatura rerum* is borrowed from John Ellistone's translation of Jacob Boehme's *Signatura Rerum, or the Signature of all Things, shewing the Sign, and Signification of the several Forms and Shapes in the Creation* (1651), but not with the intention of suggesting direct Behmenist influence on Coppe.

he hath this already learned . . . This when he can perfectly doe, and hath learned every part not by rote, but reason.[36]

The bathos of the contrast between the 'perfect' scholar who learns his cases and declensions 'not by rote, but reason' with the perfected saint who reads the signatures of the Spirit throughout creation is released through Coppe's mocking of 'university men, long-gowns, Cloakes, or Cassocks'. Whereas Coppe can read the divine 'within book, and without book, and as well without book as within book', in his introduction Lily laments how many pupils 'read the Latine in the Booke, can tell you the English thereof at any time: but when they layd away their Bookes, they can not contriwise tell you for the English the Latine again' (10).

Coppe goes on to state that 'if we were not pittiful poor Schollers, dunces, dullards' we would realize that 'the eternall God may be seene, felt, heard, and understood in the Book of the *Creatures*, as in the Book of the *Scriptures, alias Bible*' (60). This echoes the conclusion of the prayer which precedes the first section ('Of a Noun') of *A Short Introduction* and which was doubtless recited by the class before they began their grammatical exercises: 'so that thou which workest all things in all creatures, mayest make thy gracious benefits shine in me, to the endless glory and honour of thine immortall Majestie. So be it' (13). This prayer asking for divine assistance in the classroom becomes in *Some Sweet Sips* a rhapsody in praise of Coppe's new, prophetic state of being, throwing an ironic light upon the schoolboy's request in Lily's prayer that God 'beautify by the light of thy heavenly grace the towardnesse of my wit, the which with all powers of nature thou hast powered into me'. Like St Paul, Coppe's 'wit' has been perfected by the Spirit supernaturally 'powered' into his physical form—he no longer views the divine mysteries of creation through a glass, darkly. He relates this experience in the preface to *A Fiery Flying Roll*, describing how the 'visions and revelations of God, and the strong hand of eternall invisible almightinnesse, was stretched out upon me, within me, for the space of foure dayes and nights, without intermission . . . though to the utter cracking of my credit, and to the rotting of my old name, which is damned, and cast out' (83). Lily advises that the master does not proceed too quickly in teaching the rules of grammar, for 'this posting haste overthroweth and hurteth a great sort of wits, and casteth them into an amazednesse . . . and then the Master thinketh the Scholar to be a dullard, and the Schollar thinketh the thing to be unease, and too hard for his wit' (8). For Coppe, the true 'pittiful poor

---

[36] William Lily and John Colet, *A Short Introduction of Grammar; Brevissima Institutio seu Ratio Grammaticae* (1624 edn.), 9. All future references are to this edition.

Schollars, dunces, dullards' are those who seek enlightenment in, as Lily puts it, the 'continuall rehearsall of things learned' from a textbook; and, by extension, in all the facts of classical and humanist literature to which the learning of Latin grammar provided access (9).

Coppe then once again directly addresses his former cronies: 'Well, hie you, learne apace, when you have learned all that your *Pedagogues* can teach you, you shall goe to Schole no longer, you shall be (*Sub ferula*) no longer, under the *lash* no longer, but be set to the University (of the universall Assembly)' (61). We have seen in the previous chapter how the use of the rod or ferula to ensure both good grammar and good morals was endemic in the early modern grammar school, and how its place in the humanist classroom was supported by the Puritan belief that the 'teacher must work against the sinful and depraved nature of the boys if he is to succeed'. Puritan discipline 'severe as it was, was based on the premiss that children were redeemable; correction had therefore to be imposed as a duty owed to God as part of the covenant': for it was believed that even if children did turn out to be of the elect, they had not yet received the grace which would enable them not to be evil.[37] The spiritual autobiography of Richard Norwood reveals how academic failure and subsequent beating by zealous masters at grammar school in the early seventeenth century could instil a sense of reprobation and religious despair.[38] Despite his academic success at Warwick School, Coppe would doubtless have experienced the humiliation and guilt of being beaten in the front of the class for making mistakes in reciting his Latin grammar; and, given the Puritan environment in which he was schooled, of having that grammatical error linked to his unregenerate condition. In *Some Sweet Sips*, however, Coppe declines an antinomian ascent to perfection that releases the saint from the 'sinful and depraved' nature represented by the rod and renders the soteriological ethics of education irrelevant. For the centrepiece of Coppe's address to the 'Scholars of Oxford' is a parody of the declensions of verbs in *A Short Introduction of Grammar*. The visual arrangement of Lily's text, in which Latin terms and phrases were placed one to a line and then grouped together by large brackets, was central to the 'development of the spatially rationalized page' in early modern England.[39] Coppe appropriates this characteristic typographical design and redefines Lily's declensions of verbs as stages of sanctification.

---

[37] Leman Clark, *John Milton at St Paul's School*, 55, 57, 141; Morgan, *Godly Learning*, 149.

[38] Stachniewski, *The Persecutory Imagination*, 61–2.

[39] Martin Elsky, *Authorizing Words: Speech, Writing, and Print in the English Renaissance* (Ithaca, NY, 1989), 125, 128.

These declensions of the Spirit develop into an incantatory prayer for the apocalyptic dissolution of social inequality and religious difference.

Adopting his characteristic persona of the Pauline holy fool, Coppe plays on grammatical terms to add the 'Lunatick' mood to the six moods of verb listed in the Authorized Grammar. To be 'in a Lunatick Moode', to be 'accounted fooles and madmen' (61), becomes the first rule of the divine accidence, recalling Coppin's adaptation of 1 Cor. 3: 19 in *Divine Teachings*: to the regenerate 'all the wisdom of men, and the learning of men, will appear to be but meer foolishness, madness and confusion' (2). Coppe faithfully mimics the language and progression of the Authorized Grammar. He defines the optative mood of wishing or wanting: 'And (*Utina, si, o, o, si utinam*) I would to God the people of God (now) knew their interest in God, and *union in Him*' (62). The parenthetical insertion is Lily's declension of the adverbs of wishing; redeemed from their empty, formal function they become musical sounds of the spirit dwelling within Coppe, an aspect of his internalized 'Christmas Caroll'. Lily defines the optative in similar terms: 'The optative wisheth or desireth with these signs, Would God, I pray God or God Graunt . . . and hath evermore an adverbe of wishing joined with him' (42). Although following the formal rules of the Grammar, Coppe adds the whole declension of the adverbs of wishing to the optative, while the Grammar's habit of referring to verbs in the masculine singular—'joined with him'—is echoed by Coppe's desire for '*union in Him*'. Coppe reiterates the yearning for union with Christ, now playing upon the potential mood: 'Some may, can, might, should, would know it: (if they could,) there's the—*Potentiall*'. This echoes the Grammar's definition, in which the desire to love is cited as an example: 'The Potentiall Mood is knowen by these signes, May, can, would, should, or ought: as Amen, I may, or can love: without an Adverbe joined with him' (62). Next, in his version of the imperative mood, Coppe states that '[Christ] is in the Imparative moode and so are you', which recalls Coppin's insistence that 'the Lord Jesus Christ is in his people both the Teacher and the Hearer' (19).

The appropriation of grammatical form to describe the ascent to perfection finds further comic release at the climax of these spiritualized declensions, when Coppe mockingly acknowledges his temerity in breaking Lily's rules: 'And by this time I am so far beside myself, as to add an *Interjection* unto an *adverb* in the *Optative* line (now) *ha ha he—*' (62). As Coppe is drawn up into the '*Infinitive*', which is the '*infinite Love*' of God's grace, he emphasizes the irrelevance of humane learning by the pettiness of his grammatical transgression. Lily in fact lists 'ha ha he' as the correct interjection to signify laughing, and defines an interjection as 'a part of speech which betokeneth a sudden passion of the minde, under an unperfect voice' (72). The irony of comparing union with Christ to 'a sudden passion of the minde', and the regenerate language of the saint with 'an unperfect voice', seems to have appealed to Coppe. There may also be a pun on the grammatical 'interjection' and the ecstatic 'ejaculation' of the saint in praise of the Spirit's workings. Daniel Featley voiced a common complaint about the behaviour of sectarian preachers when he condemned the 'extempore ejaculations' by which they sought to conceal their intellectual inability to properly prepare and deliver a sermon. In proclaiming God's '*infinite love*', Coppe also seems to hint at Familist sympathies: it is 'that Family he is of—who is—Sweet Schollers, Your Moody Servant'. Coppe's elusiveness echoes Walwyn's provocatively playful adoption of the persona of a Familist in *The Power of Love*: 'What's here toward? (sayes one) sure one of the Family of Love: very well! pray stand still and consider: what family are you of I pray? Are you of Gods family? No doubt you are: why, God is love, and if you bee one of Gods children bee not ashamed of your Father, nor his Family'.[40] At the same time the pun on the infinitive mood and God's infinite love is again derived from Lily's definition: '[the Infinitive] hath neither number, nor person, nor nominative case before him, and is knowen commonly by this signe, To, as Amare, To Love' (79).

Coppe's laughter expresses his merry impunity from the law of the first covenant. The pedagogic rules of Lily's Grammar become symbolic of the subjection to external religious and moral forms from which Coppe has been released. Signing off his spiritual grammar as 'Your Moody Servant', Coppe plays upon the master–pupil relationship which is established in Lily's Grammar. Coppe's knowledge is instilled by the master of all creation rather than the master of the classroom: 'But no more of this till I come to (*Doctrina Magistri*) the learning of the *Master*, who is teaching me all parts of Speech, and all the Cases of Nounes, and all the Moods and Tenses of Verbs' (62). In *A Short Introduction*, under the heading 'Examples of the Cases of Nouns', examples of each case are addressed to the 'Master'. The nominative is illustrated by 'the Master teacheth', the dative by 'I give a book to the Master'. The genitive case is explained in language echoed by Coppe: 'The genitive case is known by this token, Of, and answereth to this question, Whose, thereof: as Doctrina Magistri, the learning of the Master' (18). God becomes Coppe's 'Tutor' and the 'Deane

---

[40] On 'interjection' and 'ejaculation' see the *OED*; Featley, *The Dippers Dipt*, 100; Walwyn, *The Power of Love*, in *WWW*, 79.

of *Christ-Church* Colledge' who is 'teaching his pupils his *Accidence*, a new way, new, new, new; [*Et hoc accidit, dum vile fuit*]'. The Latin tenses are also redefined as stages of the conversion process in this divine accidence: 'And there be five Tenses or Times: there is a time to be merry (*To be merry in the Lord*) and that is the present tense with some, to others the Future'. Lily's section on tenses begins identically: 'There be five Tenses or Times' (45). The address to Oxford closes as Coppe pretends to be in disputation with his 'cronies': he hears 'Interjections of Silence (such as *an* and such others) sounding in mine ears' (63). This seems at first meaningless, yet Coppe is actually using Lily's grammatically correct interjection for silence—'an'—and he plays with the paradox of having printed (and thus dumb) notation to represent sounds (and silence) by joking that his writing is halted by the interruptions of an imaginary audience (79). Coppe ends with a final statement of the transcendent knowledge revealed to the saints, ironically styled as scholars of 'divinity': 'Only I must tell my Cronies at Oxford, that such schollars who can speake with tongues more than they all—(and can understand, and interpret all Languages) know this to be sound and *Orthodox Divinity*'. This is a rewriting of Lily's declared intention in the Authorized Grammar, to 'exhort everie man to the learning of Grammar that intendeth to the understanding of tongues (wherein is contained a great treasure of wisdome and knowledge)' (5).

Coppe's address to the scholars of Oxford illustrates the linguistic ingenuity of his prose. Through the parodic impersonation of the voice of Lily's Grammar, Coppe exploits his humanist education to structure an attack on institutional learning which stylistically, if not thematically, is quite distinct from the plain-speaking anti-intellectualism of Coppin's *Divine Teachings*. The insistence of John Everard (Cambridge Doctor of Divinity) that the saint must 'know Jesus Christ and the Scriptures experimentally rather than grammatically or academically' is taken quite literally by Coppe.[41] Such close criticism of this passage is necessary because it demonstrates how intricately Coppe's prose style reflects his supra-formalism and his radical scrambling of the order of things, in a linguistic augury of the apocalyptic coming of God, 'that mighty Leveller' who has already dispensed with 'the late slaine or dead *Charles*' (71). As mentioned earlier, the Authorized Grammar possessed iconic significance: the law of standardization and uniformity in religion symbolized by the Book of Common Prayer was directly linked to the desirability for the Tudors and Stuarts of a universal and uniform grammar. Royal and

---

[41] Everard quoted in Hill, *The World Turned Upside Down*, 212.

ecclesiastical supremacy over the printed word was embodied by issuing authoritative books for public and private use such as Lily's Grammar and Nowell's Latin catechism, used in schools for language training. These texts were used as 'part of the settlement by which Crown and Church together ruled the country'. The educational statutes of 1604 state that 'No man shall teach either in Publicke schoole, or private house, but such as shall be allowed by the Bishop of the Dicocese . . . they shall teach the Grammar set forth by King HENRY the eight . . . and none other'.[42] In the 1624 edition masters are instructed 'not to teach youth and scholars with any other Grammar, than with the English Introduction hereafter . . . upon paine of our indignation and as you will answer to the contrary' (4). In its address 'To the Reader' the King's standardization of grammar is defended as maintaining discipline in both education and in the country in general. The text was also an aspect of the formal apparatus of the Church, being bound with extracts from the Book of Common Prayer and authorized by the Canons Ecclesiastical. The method of teaching Latin could thus become an expression of nonconformism. An Article from Bishop Juxon's Laudian visitation in 1640 enquires: 'Doth (the master) teach them any other grammar than that which was set forth by K. Henry VIII and hath since continued?'[43]

The identification of pedagogic, religious, and political authority was enshrined in early modern England in royal injunctions, ecclesiastical canons, and Acts of Parliament. Marchamont Nedham, Coppe's contemporary at All Souls, shrewdest of the republic's propagandists, and the government censor to whom Coppe had to apologize in his second recantation, *Copps Return to the Wayes of Truth* (1651), explicitly connected grammatical and religious uniformity after the Restoration:

They do almost in all Countries entertain the same Grammar, and go by a certain rule of teaching; *Despauter* obtains in *France*, *Alvarez* in *Spain*; and all *England* over heretofore, *Lilly* and *Camden* were in the hands of Youth. And indeed there is the same reason for *Uniformity* in School, as in Church: the variety of Methods doing very much mischief by distracting young heads . . . since these licentious times have overthrown all order, and broken us into many sects and factions, the

---

[42] Nicholas Orme, 'Schools and Schoolbooks, 1400–1550', in Lotte Hellinga and J. B. Trapp (eds.), *The Cambridge History of the Book in Britain, iii. 1400–1557* (Cambridge, 1999), 449–69 (469); Joan Simon, *Education and Society in Tudor England* (Cambridge, 1967), 307–8; Ian Green, ' "For Children in Yeeres and Children in Understanding": The Emergence of the English Catechism under Elizabeth and the Early Stuarts', *Journal of Ecclesiastical History* 37, (1986), 397–425. The statutes of 1604 are quoted in Harris Francis Fletcher, *The Intellectual Development of John Milton*, 2 vols. (Urbana, Ill., 1956), i. 169–70.

[43] Watson, *The English Grammar Schools*, 281.

Schools have been infected with that Fanatick itch; and like Independent
Congregations have bin variously administered by new lights, according to the
fancy of several Teachers, that I dare say there are as many Grammars taught as
there are Grammarians.[44]

Nedham recognizes the inscription of the order of things in grammar,
and sees a causal link between diverse grammatical teaching, the spread of
sectarianism and enthusiasm, and the overthrow of 'all order'. Grammars
were recognized by some to contain their own political rhetoric. In a
striking anticipation of modern critical ideas about the ideological functions of humanist pedagogy, Nicholas Culpeper argued in 1650 that the
combination of elaborate grammatical rules and corrective beating in the
English educational system was an insidious method of preserving the
social hierarchy and oppressing the common people:

They have imposed such multiplicity of needless rules in the learning of the Latin
tongue that unless a man have gotten a very large estate he is not able to bring up
his son to understand Latin, a dozen years expense of time will hardly do it as they
have ordered the matter, in which time, by whipping and cruel useage, the brains
of many are made so stupid that they are unfit for study, but are fain to pin their
faith upon the sleeve of that monster, Tradition . . . The poor commonality of
England is deprived of their birthright by this means.[45]

Samuel Hartlib, dedicatee of Milton's *Of Education* and intelligencer for
Commonwealth and Protectorate, sought to reform the teaching of Latin
grammar to advance his vision of the universal reformation of knowledge
and education. The preface to his edition of Richard Carew's *The True
and Readie Way to Learne the Latine Tongue* (1654), dedicated to Francis
Rous, a member of the Protectorate's Council of State, links pedagogical
to political change by representing Carew's text as a blow against
'Grammatical Tyranny'. The Authorized Grammar is part of the 'rubbish
to be removed' before a 'thorough Reformation' can be established in
England.[46] Hartlib describes grammatical reform in terms of an opposition between liberty and tyrannous custom familiar to any reader of
Milton's prose, and which recalls in particular the attack in *Of Education*
on the schooling of England's youth in 'court shifts and tyrannous
aphorismes' that instil 'barren hearts with a conscientious slavery'.

    [44] Marchamont Nedham, *A Discourse Concerning Schools and Schoolmasters* (1663), 5.
'Camden' refers to William Camden's Greek grammar, *Institutio Graecae grammaticaes
compendaria* (1595).
    [45] Nicholas Culpeper, *A Physical Directory* (1650), sigs. B$^{r–v}$.
    [46] Samuel Hartlib, 'Epistle Dedicatory' to Richard Carew, *The True and Readie Way to
Learne the Latine Tongue*, ed. Hartlib (1654), sig. A2^{r}.

Milton has been found expelling the ideological influence of Lily's Grammar from his *Accidence Commenc't Grammar* (probably written some time in the 1640s although not published until 1669) by 'unthroning' the presentation and grammatical examples of the *Regia grammatica*, often replacing references to kings, princes, and bishops with quotations from Cicero.[47] So, in redefining the signification of Lily's grammatical terms as degrees in the saint's union with the spirit, Coppe relocates linguistic and educational authority within the inspired individual and, as Nedham realizes, overturns the religious and political order as reflected in and supported by pedagogical tradition. As an aspect of his rebellion against the tyranny of forms, Coppe deforms an icon of institutional learning, and of ecclesiastical and political power: a suitable response to a royalist such as John Cleveland, who wished to silence the babble of radical voices by satirically dissecting their grammatical inaccuracies and appealing to correct grammar and definition as natural metaphors for the traditional social order.[48] Coppe's grammatical play is a quite sophisticated and self-conscious exploration of what J. G. A. Pocock describes as the linguistically inscribed paradigms of political authority, at the very moment when the paradigmatic structures of monarchical order and royalist discourse were on the verge of transformation.[49]

A LIBERTINE SYNTAX

We have seen how Thomas Edwards similarly appealed in *Gangraena* to grammatical rules as a model of underlying cultural order to set against the confusions and innovations of the times; grammar offered fixed definitions, structures of stratification, and a syntax of relationships that represented the proper, natural relations in society between clergy and laity, learned and unlearned, propertied and unpropertied. Coppe's address to Oxford can be read as a dialogue with the various polemical and representational strategies employed by the heresiographers. In choosing to parody the forms of learning Latin grammar in early modern England, Coppe—like the Lollard Walter Brut—displays his status as

---

[47] *CPW*, ii. 375; Wyman Herendeen, 'Milton's *Accidence Commenc't Grammar* and the Deconstruction of "Grammatical Tyranny"', in P. G. Stanwood (ed.), *Of Poetry and Politics: New Essays on Milton and his World* (New York, 1995), 297–312.

[48] On Cleveland see Sharon Achinstein, 'The Politics of Babel in the English Revolution', in Holstun (ed.), *Pamphlet Wars*, 14–44 (31–2).

[49] J. G. A. Pocock, *Politics, Language and Time: Essays in Political Thought and History* (London, 1972), 3–41.

litteratus and so undermines the stereotype of the heretic as illiterate; at the same time he subverts the basis of the charge of ignorance by rejecting the relevance of formal education to religious knowledge. Latin grammar was the foundation of Renaissance intellectual culture, often allegorically depicted as a teacher unlocking the tower of knowledge to allow children to enter. As one Latin grammarian of the 1650s put it: 'to be an Ignoramus [is] to erre in Grammar, which is the foundation on which the super-structure of Arts and Sciences is grounded'.[50] Coppe's spiritual grammar, with its added 'Lunatick moode', appeals precisely above disputative reason and the formal logic of the syllogism to the anti-logical workings of the Spirit, the experience of which transforms the saint into a fool for Christ's sake (1 Cor. 4). Beside the infused knowledge of the Spirit, 'to erre in Grammar' is a laughable irrelevance. Indeed in terms of Paul's inver-sion of the definitions of wisdom and folly in Corinthians, to be regarded by the learned as 'an Ignoramus' in grammar, rhetoric, and logic is a testament to sainthood. In *A Fiery Flying Roll,* Coppe prophesies that in 'but a little while . . . the strongest, yea, the seemingly purest propriety, which may mostly plead priviledge and Prerogative from Scripture, and carnall reason; shall be confounded and plagued into communality and universality' (109). This vision of the confounding of 'purest propriety' scrambles the categories of evaluation in John Brinsley's advice to the schoolmaster in *Ludus Literarius* on the correct method of teaching Latin. The boys should strive 'to expresse whatsoever they construe, not onely in proprietie, but in varietie of the finest phrase, who can give the best. This chiefly in the higher fourmes: So reading forth of Latine into English; first in proprietie, then in puritie' (23).

The propriety of grammar in the humanist pedagogical economy, which worked to divide society into *litteratus* and *illitteratus,* reflected and supported not only the propriety of the religious hierarchy of clergy and laity but the social hierarchy of gender. The learning of Latin grammar marked the separation of the male child from 'both "the mother tongue" and domestic family life'; from a ' "popular" English culture that [was] transmitted through female speech'. Humanist train-ing in an all-male environment was thus enlisted to 'correct the faults inculcated in the female and vernacular world of early childhood' and prepare the boy for the public world of the professions, the Church, and the Court.[51] This hierarchical division of the genders was written into the

---

[50] Clark, *John Milton at St Paul's School,* 5; Thomas Merriot, *Grammatical Miscellanies* (1660), sig. A3^v.

[51] Wendy Wall, ' "Household Stuff" ', 4, 13.

very rules of the grammar textbook. Directly following the rule in the Authorized Grammar that an adjective 'agreeth with his substantive, in case, gendre, and numbre', Lily asks the boys to '[h]ere note, that the masculine gendre is more worthy than the feminine'. For the heresiographers, as we have seen, popular revolt and the overturning of social hierarchy were presaged by the collapse of the institutional structures securing the relationship between masculinity, education, and knowledge; by the appearance of 'swarms . . . of all sorts of illiterate Mechanick preachers, yea of Women and Boy preachers!'.[52] Coppe's confounding of the propriety of Latin grammar is an appropriate expression of his confounding of hierarchies of gender, as well as of education, wealth, and status, into 'communality'. In *Some Sweet Sips* he prints a letter from 'Mrs. T. P.' asking him to interpret her dreams. In response to her doubts about her capacity as a woman to receive the Spirit's teachings, he responds: 'Deare friend, why doest in thy letter say, [what though we are weaker *Vessels*, women? &c.] I know that Male and Female are all one in *Christ*, and they are all one to me' (66).

Coppe explodes the clerical identification of religious knowledge with the humanist practices of philology and textual scholarship: his regenerate scholar in *Some Sweet Sips* 'can reade [God] from the left hand to the right, as if they were reading *English*, or from the right to the left, as if they were reading *Hebrew* . . . can reade God as plainly in the *Octavo* of a late converted JEW, as in a Church Bible in *Folio* . . . can reade him within book, and without book' (61). The inner Word renders the categories of knowledge ordered by grammar, syntax, translation, typography, by the written word itself—even by the text of Scripture—irrelevant. Coppe makes this point by inverting the act of persecution represented by the burning of 'blasphemous' books into an ecstatic act of devotion: 'then you will fall upon your books (as if ye were *besides* your *selves*) and bring your books together, and burne them all before men; so mightily will (ό λόγος—) the word grow in you, and prevaile upon you'. In reply to the clergy's accusations of ignorance, Coppe assures the scholars of Oxford that 'you will heare no Mechanick Preach; (no not a *Peter*, if he be a Fisher-Man) but the learned Apostle, who speaks with Tongues more then they—all' (48). Calling upon his linguistic education, Coppe demonstrates how he, like St Paul, hears 'the fathers voyce, in all voyces, and understand[s] him in all tongues' by inserting Latin, Greek, and Hebrew phrases into his prose. Divine shapes—the *signatura rerum*—are

---

[52] On the treatment of gender in Lily's Grammar see Anne Ferry, *The Art of Naming* (Chicago, Ill., 1988), 37–8; *Gangraena*, i. 8.

revealed to the saint in the ancient languages as in the entirety of creation, in Latin declensions as in the sun and the moon: 'Mine eare hast thou opened indeed . . . That can heare (*Verbum Dei, in verbis dei, noctisque sermone*—) the Word in the dayes, and nights report . . . For the heavens [מספרים] are telling declare the glory of God . . . so mightily will [ὁ λόγος—] the word grow in you' (61).[53]

John Webster's *Academiarum Examen* (1654) provides a gloss on Coppe's often elliptical, incantatory style. In response to the argument that 'Schools teach the knowledge of tongues, without which the Scriptures (being originally written in the *Hebrew* and *Greek*) cannot be truly and rightly translated, expounded, nor interpreted', Webster maintains that 'while men trust to their skill in the understanding of the original tongues, they become utterly ignorant of the true original tongue, the language of the heavenly *Caanan*, which no man can understand or speak, but he that is brought into that good Land that flowes with milk and honey, and there to be taught the language of the Holy Ghost' (5–6). Consequently

he that is most expert, and exquisite in the *Greek* and *Oriental* tongues, to him notwithstanding the language of the holy Ghost, hid in the letter of the Scriptures, is but as *Hieroglyphicks*, and *Cryptography*, which he can never uncypher, unless God bring his own key, and teach him how to use it, and otherwise the voice of Saints will be but unto him as the voice of *Barbarians, even as a sounding brass, and a tinkling Cymbal*, as not giving any *perfect or distinct sound*. (8)

Webster concludes with a reference to Paul's description of the voice of the holy fool, and then quotes (in Latin) from St Chrysostom's commentary on Corinthians: Plato's eloquence was superior to Paul's, but this merely demonstrates that knowledge of God is given by divine grace rather than obtained through humane learning.[54] Speaking with the 'voice of Barbarians' is precisely the charge that Daniel Featley directed at the Anabaptists in *The Dippers Dipt*. Arguing that the sectarians' irreligious beliefs are reflected in the barbarisms of their grammar, Featley turns to etymology to associate heresy with *catachresis*, a rhetorical term for the abuse of speech whereby 'one matter [is expressed] by the name of another which is incompatible with it, and sometimes

---

[53] Coppe incorporates 1 Cor. 14: 19: 'I thank my God, I speak with more tongues than ye all', and 1 Cor. 14: 10: 'There are, it may be, so many kinds of voices in the world, and none of them is without signification'. The Hebrew is from Psalm 19: 1: 'The heavens declare the glory of God; and the firmament sheweth his handywork'.

[54] See 1 Cor. 14: 11: 'Therefore if I know not the meaning of the voice, I shall be unto him a barbarian, and he that speaketh shall be a barbarian unto me'.

clean contrary'.[55] Featley argues on the grounds of 'the preposition κατα which is commonly taken in the worst sense, as in Catachresis, *Cataphryges, Catabaptists*' (163). As the Baptists are '*Anomalaes* themselves' their language does not conform to 'any Rules', and further etymological association allows Featley to identify this abuse of language with attempts 'to abuse the Magistrates power' (175).

In response Coppe, as we have seen, mocks the identification of religious truth with correct grammar by flaunting 'Lillies rules' and delighting in the solecism of adding 'an Interjection unto an adverb in the Optative line'. Featley's disqualification of the radicals' right to dispute religious matters on the grounds that they 'understand not the Scripture in the Originall languages' is reversed by Coppe, for the saints speak the 'true original tongue... the language of the holy Ghost', which those who are 'exquisite' in the original languages 'can never uncypher':

> That which is here (mostly) spoken, is inside, and mysterie. And so farre as any one hath the mysterie of God opened to him, *In Him*, can plainly read every word of the same here.
>
> The rest is sealed up from the rest, and it may be the most,—from some. (49)

Coppe thus maintains his prose will remain 'a Riddle' to those who are 'Strangers to a powerfull and glorious manifestation of their union with God'. He uses the same image as Webster of the 'true original language' as a cipher to which only God can provide the key: 'Thus you have one Claval hint; if the Lord come *in*, it may be an instrumentall key to open the rest. But the Spirit alone is the incorruptible Key' (ibid.). The regenerate Coppe, restored to a condition of Adamic purity, communicates in what Webster describes as the '*Paradisical* language of the outflown word which *Adam* understood while he was unfaln in *Eden*, and lost after'. This language transcends the 'Grammatical rule' and 'Rhetorical order' that men seek to master by studying 'the dead paper idolls of creaturely-invented letters'. Ironically explaining this supragrammatical language in terms of a grammatical case, Webster describes the Adamic ability to decipher the 'preaching *Symbols*' of creation, as 'not inventive or acquisitive, but meerly dative from the father of light'.[56]

Coppe's ridicule of institutional learning extends to his use of Latin tags to parody academic discourse and the intellectual condescension of the heresiographers. He begins a marginal comment explaining that

---

[55] John Hoskins, *Direccions for Speech and Style* (1599), 11.

[56] Webster, *Academiarum Examen*, 27–9. On Webster's understanding of the paradisal language and his wish to 'relocate grammar . . . closer to the reality of the divinely interpenetrated nature' see Smith, *Perfection Proclaimed*, 279–82, 284, 288 (288).

'every forme is a persecutor' with '*experientia docet*' (55), recalling
Featley's use of such phrases to dismiss Anabaptist arguments: 'This
argument is fallacious and childish; called in the Schools *fallacia acci-
dentis*' (77). Coppe tends to use these rhetorical Latin tags particularly
when referring dismissively to religious and educational authority: in the
preface to Coppin's *Divine Teachings* he describes his words as 'to the
Greek foolishness: To the scribe folly; To the Pharisee blasphemy, who
hath (*ad unguem*) at's fingers ends' (75).[57] While this line initially echoes
1 Cor. 1: 20, the final phrase in fact illustrates how deeply the rejection of
institutional learning, as iconically represented by Lily's Grammar,
pervades Coppe's prose. After the section on the eight parts of speech in
A Shorte Introduction of Grammar there followed (in all editions throughout the centuries) Lily's 'Carmen de moribus', a code of manners and
morals for pupils composed in Latin verse. In early modern English
grammar schools the 'Carmen de moribus' was 'construed in the first or
second form and memorized by the little boys and read aloud'. This verse
meditation enshrined the humanist philosophy that a classical and
linguistic education should teach 'both pure Latin and clean morals'. The
pupils are instructed to 'be mindful that thou speakest in Latin and avoid
barbarous words, as things very dangerous', and to regard their tongue as
'the gateway of life and of death too'. The verse then outlines the etiquette
of learning in the classroom, including the command that 'whatsoever
thou repeatest to me, let them be learned at thy finger's ends, and thy
book laid aside, rehearse every word'.[58] So Coppe's reference to the
'Pharisee, who hath (*ad unguem*) at's fingers ends', which looks likely to
be scriptural in provenance, is actually an echo (and translation) of the
'Carmen de moribus', which he would have learned by heart at Warwick
School. The allusion to Lily's code of moral conduct emphasizes Coppe's
scorn for the humanist philosophy that a classical education instils
Christian virtue. The specific association of the phrase 'at his fingers ends'
with language study is confirmed by its use in Overton's *The Araignement
of Mr. Persecution* to ridicule the Presbyterians' identification of linguistic
scholarship and religious knowledge: 'Oh, Martin, hath it at his fingers
ends, he's a university man, skilled in the tongues and the sciences, and
can sophisticate any text, oh he is excellent at false glosses and scholastic
interpretations, he can wrest the Scriptures most neatly, tell the people it
thus and thus in the original, an excellent man to make a presbyter!' (3).

[57] In *CRW* 'unguem' is incorrectly transcribed as 'unquem'.
[58] Clark, *John Milton at St Paul's School*, 51, 54; William Haine, *Lillies Rules Construed*
(1638), 92–4. See also the notes to *Of Education* in *CPWM*, ii. 197.

Both the grammatical and moral rules codified in Lily's Grammar symbolize for Coppe the fallen, hypocritical religious formalism that he has transcended.

Once we become accustomed to reading Coppe in the context of a dialogue with the 'priests and professors' and regard him as intellectually capable of engaging with them in their own terms, the parody of learned forms of expression becomes apparent throughout his writing. He plays upon the academic tendency to follow lines of vernacular prose with a Latin tag—a continual rhetorical tactic of Featley to confuse the Anabaptists and emphasize his intellectual superiority in the debate—by adding lines of Latin associated with the English only through phonetic resemblance, as in 'accidence' and 'accidit': 'teaching his pupils his *Accidence*, a new way, new, new, new; [*Et hoc accidit, et dum vile fuit*]' (62). In *A Fiery Flying Roll* the use of etymological proofs, such as Featley's discussion of the Greek derivations of 'baptize' and 'catabaptist', is comically exploited during one of Coppe's attacks on social injustice: the words 'A Rogue should ask for it' set off a spurious phonetic coincidence with Latin in the margin: 'A *rogo*, to ask' (110). In both *Some Sweet Sips* and *A Fiery Flying Roll* even the bibliographic conventions of publication are undermined. The contents list of *Some Sweet Sips* constitutes more than 10 per cent of the entire pamphlet, with over sixty points, some of which have only a tenuous relation to what follows. Coppe ends the contents list with the first of his parodic Latin phrases, '*Cum multis aliis, quae nunc prescribere longum est*' (40). This phrase (though a commonplace) is repeatedly used by Thomas Edwards in *Gangraena* after listing examples of recent heretical publications, so Coppe may be making a deliberate reference here (see e.g. the 'Epistle Dedicatory', sig. A4ʳ). The division of the contents of 'A Second Fiery Flying Roule' is printed on the same page as that of *A Fiery Flying Roll*, and the 'separate' pamphlets are printed as one, despite having individual title pages. Coppe plays with authorship and anonymity, but not with any apparent purpose of self-protection. The title page of *A Fiery Flying Roll* names the author as 'his most Excellent MAJESTY, dwelling in, and shining through AUXILIUM PATRIS, כל alias, *Coppe*' (80). Yet at the beginning of chapter 1, in a marginal aside to the reader, Coppe apologizes for 'the Authors' obscure references to himself, explaining that 'not one in a hundred, yea even of his former acquaintance, now know him, nor must they' (86). In his broadsheet of 1657 *Divine Fire-Works* Coppe breaks off in mid-sentence amidst exclamatory celebrations of the inscrutability of God, declaring, 'The rest is torn out'. After a blank space of several lines, he continues, 'yet it is written'. 'The End' of *Divine Fire-Works* is followed by the coda, 'Is not yet', so that the printed progression of the broadsheet embodies the apocalyptic narrative which it describes. There seems to be a deliberate subversion of the conventional structures of publishing religious polemic as an aspect of Coppe's wider parody of official, formalized expression. James Rigney has shown how both Anglican and Puritan clerics, concerned about the vulnerability of their sermons to distortion when disembodied in print and exposed to the market place of readers in revolutionary England, tried to maintain the integrity of their texts by binding them to 'certain decorums of production . . . [the text] was the product of a system of education and clerical community in and by which it had been evaluated, approved, and supported. As such, this printed sermon stood in opposition to the highly personal and inspired discourse of radical religion'.[59] It is these 'decorums of production' that Coppe seems to be consciously subverting.

Characteristically Coppe puts his knowledge of classical literature to unorthodox and provocative use. In *Some Sweet Sips*, amongst a tissue of scriptural references to the sufficiency of divinely revealed knowledge, he has God speak through a line from Juvenal's *Satires*: 'Amen. Amen say I. Amen, Amen, saith the Lord.—(*sic volo, sic jubeo, stat pro ratione voluntas*)' (59). According to John Tickell's account of his debate with Coppe over God's arbitrary abolition of his own ordinances, Coppe again used this phrase from the *Satires* to express the divine will: 'to this Mr. *Coppe* brought in (as I have heard of Jugglers) his *sic volo sic Jubeo*'.[60] In *A Fiery Flying Roll* God's direct, first-person 'admonition to great ones' is accompanied by the marginal quoting of the Latin commonplace, '*Sero sapiunt Phryges, sed nunquam Sera est ad Bonos mores via*', the latter half of which is from Seneca's *Agamemnon* (89–90). Senecan moral philosophy was particularly popular amongst the Puritan clergy.[61] Here the use of the classics as a learned comparative source to denigrate the radicals—as in Featley's reference to the Ovidian metamorphoses of mechanics into preachers—is redeployed as the direct sanction by God of the inspired wisdom of his prophet. Tickell was closer to the truth than

[59] James Rigney, 'The English Sermon, 1640–1660: Consuming the Fire', D.Phil. thesis (Oxford University, 1994), 208.

[60] See Juvenal, *Satires* 6.223: 'That is my wish, my order; my will is reason enough' (Coppe substitutes 'stat' for 'sit'); Tickell, *The Bottomless Pit Smoaking in Familisme*, 86.

[61] The phrase is in fact an amalgam of Sextus Pompeius Festus, *De verborum significatu*, 343M, and Seneca, *Agamemnon*, 242: 'The Trojans understood too late, but it is never too late to follow the way to good'. On the Puritan taste for Seneca see Margo Todd, 'Seneca and the Protestant Mind: The Influence of Stoicism on Puritan Ethics', *Archiv für Reformationsgeschichte*, 74 (1983), 182–99.

perhaps he realized when he accused Coppe of 'care[ing] no more for Scripture, than *Gesta Romanorum*, and scarcely like as much'. The *Gesta Romanorum* (first printed c.1472) was a Latin collection of accounts of saints' lives, romances, and classical myths often used by the Catholic clergy for exempla.[62] This declaration of the divine will through the words of Juvenal and Seneca seems intended to shock and relates to Coppe's dramatic sense of voice which, like Overton's polemical style in the Marpriest tracts, perhaps owes something to the transfer of dramatic performance to satirical pamphlets after the theatres had been closed. Coppe's impersonations tend to have, however, a specifically textual resonance.

A striking moment occurs in *A Fiery Flying Roll*, where he presents God as a highwayman: 'Thou hast many baggs of money, and behold I come as a thief in the night, with my sword drawn in my hand, and like a thief as I am,—I say, deliver your purse, deliver sirrah! deliver or I'll cut your throat!' (100). These lines have caught the attention of Christopher Hill, who attributes them to 'a radical antinomian tradition [of] aggressive lower-class Robin Hoodery'.[63] While the description of God as a 'thief in the night' is scriptural in provenance (1 Thessalonians 5: 2), the interjection of the highwayman may also be explained as another expression of Coppe's anticlericalism.[64] In John Fry's *The Clergy in Their Colours*, which is bound with one of the copies of *Some Sweet Sips* in the Bodleian (both were published by Giles Calvert), the pride of the clergy in their learning is denounced with a reference which perhaps points to the origins of Coppe's divine cut-purse: 'so if many of our profound Parsons would but speak plainly, they would tell us, that none are qualified to preach, or write, but such as are in their Order; and that for such, as by a fine distinction they call Laity, they should spend their time in reading tales of *Robin Hood* and following their worldly affairs'. Coppe assumes the voice of the texts condescendingly granted to the unlettered, the popular chapbooks and 'penny merriments' featuring the adventures of Robin Hood, and has it convey the apocalyptic threat of God to the priests and professors.[65] Coppe's prose is a ludic yet polemically purposeful instance

---

[62] Tickell, *The Bottomless Pit*, 39; on the *Gesta Romanorum*, see J. A. Cuddon, *A Dictionary of Literary Terms* (rev. edn., Harmondsworth, 1987).

[63] Hill, *The English Bible and the Seventeenth Century Revolution*, 445.

[64] See also 'I. F.', *John the Divines Divinity* (1648), 45–6: 'The workings of God in, & with souls, are divers: His Grace and Love commeth to some as a Thief, when they are asleep'. Coppe's first publication was a preface to this work; this and other anticipations of the later works in the main body of the text suggest he might have had a hand in writing the pamphlet.

[65] Fry, *The Clergy in Their Colours*, sig. A4ʳ. Fry was accused of 'Rantisme' by Anthony

of the 'libertine syntax' that has been ascribed to Milton: 'a language which appropriates the voice of other, sometimes opposite speakers, in order to . . . mock the order of the appropriated voice itself'. The term is all the more appropriate considering Coppe's deliberately provocative description of service to God as 'pure Libertinisme' (86).[66]

THE HERETIC'S ABC

Despite Coppe's ridicule of the notion that mastery of the 'original' languages confers spiritual insight, one aspect of his systematic sub-version of clerical and educational authority is the use of Hebrew and Hebraisms. Coppe evidently had some Hebrew, probably from his uni-versity tutor Ralph Button who, as we have seen, was noted in Oxford as a Hebraist. However, the better grammar school pupils—Milton, for instance—were often introduced to the rudiments of Hebrew in their final year.[67] Coppe may also have seen one of the several Hebrew grammars in English which appeared in the late 1640s, and was perhaps attracted in particular to the perfectionist implications of Christian Rave's discussion of the direct access to the divine offered by the language. Rave (or Ravius) was a German emigré who briefly held a fellowship at Magdalen Hall, Oxford, in 1648–9. In the early 1640s Rave taught Hebrew to Laurence Clarkson's acquaintance, the Particular Baptist Hanserd Knollys (Clarkson and Knollys were arrested together in 1645 on charges of public 'dipping'). In *Discourse of the Orientall Tongues* (1648; 2nd edn. 1649) Rave opposes the 'fundamentall unity' of the 'holy tongue of God' to the complexities of Latin, with its 'six cases in singular, and as many in plurall, so many Declensions in nouns, and Conjugations in verbs, divers terminations for all persons, various both in Active and Passive, and an infinite of such like conceits' (51). The 'singleness' of Hebrew, however, is 'seen in many things': 'First, in a constant Triunity (representing the nature of its author) in having for a union to a root, a trinity of letters: for a unity of a conjugation, a trinity of tenses: for a unity to a tense (of things past or to come) a trinity of persons' (17, 63). For Rave, the very grammatical structure of Hebrew embodies its divine origins; the

Wood (see *DNB*). The Bodleian shelf-mark is 8⁰C 75 Linc. On chapbook tales of Robin Hood published in the 1630s see Watt, *Cheap Print and Popular Piety*, 298.

[66] Nigel Smith uses the phrase to describe Milton's manipulation of texts opposed to his argument in '*Areopagitica*: Voicing Contexts, 1643–5', 112.

[67] Clark, *John Milton at St Paul's School*, 18, 121, 145–7.

'Triunity' found in every aspect of Hebrew grammar signifies 'the nature of its author'. The opinion that Hebrew was, or was descended from, the language that Adam spoke in Eden was a commonplace of medieval and Renaissance thought. Eschatological symmetry suggested that a form of Hebrew would again become the natural language of men with the second coming of Christ. David S. Katz has argued that interest in Hebrew intensified in revolutionary England with the millennial expectations aroused by the reformation of Church and State, 'help[ing] to put Jews in a favourable light as guardians of that sacred heritage' and to facilitate their readmission to the country in 1655.[68] Indeed Rave corresponded with Samuel Hartlib over the benefits of establishing a Hebrew academy in England; the desire of Hartlib and his close colleague John Dury to reform learning and education at the moment of religious and political reform was driven by 'a powerful millenarian impulse'.[69]

Yet in Rave's *Discourse* the notion that learning Hebrew involves recovering something of the paradisal language develops into a form of anti-intellectual argument: '*Adam* (the first speaker of it) in his state of innocence (when it was given to him) was the most true and simple Grammarian, Rhetorician, Logician, and Metaphysician that lived in the world and the church' (62). A knowledge of Hebrew thus renders irrelevant the linguistic arts of the trivium—grammar, rhetoric, and logic—that comprised the basis of a formal education in the Renaissance. 'We smart at school', Rave suggests, 'for our parents and masters foolery, not our ancestor's rebellion at Babel' (67). The rules of Latin and Greek grammar become equated with a fallen formalism which is transcended by the supernatural force of Hebrew, restoring original perfection to its speaker: 'In one word it [Hebrew] makes us (when by the *Greec* and *Latine* wee were become beasts) to become *Adam* our selves; to be no more under the law' (18). Rave identifies Hebrew not with the Mosaic law of the Old Testament, but with the transcendence of that law and the earthly perfectibility of man—the definition of antinomianism.

In *Some Sweet Sips* the rehearsal of the declensions of Latin verbs is finally transfigured into Psalmic song in a celebration of the saint's union with God, echoing Rave's contrast between the complexities of Latin grammar and the divine unity of Hebrew:

---

[68] David S. Katz, *Philo-semitism and the Re-admission of the Jews to England, 1603–55* (Oxford, 1982), 45–88 (87–8).

[69] Letter from Rave to Hartlib, British Library, Add. MSS 4365, fo. 172; Stephen Clucas, 'Samuel Hartlib's "Ephemerides", 1635–59, and the Pursuit of Scientific and Philosophical Manuscripts: The Religious Ethos of an Intelligencer', *The Seventeenth Century*, 6 (1991), 33–55 (34).

> —your selves, when you are
> non-entities, walk with God and are not, because the
> Lord hath took you, then (I say) you will sing one of the
> Songs of *Sion*, an *Hebrew* Song and say (אבי אהואלי)
> thou art my Father, my God, *Psal.* 89. 26 (62)

Coppe validates his prophetic identity as a 'late Converted JEW' by the assumption of a Hebrew title, אביצור, 'the Lord is my strength'. This use of Hebrew does not depend on its correctness: the simple strangeness of the Hebraic characters is used to fragment conventional linguistic sense, while evoking at once the voice of the Old Testament Jehovah and the apocalyptic God of Revelation, 'that mighty Leveller' coming to dissolve all 'humane' forms. Echoing Habakkuk 3: 1, 'Chapter II' of 'Epistle II' of *Some Sweet Sips* is entitled '*A Prayer of* אביצור *upon Siginoth*'. 'Shigionoth' is a Hebrew term for a type of psalm, and Coppe celebrates his conversion in the language of Hebrew liturgy: 'Who is the *King of glory?* the *Lord of hosts*, he is *the King of glory. Selah*' (51–2). John Spencer, looking back in 1665 on the 'many giddy Fancies and Errors of the late Times', noted the 'many *Selah*'s' that enthusiasts would 'affix to their Prophetick speeches'. Spencer regarded such use of Hebraic language as a feature of their 'bold pretences' to the 'greater intimacy with the Divine Spirit' enjoyed by the ancient Israelites; as an attempt to lend authenticity to their false claims to be the earthly vessels of 'an interpretative voice from Heaven, a kind of *Bath Kol* to supply the defect of Scripture-prophecy in Dispensations dark and enigmatical'. According to John Selden, 'Bath Kol' was the term used in the Talmud for 'that voice [which] utters the statements of the living God ... which in that era they say took the place of the holy spirit'.[70] Hebrew and Hebraisms in *Some Sweet Sips* thus signify personal perfection and unity with the divine, providing linguistic expression of the prophet's internalized apocalypse. Hebrew is explicitly opposed to the rules and stratifications of Lily's Grammar, which become a sign of man's fall into sin and are identified with the formalism of the Mosaic law. A similar opposition between Hebrew and Latin is found in the writings of John Brayne, the Winchester minister, Oxford graduate, and advocate of free grace who called for the abolition of the universities and their replacement with schools that would 'teach the Hebrew reading to some'

---

[70] John Spencer, *A Discourse Concerning Vulgar Prophecies* (1665), sigs. A2ᵛ–A3ʳ, 46; John Selden, *Uxor Ebraica* (1646), trans. Jonathan R. Ziskind (Leiden, 1991), 388–9. On the attraction of some radicals, especially autodidacts, towards Hebrew as an alternative form of signifier that brought them closer to the divine signified see Nigel Smith, 'The Uses of Hebrew in the English Revolution', in Peter Burke and Roy Porter (eds.), *Language, Self, and Society* (Cambridge, 1991), 51–71.

and 'the Prophets to others, and their meaning' in preparation for the millennium. Brayne condemned Latin as 'a badge of the Roman conquest' and proclaimed that the 'time is coming' when Hebrew would become the vernacular and 'knowledge shall cover the earth, as water the seas: and all those mighty Libraries [will be] but as lost matter'.[71]

In the Hebrew linguistic tradition as transmitted to Renaissance culture by such controversial figures as Johannes Reuchlin and Cornelius Agrippa (although something of it was probably known to anyone in the seventeenth century who was familiar with scholarly discussions of biblical translation) the very characters of the Hebrew alphabet were perceived as divinely instituted hieroglyphs, disclosing the secrets of creation.[72] In his 'Additional and Preambular Hint' to Coppin's *Divine Teachings* Coppe appears to be influenced by this Hebraic conception of language in which words and letters are 'conceived of as material things that belong to the same network of resemblances that endows natural objects with allegorical meaning, a conception of language clearly connected to hieroglyphs and emblem literature'.[73] In the right-hand margin of his preface Coppe explains the '*hiroglyphical divinity*' of the first letter of the English, Greek, and Hebrew alphabets by revealing how their spatial design manifests the paradox of the unity of the Trinity. He takes God's self-defining declaration of omnipresence in Revelation 1: 8—'I am Alpha and Omega, the beginning and the ending'—and expounds it literally, geometrically dividing the printed characters of 'A' and 'א', so that each line of the character is shown to represent the Father, the Son and the Spirit. This demonstrates the 'Effluence or outspreading of Divinity. Or out-going of God into ALL THINGS' (74–5). The letters are revealed to be hieroglyphs of God, recalling Rave's discussion of the 'Triunity' of Hebrew grammar which represents 'the nature of its author'.

John Webster proposed that the study of the classical languages be replaced in the universities by efforts to develop a '*Hieroglyphicall* (or *Emblematicall*) and *Cryptographicall*' language that would express the immanence of the divine in nature in its very lexical and grammatical structure. Seth Ward attributed such notions to occult and cabbalist

71 John Brayne, *The New Earth or, The True Magna Carta* (1653), 90–1. Brayne had a very sophisticated level of Hebrew, and he consistently refers to patristic and humanist sources; it seems likely that he was the John Brayne listed as matriculating at New Inn Hall, Oxford, in 1636; see *Alumni Oxonienses: the Members of the University of Oxford, 1500–1714*, ed. Joseph Foster (Oxford, 1891–2).

72 Popkin, 'Theories of Knowledge', in Charles B. Schmitt and Quentin Skinner (eds.), *The Cambridge History of Renaissance Philosophy* (Cambridge, 1988; repr. 1996), 676–7.

73 Elsky, *Authorizing Words*, 149.

theorists who 'have made Symbols of the Letters of the Alphabet, so that
א signifies with them *God*: ב the Angelicall Nature &c'.[74] According to one
version of the cabbalist tradition the letters which compose the text of the
Bible were scrambled after the Fall to spell sin, death, and the Mosiac law,
concealing their original divine sense. In his discussion of the cabbalist
conception of the biblical text in *Moses and Aaron* Thomas Godwin states
that 'the text they terme *Cethib, Scriptionem*, the writing; the difference in
the margine they terme . . . *keri, Lectionem*, the reading; because they doe
reade according to that in the margine. The difference . . . is of *divine
authority*, containing many mysteries knowne to *Moses* and the *Prophets*
successively.'[75] The right-hand margin of Coppe's preface reveals the
'*Hiroglyphical Divinity*' of letters, acting as a commentary on the inner,
mystical significance of the tissue of scriptural references in the main text.
So Coppe could be displaying his prophetic insight into the true spiritual
order of the letters of the scriptural text. Yet while Coppe's play with
the alphabet in the preface to *Divine Teachings* may be connected to
cabbalistic theories of language, he is concerned above all to rewrite the
discursive forms of institutional religion, instruction in which was bound
up with the experience of learning to read in seventeenth-century
England. Although J. C. Davis dismisses Coppe's preface as 'innocuous
and bafflingly mystical' and Thomas N. Corns believes it 'operates to
obscure Coppin's argument', it in fact develops into a complex ridicule of
educational practice and is thus an appropriate preparation for Coppin's
arguments for the sufficiency of revealed knowledge in *Divine Teachings*.[76] On this occasion the focus of Coppe's parody is the conventional
method of instilling vernacular rather than Latin literacy—the ABC.

After his demonstration of the divine structure of the letter 'A', Coppe
concludes: 'And thus much for A. which no man knows, yet poor, proud
man would be called Rabbi, and pretends he knows the ORIGINAL, when
he hath not learned his Primer, nay his ABC, not yet knows great A' (74).
According to A. W. Tuer's compendious history of the hornbook, in the
typography of early modern ABCs an upper case 'A' preceded the lower
case 'a' and the rest of the letters. The child was taught to call this letter
'Great A'.[77] Coppe's precise meaning here is clarified by this knowledge.
The 'rabbis', the university-trained clergy who claim exclusive access to

---

[74] Ward and Wilkins, *Vindiciae Academiarum*, 212–13.

[75] Gershom H. Scholem, *On the Kabbalah and Its Symbolism* (Boston, Mass., 1965),
32–86; Thomas Godwin, *Moses and Aaron. Civil and Ecclesiastical Rites, Used by the Ancient
Hebrewes* (1634), 279.

[76] Davis, *Fear, Myth and History*, 38; Corns, *Uncloistered Virtue*, 189.

[77] A. W. Tuer, *History of the Horn-Book* (London, 1897), 97.

divine truths through their command of Latin and Greek ('the Original') are unable to read God's presence even in 'Great A', the first letter of the ABC, the most basic educational text. They are spiritual illiterates. The intellectual condescension of a heresiographer such as Featley, who structures his condemnation of the Anabaptists around their ignorance of the 'Original', is satirically reversed. Coppe mimics the manner of the minister who chastises his congregation for their inability to understand his sermon: 'Well! there are some things in these, somewhat (and in mine muchly) hard to be understood' (74). Although Hebrew is given the status of *lingua sancta* in *Some Sweet Sips*, Coppe seems to deny any particular language to be the 'Original' in his preface: 'This א Aleph, or A, is (in lingua sancta) an aspiration. And in its ORIGINAL and in truth, is the out-breathing, or emanation of Divinity, into Father, Son and Spirit'. Yet the Hebrew character is 'only a further hint of the A. in another figure, name and language (though one and the same is truth, and the inward ground)' (ibid.). The contradiction here may be a consequence of Coppe preparing the way for Coppin's denial at the beginning of *Divine Teachings* that Hebrew, Greek, or Latin disclose the divine any more than the vernacular. Coppin describes rather 'How God is the ORIGINAL, and they that know him know the Original' ('Contents'). Characteristically, however, Coppe emphasizes his point through learned grammatical play: 'aspiration' is at once a notation of Greek grammar which precedes alpha, the 'out-breathing' of God into all creation, and the desire of the saint for union with the divine.

The early modern ABC became virtually a rite of orthodox religion through the regally authorized issue of the *ABC and Catechism* at Elizabeth's accession, which differed from earlier primers only by being cast in question and answer form. The alphabet was followed by the Creed, the Commandments, the Lord's Prayer and, from 1604, the sacraments; it has been estimated that by the early seventeenth century there were around half a million copies of the *ABC and Catechism* in circulation in a population of four million.[78] As Margaret Spufford has emphasized, 'those who had learnt to read had also learnt basic Christian tenets . . . [i]f you could read, you were also religiously indoctrinated'. In early modern England no less than in late medieval Europe 'the very acquisition of literacy was often part of the acquisition of [religious] orthodoxy—in so far as the primer was the fundamental book of instruction for those

---

[78] Green, 'The Emergence of the English Catechism' 399, 405, 425. Green has expanded his study of the catechism in *The Christian's ABC: Catechisms and Religious Instruction in England, c.1530–1740* (Oxford, 1996).

learning to read'.[79] Mastery of the catechism was supposed to precede confirmation, which in turn preceded first communion and incorporation into the body of the Church. A striking feature of the alternative catechisms which appeared in the early seventeenth century, many of which were composed by those we would now describe as Puritans, is that they were aimed at the unlearned and illiterate (in the vernacular) as much as the young, at 'the vulgar sort', the 'ignorant', at both 'children in yeeres and children in understanding'. The composers of these catechisms sought to encourage not merely memorization of basic religious principles but an ability to read, understand, expound, and apply this knowledge. They virtually equated illiteracy with irreligion, grouping the illiterate with fools, madmen, and children.[80]

The question and answer form of the catechism is used by Coppe to confirm his orthodoxy in *Copps Return to the Wayes of Truth*, as he answers point by point the questions of John Dury and Marchamont Nedham and denies the heresies for which he has been indicted by the Blasphemy Act:

> Prop. I. *What do you understand sin to be?*
> *Answ.* In general, I understand sin (which is my most unsupportable burden) to be the transgression of THE Law. (149)

Languishing in Newgate, Coppe declares the 'day of my new-birth' as 30 May 1651, and this conversion from his previous blasphemy is followed by a relearning of the catechism of orthodox belief. This use of the catechetical form to structure his recantation indicates once more Coppe's sensitivity to the relationship between the content and visual arrangement of the printed page. The typography of Coppe's preface to *Divine Teachings*, with its verbal pictures of the Trinity and schematic, three-column design, seems to be a parody of the page design of contemporary ABCs which were circulated in the form of ballads and broadsides. Tessa Watt has described how print was exploited to craft the ABC into a visual form for religious as well as linguistic instruction:

> The practical rules and values of ABCs were predicated on a larger religious framework, the teaching of which was also the job of the good householder. Many of the godly tables tried to give visual expression to the more abstract structure of salvation and damnation. In these broadsides one can sense a drive to encompass

---

[79] 'The Importance of Religion in the Sixteenth and Seventeenth Centuries', in Margaret Spufford (ed.), *The World of the Rural Dissenters, 1520–1725* (Cambridge, 1995), 1–102 (73–4); Swanson, 'Literacy, Heresy, History, and Orthodoxy', 287.

[80] Green, 'The Emergence of the English Catechism', 408–11.

as much of Christian wisdom as possible within the boundaries of the page; to package it neatly into lists, diagrams, memorizable sayings, polarities of good and bad . . .

One feature was the use of 'verbal schematizing' in the form of 'diagrammatic half-word half-pictures', particularly of the Trinity.[81] Coppe appropriates the typographical design of these 'godly tables' to re-educate the pedagogues, the composers of the catechisms; his antinomian ABC, however, subverts their 'abstract structure of salvation and damnation' and collapses 'polarities of good and bad'.

This point is once more made through complex linguistic play. In relating the significance of the geometric construction of 'A', Coppe explains that the central line of the character is an '*overthwart* I' which is '*In name*, God'. The 'I' is literally 'overthwart' in its horizontal position in the letter; at the same time there is a self-referential pun, for Coppe's own behaviour is, in conventional terms, 'overthwart' or deviant. He is '*In name*, God' because of the presence of the indwelling Spirit, sanctifying his actions. Coppe refers to the letter's other two lines of 'Obliquity' which 'step out' from 'rectitude': '(In which two-fold Obliquity is no pravity but purity it self)' (73–4). The deciphering, as Coppe calls it, of the hieroglyphic significance of the letter 'A' becomes, by the legerdemain of wordplay, simultaneously a sanction of Coppe's divergence from moral rectitude, of his deviation from orthodox values of action, conduct, and speech. 'Oblique' also signifies a case inflexion other than nominative or vocative; so once more grammatical form, which seems to symbolize for Coppe the external laws which bind the unregenerate, is made to disclose an anti-formal, anti-intellectual meaning. Such tricksiness anticipates his blunter statement of moral impunity in *A Fiery Flying Roll*: 'sinne and transgression is finisht, its a meer riddle, that they, with all their humane learning can never reade' (91). Whereas the Puritan pedagogues increasingly aimed their catechisms at the ignorant and those with 'weak or crazed memories' in an effort to reverse what they saw as moral backsliding, Coppe emphasizes the irony of his parody by insisting that only 'he that hath (a * soft place in's head, thats out of his wits, and besides himself, besides his own will, knowledge, wisdom and understanding: that is become or made a fool, that he might be made wise can understand this, and this ensuing Treatise' (75). The scriptural references are to 2 Cor. 5: 12 and 1 Cor. 3: 18, invoking Pauline holy foolishness, while '*' refers to a phrase in Coppe's left-hand margin, 'Admonition given to fools'. The

---

[81] Watt, *Cheap Print and Popular Piety*, 235–8 (including illustrations), 244.

mocking reference to the inability of the 'rabbis' to progress to a primer when they have failed to read the divine significance of 'Great A' recalls Coppe's description of the rewriting of Lily's Grammar in *Some Sweet Sips* as a primer for the saints. The preface to *Divine Teachings*, with its 'diagrammatic half-word half-pictures' of 'A' and 'א', is a companion piece to the parody of the Authorized Grammar: an ABC of free grace alongside a grammar of perfection. The ABC was also known as the 'Christ Cross Row' because of the cross placed before the 'Great A'; despite being a remnant of Catholic practice, it remained on ABC texts until the eighteenth century. This cross is relocated within the heart of the regenerate Coppe, signifying the release from sin and religious formalism brought about by the internal resurrection: 'internally, or in the eye of eternity † which is seated in the soft, undone, contrite, ie, the heart shattered to shivers, ground down to meal, pounded to dust, and made up of a new one, of a humane, a divine one: This A. is a hundred times more clearly seen to be' (74). The cross-row ended with 'Amen est.', which seems to have been derived from the formula closing the Latin mass, 'Ite missa est, Amen'; Coppe concludes his discussion of '*Hiro-gylphical Divinity*' with '*Amen.* Hoc Scriptum est, est Scriptura, et in Scriptura' (ibid.).[82]

This reading of the preface to *Divine Teachings* explains Coppe's sub-title, 'a general Epistle written by ABC'. Coppe's play with the initials of his name validates his prophetic authority, for the form of AB[iezer] C[oppe] becomes a physical hieroglyph embodying divine teachings. In *John the Divine's Divinity*, for which Coppe wrote a brief preface, 'I. F.' declares that 'the Saints are said to be an *Epistle read* and *viewed of all*' (16). Evidently Coppe did not distinguish between his public and private personae. In the one extant example of his correspondence, written from Newgate in 1650, he signs himself 'Alpha and Omega ABC'.[83] As the priests and professors are unable to read the '*Hiroglyphical Divinity*' of 'ABC', they dismiss Coppe's words and behaviour as blasphemous or crazed or foolish. The 'holy man (whose holiness stinks above ground)' is unable to interpret what Coppe calls his 'transgressive pranks', regarding them as 'at least whimsey, if not Blasphemy' (104, 79). While Coppe seems to have envisaged an audience of the university-educated in his address to the 'Scholars of Oxford' in *Some Sweet Sips*, in the preface to *Divine*

---

[82] Tuer, *History of the Horn-Book*, 62–6. The hardened heart was regarded by Calvinists as a divine punishment on the reprobate.

[83] Letter from Coppe to Joseph Salmon and Andrew Wyke, Worcester College, Oxford, Clarke MSS, vol. 18, fo. 24ᵛ, printed in *CRW*, 117.

Teachings he appropriates a discursive form known to any literate or semi-literate person in early modern England, perhaps assuming that Coppin's pamphlet would circulate amongst a less educated audience. Nonetheless Coppe still makes use of Hebrew and puns on Greek grammar, while his attention to the rhetorical potential of the printed page also provides an obvious visual contrast with the plain, uniform text of Coppin's work, and indeed of most controversial writing published in this period.

Coppe's typographical parody of 'godly tables' in the preface to *Divine Teachings* anticipates by over a decade one of the most remarkable of the early Quaker pamphlets, George Fox's *A Battle-Door for Teachers and Professors* (1660). Fox organized the typographical design of some of his pages in the shape of the hornbook, also known as the 'battledore', to mock the spiritual ignorance of the learned: 'But you Teachers, Professors, Scholars and Magistrates . . . who pretend that you know Accidence and Grammar, Logick, Rhetorik and Divinity; yet in practice you must have your BATTLE-DOOR again' (first pagination, 3). By incorporating the physical form of the hornbook into his text, Fox is able to play satirically upon his own lack of formal education while representing the learned clergy as spiritual illiterates: 'Come you Priests and Professors, have you not learnt your Accidence . . . and do you not deserve the rod as children?' (4). However, the main point of Fox's polemic is to defend the pronominal usage of 'thee' and 'thou' adopted by the Quakers as a badge of their divinely sanctioned 'plain speech' and as a demonstration of their disregard for hierarchies of birth, education, and rank. He argues that the teachers and professors have 'degenerated from their own words and doings as they have from their owne Tongues' (37). Their incorrect pronominal usage allows him to identify grammatical and spiritual barbarism. The solecisms of the learned reveal them to be 'far degenerated from *Divine* things and *Spiritual* things'. Here Fox appropriates the polemical strategy of the heresiographers such as Featley. However, Fox's argument that the 'Priests and Schollers' do not 'practise what they preach in their Grammars' leads him to debate in the learned terms of his opponents—he lists the correct grammatical form of pronominal address from an array of languages, from Latin, Greek, and Hebrew to 'Aethiopick', Samaritan, and Coptic (42).[84] Fox's polemical method traps him into citing linguistic proofs in the manner of orthodox

---

[84] It is known that Fox was assisted by John Stubbs and Benjamin Furly, although it seems likely that the Oxford MA Samuel Fisher, who certainly knew Latin, Greek, and Hebrew and who is the subject of Chapter 5, was involved.

religious dispute. Coppe's rhetorical strategy anticipates that of Fox, but is more complex and more radical. The language and visual form of the ABC and the authorized Latin grammar are appropriated to confound orthodox religious and cultural values; their conventional, authorized signification is transformed as they become expressions of an internal prophetic experience that renders external instruction—whether linguistic, religious, or moral—irrelevant. While the Puritan clergy identified Latin literacy with ordination and vernacular illiteracy with reprobation, Coppe seems to have regarded neither Latinate nor vernacular literacy as a means of approaching or comprehending the divine. Yet his writings are not self-consuming artefacts, solipsistic 'expositions of the inadequacy of language for communication by the Saints'.[85] Their message is conveyed through an elaborate rhetorical manipulation of the discursive shapes of orthodoxy.

ELOQUENT NONSENSE

In *The Dippers Dipt* Daniel Featley initially represents his use of print as a necessary but second-best option, maintaining his preference for the spoken word of the sermon: 'Now therefore since I cannot *lingua*, I must be content as I am able to *evangelizare calumo*, to preach with my pen' (sig. C2^r). However, the polemical strategy of Featley's subsequent account of his debate with 'a company of Anabaptists', which he claims to be a true record of events which took place in Southwark on 17 October 1642, relies heavily on the typographical arrangement of the syllogism to represent his opponents' intellectual inadequacy. Coppe's parodic application of the typographical design of Lily's Grammar and the ABC demonstrates that such polemical exploitation of the space of the printed page was not one-sided. Only in his recantations does Coppe use syllogisms, Featley's vehicle of 'dispute by Reason', as a formal expression of his orthodoxy:

> Fourthly, the meer creature is finite.
> But God is infinite. *Ergo,*
> The meer creature is not very God.[86]

---

[85] Corns, *Uncloistered Virtue*, 182. The argument that Coppe despaired at the inefficacy of language to communicate his beliefs is central to Byron Nelson, 'The Ranters and the Limits of Language'; it is also to be found in Noam Flinker, 'Milton and the Ranters on Canticles', in Mary A. Maleski (ed.), *Fine Tuning: Studies in the Religious Poetry of Herbert and Milton* (New York, 1989), 273–99.

[86] Coppe, *Copps Return to the Wayes of Truth* (1651), in *CRW*, 140. On Featley's

For John Webster the syllogism embodied not only the hold of corrupt
Aristotelian logic over the universities but the constriction of the free play
of the supra-rational spirit by religious and educational forms:

> they have laid down positive definitions of God, who cannot but be defined by his
> own Logick . . . as though the holy Ghost had not an higher and more heavenly
> method and way to teach divine things in and by, than the art of *Logick* (which is
> meerly humane, and mans invention) seeing *the foolishness of God is higher than
> the wisdom of men, and the weakness of God is stronger than men* [1 Cor. 1: 25], when
> indeed the Spirit of God hath a secret, divine and heavenly method of its own, and
> onely proper to it self, which none can know but those that are taught it of God
> . . . But these men accumulating a farraginous heap of divisions, subdivisions,
> distinctions, limitations, axioms, positions and rules, do chanel and bottle up
> the water of life (as they think) and again powre it forth as they please . . .
> (*Academiarum Examen*, 13–15)

As the operation of the Spirit 'doth supereminently transcend [the] whole
praedicamental scale', there may be a degree of irony in Coppe's use of the
syllogism in his recantation to define a God 'who cannot but be defined
by his own Logick'. Indeed when Coppe declares in his second recantation that the 'pure spark of Reason (was for a season) taken from me. And
I driven from it; from men, from *RATIONALITY*', a statement that seems
like an acknowledgement of sin can, in the context of Coppe's adoption
of the persona of the Pauline holy fool, be read as a reiteration of his privileged grace while in the 'Lunatick moode'. The relevant text is quoted by
Webster in his attack on the syllogism: 'the foolishness of God is higher
than the wisdom of men'. In his first, more defiant, recantation, Coppe,
quoting '*1 Cor.' in the margin, refers to how he 'formerly . . . (and in the
time of my fleshly wisdom, which was *enmity to God*) spake of formally,
ignorantly, notionally (onely) like a Parot in a cage'.[87] The rational progression of the syntax in these extracts seems itself to be about to break
down with the rhyme of 'reason' and 'season' and the pun on 'formerly'
and 'formally'. The image of the 'Parot in a cage' is used by Webster to
represent the empty forms of 'fleshly wisdom': schoolboys emerge from
years of grammatical study 'like Parrats to babble and prattle', while
undergraduates repeat '*Parrat*-like' meaningless syllogisms (22, 40).[88]

---

polemical use of the visual design of the printed page, see Lucasta Miller ' "The Shattered
Violl": Print and Textuality in the 1640s', in *Essays and Studies, 46 (Literature and Censorship)* (1993), 23–38.

[87] Coppe, *Copps Return*, 130; *A Remonstrance of the Sincere and Zealous Protestation of
Abiezer Coppe* (1651), in *CRW*, 121.

[88] For an example of the exercise of 'posing the parts', in which the pupil answers
grammatical questions under the threat of the rod, see Brinsley, *Ludus Literarius*, 74–6.

Nigel Smith has argued that ideally 'Ranter discourse would dispense with all forms of order imposed by convention', but that such an aspiration was unavoidably compromised by the necessity of communication; as a consequence, religious radicals had to adapt orthodox soteriological and disputative forms.[89] This is actually a variation on one of Featley's shrewd criticisms of enthusiastic 'ejaculations' in *The Dippers Dipt*: 'though the Prayer of the Preacher be no set form to him, but meer voluntary and extemporary; yet it is a set form to the hearers' (105). Here Featley tries to undermine the radicals' claims for the uniqueness of their inspired experience. In his recantations Coppe signals his orthodoxy by tying his prose to the catechetical form and the syllogism; in his radical writing he evades the problem that Featley and Smith identify by using authoritative pedagogical forms as vehicles for the dissemination of heterodoxy. It is through parody that Coppe is released from the repression of forms. There is an important final point which arises from Featley's reference to 'hearers'. In his lecture on radical prose style Christopher Hill argues that Coppe's publications are 'almost certainly an attempt to reproduce his pulpit style'.[90] Yet it is difficult to see how Coppe's parodies of Lily's Grammar and the ABC could ever have been intended for oral performance. Along with Coppe's subversion of publishing conventions, they suggest rather his acute awareness of the rhetorical potential of the printed page to rewrite hegemonic languages and values. Whereas Richard Coppin turned to print only because he was physically prevented from preaching in Oxfordshire and Berkshire and apologizes for communicating through print and 'not in bodily presence', Coppe represents the process of writing and publishing as divinely sanctioned (*Divine Teachings*, 'Preface'). The account of his conversion that prefaces *A Fiery Flying Roll* culminates in God's command that Coppe 'Go up to *London*, to *London*, that great City, write, write, write', echoing Ezekiel's vow to 'overturn, overturn, overturn' (83). The intricacy of the typographical and bibliographical design of Coppe's pamphlets suggests he had close control over the page layout and presentation, casting doubt upon suggestions that the elliptical style and unorthodox punctuation of his prose are the result of poor compositing.[91] Both *Some Sweet Sips* and the preface to *Divine Teachings* were printed by Giles Calvert, who was involved in the publication of many of

[89] Smith, *Perfection Proclaimed*, 326.

[90] Hill, 'Radical Prose in Seventeenth Century England', 115.

[91] Smith speculates that the irregularities may have been the result of compositing errors or a habit of oral delivery, in *Perfection Proclaimed*, 336. A. D. Nuttall observes that Coppe's use of dashes is 'as extreme as Sterne's in *Tristam Shandy*' (*The Alternative Trinity*, 209).

the radical tracts circulating in England in the late 1640s and 1650s. According to Laurence Clarkson, Calvert was associated with the 'Ranter' group 'My One Flesh'. On introducing Clarkson to this group Calvert told him that if he had 'come a little sooner, [he] might have seen Mr. Copp . . . in a most dreadful manner', so Calvert and Coppe may have been acquainted.[92]

Coppe's parodic application of his learning also raises the problem of his intended audience. The echoes of Lily would have had significance only for an audience with a degree of Latin literacy; those who at least had some grammar school education. They would surely have meant little to the majority of Hill's projected popular readership of 'craftsmen and yeo-man', and even less if 'read aloud to illiterate audiences'. The origins and writings of Abiezer Coppe, the most important of the Ranters, seem difficult to reconcile with the argument that those called Ranters spoke for and to a constituency of 'the slum dwellers of London'; that their writings 'gave ideological form and coherent expression to practices which had long been common among vagabonds, squatter-cottagers, and the in-between category of migratory craftsmen'.[93] Coppe's satires on learning might rather be linked with the collegiate tradition of playing with the curriculum to impress one's fellow students featured in Milton's *Prolusions* and 'At a Vacation Exercise in College' (1628). Coppe describes his address to his ex-cronies at Oxford as 'a Christmas Caroll at the famous University'. Parliament had sought to prohibit observance of Christmas from 1648 so this might be interpreted as a hostile gesture towards Puritan rule similar to the celebration of traditional festive ritual in Cavalier verse. However, the varsity context suggests that Coppe's academic parody is designed to evoke the kind of Christmas festivities experienced by Anthony Wood in his first term at Merton College in 1647: 'a little after five of the clock, the senior undergraduates would bring into the hall the juniors or freshmen between that time and six of the clock, and there make them sit downe on a forme in the middle of the hall, joyning to the declaiming desk: which done, every one in order was to speake some pretty apothegme, or make a jest or bull, or speake some eloquent nonsense, to make the company laugh'.[94] That the theme of such 'eloquent nonsense' was often the intensive and painful training in Latin grammar that everyone in the audience had experienced is suggested

---

[92] Clarkson, *The Lost Sheep Found*, in *CRW*, 180–1.

[93] Morton, *The World of the Ranters*, 71, 114; Hill, *The World Turned Upside Down*, 258.

[94] Anthony Wood, *The Life and Times of Anthony Wood, Antiquary, of Oxford, 1632–1695, as Described by Himself*, ed. A. Clark, 5 vols. (Oxford, 1891–1900), i. 133.

by Francis Beaumont's mock 'Grammar Lecture', delivered at the Christmas revels of the Inner Temple sometime between 1601 and 1605. Beaumont's comic lecture follows the plan of Lily's Grammar, parodically applying the rules to absurd contexts and impersonating the distinctive textual voice of the *magister*.[95] The tradition of the academic grammar play in England can be traced back at least to a Latin version of Andrea Guarna's *Bellum Grammaticale* performed at Christ Church in 1592. A grammar play in English dating from the early seventeenth century, *Heteroclitanomalonomia*, features a character called William Lily, who settles a dispute between Noun and Verb over precedence. Lily acts as a force of political as well as grammatical order, spreading peace throughout the land of Queen Oration by sending the rebellious 'anomalaes' and 'heteroclites' to 'grammar prison'.[96] Featley, we might recall, urged his readers to pay no heed to the 'fancies and dreames' of sectarians and enthusiasts 'who because they are *Anomalaes* themselves, would have not by their good will there should bee any Rules' (*The Dippers Dipt*, 175).

So Coppe's address to the 'Scholars of Oxford' is in fact a parody of the parodic festivities that were a regular feature of life in the universities and Inns of Court. The mock encomium to foolishness which was characteristic of these collegiate revels becomes both a real satire on the folly of those who place value on their learning and a real encomium on the holy simplicity of the saints. The elite cultural context of this passage sharply qualifies claims that the 'rhetoric of mania' in Coppe's writing represents 'a subcultural ethos' that was 'constituted by the process of plebeian struggle'.[97] The pose of madness frequently adopted in radical texts needs to be related not only to scriptural models which were available to anybody who was literate, but to the specific theme of Christian folly in early modern intellectual culture. The Pauline language of inversion that licensed much of the anti-intellectual rhetoric of radicalism in this period was an oppositional presence within Erasmian humanism almost from its inception. In the *Encomium Moriae* (1509; first published, 1511) Erasmus seems to subvert the identification of education, virtue, and religious knowledge that he played such a central role in disseminating, or at least

---

[95] The text is printed in Mark Eccles, 'Francis Beaumont's *Grammar Lecture*', *Review of English Studies*, 16 (1940), 402–14. Milton wrote a 'theme' on Lily's Grammar as a schoolboy (*CPWM*, i. 1036–9).

[96] The text is printed in *Jacobean Academic Plays: Malone Society Collections, xiv,* ed. Suzanne Gossett and Thomas L. Berger (Oxford, 1988), 57–97.

[97] Hawes, *Mania and Literary Style*, 9, 28. On the various forms of parodic literary and academic humour which were developed in the revels at the universities and the Inns of Court see Noel Malcolm, *The Origins of English Nonsense* (London, 1997), 1–51.

he satirically explores the dangers of dislocating reason from faith in the pursuit of secular knowledge. The condemnation by Folly of the empty rhetorical and logical constructs of academics, clerics, and theologians, which she connects to the abuse of ecclesiastical hierarchy as a source of power and wealth, is followed by her genuine praise of unlearned piety in the final pages. The text increasingly dwells on the theme of Christian folly, concluding 'with a remarkable feat of double irony as it transforms itself from a mock encomium into a real one'.[98] Quoting extensively from Ecclesiastes, Acts, and Corinthians, Folly describes the unification of the soul with the divine as 'nothing other than a certain kind of folly and madness'. The holy fool 'who has gained understanding pities his companions and deplores their insanity which confines them to such an illusion, but they in their turn laugh at him as if he were crazy and turn him out'. The speech of the holy lunatic is the converse of the rhetorical fluency which was the prime objective of humanist pedagogy: they 'speak incoherently and unnaturally, utter sound without sense'. Coppe represents his regenerate self as a type of '*Paul*, the *Athenians* Babler', who speaks 'with a stammering tongue'. Although he is 'not eloquent' and cannot 'write that smoothly', he 'rejoyce[s] exceedingly' that he speaks and records '*the Fathers voyce*'. The same arguments are employed by Folly that were used by those accused of heresy throughout the Middle Ages to subvert and reverse clerical charges of ignorance—a fact of which Erasmus can hardly have been unaware. Christ chose 'simple, ignorant apostles, to whom he unfailingly preached folly', because the 'mystery of salvation had been hidden from the wise'.[99] Given Erasmus' own celebrated learning and concern with educational advancement, the final praise of Pauline folly 'sounds a harsh note of self-parody'. Erasmus himself professed surprise at the controversy provoked by a work that he claimed to regard as a slight exercise in irony, and defended his intentions in a formal letter to Martin Dorp (1515), subsequently printed with the text. Nonetheless, as David Weil Baker has recently shown, Erasmus was anxious about the dissemination of the *Encomium Moriae* in print and about the radical uses to which insufficiently sophisticated readers might put his anticlerical satire.[100]

---

[98] Erasmus, *Praise of Folly*, ed. A. H. T. Levi, trans. Betty Radice (Harmondsworth, 1971), 186 n. 122.

[99] Ibid. 203, 199, 197, 207; *CRW*, 60, 70. The tradition of religious ecstasy and Christian madness that Erasmus draws upon is comprehensively discussed in M. A. Screech, *Erasmus: Ecstasy and the Praise of Folly* (1980; repr. Harmondsworth, 1988), esp. 63–74.

[100] Erasmus, *Praise of Folly*, 41; David Weil Baker, *Divulging Utopia: Radical Humanism in Sixteenth Century England* (Amherst, Mass., 1999), 22–47, 126–30.

A striking instance of the radical appropriation of a specifically
Erasmian mode of folly is found in a work written by John Rogers while
imprisoned in Carisbrook Castle on the Isle of Wight. Rogers was one
of the leaders of the Fifth Monarchists, a loose collection of Baptists
and radical Independents who sought to establish a theocratic republic
in England in the 1650s. They envisaged rule by an oligarchy of regenerate
saints who would impose the law of the first covenant upon the
unregenerate multitude in preparation for Christ's millennial kingdom
on earth. Rogers identifies his exile on the Isle of Wight by the
Protectorate with St John's exile on Patmos and looks forward to the
apocalyptic overturning of the great and wise by the foolish and the base.
His introduction is an explanation of why the Fifth Monarchists are
'accounted Fools and Madmen; and how we are so'. Rogers, who was an
undergraduate at King's College, Cambridge, in the early 1640s, relates
how he has 'studied to be *wise* (as well as others) but now I am learning to
be a *Fool*, which none will look after, because such are the Lords
Instruments, and by such he will confound the *wisdom* of the *wise*'.
Amongst a tissue of quotations from Ecclesiastes and Corinthians, Rogers
declares that 'the *Prophet* is a *fool*, and the *spiritual* man is *mad* (so
accounted at this time). And who but such *Mad-men* and *Fools* would
oppose *Powers, Armies, Kings, Councels, Priests, Lawyers?*'. He is
influenced not only by the scriptural topoi of holy madness but by the
figure of the Court fool who is given licence to speak the unspeakable and
criticize the king: 'let our *Wise-enemies* at Court, or in Country, give me
leave, for once, to speak like a *Fool*, without stirring up their *anger*'.
Rogers represents himself as fool to the Court of Cromwell, who was
accused by the Fifth Monarchists of having merely replaced the reign of
one tyrannous monarch with that of another. As one would expect,
Rogers appropriates the hostile stereotype of the heretic as ignoramus by
citing the example of the lowly status of the Apostles; however, he refers
not to Scripture but to another source: 'as one says, *Asinos & Ideotas
Christus eligit* [Christ chose asses and idiots]... and indeed, I write to, and
for, such *Fools*'.[101] In the *Encomium Moriae* Folly speaks not only of how
Christ chose 'simple, ignorant apostles' but of his 'delight in little
children, women, and fishermen, while the dumb animals who gave him
the greatest pleasure were those furthest removed from cleverness and
cunning. So he preferred to ride an ass, though had he chosen he could

---

[101] John Rogers, *Jegar-Sahadutha: An Oyled Pillar. Set up for posterity, against Present
wickednesses, hypocrisies, blasphemies, persecutions & cruelties of this serpent power in England*
(1657), 44–5.

safely have mounted on a lion'. Rogers always quotes Scripture in the vernacular and classical and neo-Latin texts in their original; several lines after this he quotes in Latin from a sermon by Erasmus and later tells us that '*Erasmus* did the enemy more mischief by jesting, than *Luther* did by his angry stomachfull and yet more solid resisting of him'. Rogers's preference for the 'jesting' method of Erasmian satire suggests that he found in the *Encomium Moriae* both a celebration of the supra-rational insight of the Fifth Monarchist saints and a polemical language of inversion with which to engage the Protectorate from his powerless position of exile. Presumably Rogers was working from memory, as it seems unlikely that he had access to many books in Carisbrook Castle. Nonetheless he assumes the characteristically disingenuous voice of Folly in his insistence that his captors keep decorum: 'Therefore, for shame, take not such *counsel*, as ye do, how to deal with a *fool* or *mad-man* (as you say I am) who surely should not offend the *wise*, if he play the *fool*'.[102]

Anthony Wood described the Christmas revels in Merton to illustrate 'the folly and simplicity of those times' before the dark years of Puritan rule over the universities. Coppe—who transferred to Merton from All Souls in the late 1630s—presents his address to Oxford as one of these freshmen's Christmas jests. His 'eloquent nonsense', however, is designed less to 'make the company laugh' than to attack the very basis and function of the academic institution in early modern English society; to rupture the connection securing formal education and social and religious hierarchy. Wood records his own piece of 'eloquent nonsense' at the festivities in Merton in 1647: 'Most reverent Seniors, may it please your Gravities to admit into your presence a kitten of the Muses, and a meer frog of Helicon to croak the cataracts of his plumbeous cerebrosity before your sagacious ingenuities'.[103] There may be something of this sense of collegiate familiarity and playfulness in Coppe's address to Marchamont Nedham, who was at All Souls when Coppe came up in 1636 and whom Coppe had to convince of the sincerity of his recantation to secure his release from Newgate: 'For his much Honoured friend, *Mr. Marchamont Nedham*: M. Nedham! My humble service, sincere respects, and hearty commendations to you presented, &c' (156). Whether or not Nedham remembered the young Coppe, it is evident that the apparently rambling, irrational progress of Coppe's pamphlets masks a complex

---

[102] Erasmus, *Praise of Folly*, 198–9; Rogers, *Jegar-Sahadutha*, 45, 47, 60. In his prefatory letter to Thomas More, Erasmus had excused Folly's attacks upon the clergy on the grounds of literary decorum (60–1).

[103] Wood, *The Life and Times of Anthony Wood*, i. 139.

polemical strategy, the purpose of which becomes clearer if interpreted as a dialogue with heresiographic writings of the period. While Coppe at first appears to present himself as conforming to the polemical stereotype of the ignorant and crazed libertine, through careful parody he subverts the institutional link between educational status and religious authority, and transfers the image of illiterate heretic on to the university-educated clergy. Ironically it was in part his own experience in 'the Schools of Anti-Christ', under Thomas Dugard and Ralph Button, that allowed Coppe to express his anti-intellectual arguments in terms of the categories of educational attainment used by the clergy to divide and rule English society. One might even argue that his parody of Latin grammar reinstates in his readership the very hierarchy of literate and illiterate that he seeks to destroy. Yet far from being the invention of anti-sectarian polemic, Coppe can be read as appropriating and dismantling these projected images. Such a reading lays to rest the enduring perception of Coppe's prose as the printed record of a 'mechanick' preacher.

5
Washing in Cabalinus' Well: Quakerism, Scepticism, and Radical Enlightenment

More items were published in England between 1640 and 1660 than in the whole of the previous two centuries. The Bible remained, however, the authoritative text in any matter of religious, political, or moral controversy. As David Wootton observes: 'When questions of order arose, people in seventeenth-century England immediately thought in biblical terms. Political authority and private property, they were told from the pulpits, had been established as a result of the Fall'. Gerrard Winstanley reversed this argument in seeking to establish his Digger communes: man would be restored to the Edenic state of perfection by the abolition of political authority and private property. The example of Winstanley, the most socially radical thinker of the period, demonstrates how 'both the defence and the subversion of authority were naturally conducted in language drawn from the Bible'.[1] A short chapter on radical attitudes to Scripture in Christopher Hill's *The World Turned Upside Down* is entitled 'Samuel Fisher and the Bible'. For Hill, Fisher's *Rusticus ad Academicos* (1660), a lengthy reply to Presbyterian and Independent attacks on Quakerism, represents the fullest expression of one aspect of these attitudes, an approach which 'denied the infallibility of the Bible, or submitted it to close textual criticism'. Hill believes *Rusticus ad Academicos* marks 'the end of an epoch, the epoch of Protestant Bibliolatry'. He even goes as far as to say that 'Fisher deserves greater recognition as a precursor of the English enlightenment than he has yet received'. Fisher's location of revealed religious knowledge in the light within each individual and systematic rejection of the spiritual authority of Scripture on the grounds of historical and textual proofs can be seen as 'very difficult to differentiate in practice from simple human reason'.[2]

---

[1] Wootton, *Divine Right and Democracy*, 27.
[2] *The World Turned Upside Down*, 261, 266–8.

Elsewhere Hill has argued that Fisher 'applied Renaissance standards of textual criticism to the Bible' but that *Rusticus ad Academicos* was nonetheless 'a lower class response to established religion': 'If it had appeared earlier, then it could have been discussed by rustics and artisans and the undermining effect on the Bible might have been more serious'.[3] While only a couple of pages are devoted to Fisher in *The World Turned Upside Down*, Hill's brief elevation of a writer hardly noticed outside Quaker circles to a position of some interest in the history of ideas has been developed by Richard Popkin. When Fisher arrived in Amsterdam in 1658 as part of a conversion mission which later took him to Rome and Constantinople, he gave the job of translating two of Margaret Fell's pamphlets into Hebrew to an excommunicated Jew, whom Popkin believes was the young Benedict Spinoza. The first Quaker missionaries in Holland—John Stubbs, William Caton, and William Ames—had developed links with the radical spiritualist sect known as the Collegiants, whom Spinoza had joined after being expelled from the Jewish community in Amsterdam in 1656. The Hebrew translation of Fell's *A Loving Salutation to the Seed of Abraham* was published in Amsterdam in 1658 and in London in 1660; to both editions was appended a short exhortation to the Jews to convert to Quakerism, composed in Hebrew by Fisher. Popkin shows that the arguments advanced by Fisher and Spinoza to reject the identification of God's Word with Scripture and to make the case for absolute liberty of conscience bear some comparison, and speculates on a mutual influence emerging from their acquaintance in Amsterdam in 1658: 'Fisher was moved by the Spirit, Spinoza by reason, but eventually they come to a somewhat similar vision, as expressed at the end of Spinoza's *Ethics*'. Popkin shows how the historical and textual arguments produced by Fisher concerning the ambiguity of the Mosaic authorship, the authority and origin of the biblical canon, and the development of the Hebrew and Greek languages since biblical events were first recorded are 'strikingly novel for the time, and contain much of the material that Spinoza used in challenging the world of Jewish Bible interpreters' in the *Tractatus theologico-politicus* (1670).[4]

Such arguments had some precursors in post-Reformation Europe.

[3] Hill, 'Freethinking and Libertinism: The Legacy of the English Revolution', in Lund (ed.), *The Margins of Orthodoxy*, 54–72 (57–8); 'The Problem of Authority', in *Collected Essays of Christopher Hill*, ii, 37–50 (46); see also Hill, *The English Bible*, 420, 427–8, 438, 441.

[4] Richard H. Popkin, 'Spinoza's Relations with the Quakers', *Quaker History*, 73 (1984), 14–28; Popkin, 'Spinoza and Samuel Fisher', *Philosophia*, 15 (December 1985), 219–36 (231–2); Richard H. Popkin and Michael J. Signer (eds.), 'Introduction' to *Spinoza's Earliest Publication? The Hebrew Translation of Margaret Fell's 'A Loving Salutation'* (London, 1987).

Jesuits such as François Verron had deployed Pyrrhonian techniques to undermine Calvinist arguments for Scripture as the supreme rule of faith. They argued firstly that rational procedures alone cannot establish the Bible to be the Word of God and secondly that appeals to inner persuasion by the Spirit can, in the absence of miracles or direct revelation, never be satisfactorily distinguished from fancy (a virtually identical argument to that used by Calvinists to discredit the enthusiasm of their radical opponents such as the Anabaptists). Sceptical treatment of the Bible as a rule of faith was thus deployed to argue for fideistic reliance on the traditions of the Catholic Church. Developing French sceptical humanism, the *libertin érudit* Isaac la Peyrère called the Bible 'a heap of copie upon copie' in *Prae-Adamitae* (1655; translated into English as *Men Before Adam*, 1656), arguing that Moses could not have written the Pentateuch and that we no longer possess an accurate text of the Bible. In England Thomas Hobbes had similarly raised the problem of the apparently non-Mosaic lines of Deuteronomy recording Moses's own death and burial, throwing into doubt the whole question of who decided the composition of the biblical canon. Hobbes's solution, in the absence of revelation, was to delegate the formation and authority of the text to the 'Sovereign Prophet', to the Leviathan.[5] In the immediate context of English radical religion we have seen how William Walwyn had adapted the Catholic scepticism of Montaigne and Charron to deny, at least implicitly, the objective authority of any particular interpretation of Scripture regardless of scholarly proofs. His friend Clement Writer, a Worcester clothier accused by Thomas Edwards of being 'an anti-Scripturist, a Questionist and Sceptick, and I fear an Atheist', had maintained the impossibility of locating truth in a text which had passed through so many transcriptions and translations; Writer argued that faith must be established upon the 'infallible evidence' of personal spiritual experience rather than 'any history of words from men fallible and liable to error'.[6] Fisher's *Rusticus ad Academicos* is, however, the most strident and comprehensive rejection of the Bible as a framework for understanding man and the universe written in early modern England.

Spinoza wrote in Latin for a scholarly, European audience. Hill makes much of Fisher's prose style, which he argues has 'something of Rabelais

---

[5] Popkin, 'Spinoza and Samuel Fisher', 225; Popkin, *The History of Scepticism*, 70–8, 214–28; Richard Popkin, 'Spinoza and Bible Scholarship', in J. E. Force and Popkin (eds.), *The Books of Nature and Scripture* (Dordrecht, 1994), 6; Jonathan I. Israel, *Radical Enlightenment: Philosophy and the Making of Modernity 1650–1750* (Oxford, 2001), 447–56.

[6] Edwards, *Gangraena*, i. 96; Clement Writer, *Fides Divina* (1657), 77; see also Writer, *The Jus Divinum of Presbyterie* (1646; 2nd edn. 1655), 66–9.

and something of Martin Marprelate in it—buffooning and alliterative
. . . [w]hat is important is that Fisher wrote in the vernacular, in a racy,
popular style'. For Hill the example of Fisher illustrates that 'mechanick
students of the Bible were more creative, more boldly innovating, *because*
they were selective in their approach, more responsive to problems of
their own world which demanded new solutions'. However, Fisher was
hardly *laicus illitteratus*. He had spent seven years at Oxford and was,
according to the *DNB*, 'dextrous and well-skilled in the ancient poets and
Hebrew'. Indeed Popkin tells us that Fisher wrote in Hebrew much as he
did in English, 'in his inimitable, run-on, rambling style, that came to
encompass all sorts of messages and digressions'.[7] The aim of this chapter
is to reconcile these divergent reactions to Fisher as on the one hand a
'mechanick' heretic writing popular polemics aimed at 'rustics and
artisans' and on the other a sophisticated textual critic who was con-
versant in Hebrew and may have influenced the development of
Spinoza's scepticism. Fisher's text is in large part a satire on the clerical
application of logical, philological, and rhetorical skill to biblical exegesis.
Fisher draws on his own considerable learning and formal education for
the sources and resources of his anti-intellectualism. As with the
Marprelate tracts themselves, the use of a 'buffooning' style and a rustic
persona is in fact governed by the humanist tradition of satirical mock
scholarship. *Rusticus ad Academicos*, written at the moment of the
Restoration, is a Janus-like text which fuses a satirical mode of religious
dissent which looks back to the 1580s with a rational treatment of revealed
religion which looks forward to the deistic arguments espoused at the end
of the century by figures such as John Toland and Charles Blount. Fisher's
version of Quaker enthusiasm may indeed tell us something new about
the origins of the 'radical Enlightenment' in England, putting flesh on the
bones of J. G. A. Pocock's suggestion that eighteenth-century deists and
freethinkers rationalized enthusiastic visions of the unified relationship
between man, nature, and the divine which they inherited from the
radical traditions of the mid-seventeenth century.[8]

From the original reformers to the heresiographers of revolutionary
England, the central theme of Protestant efforts to delegitimate claims to
direct divine inspiration was that revelation had ceased in the post-
Apostolic age and that Scripture was sufficient for delivering God's

[7] *The World Turned Upside Down*, 260, 263, 268; Popkin and Singer (eds.), *Spinoza's
Earliest Publication?*, 9.

[8] J. G. A. Pocock, 'Post-Puritan England and the Problem of the Enlightenment', in Perez
Zagorin (ed.), *Culture and Politics From Puritanism to the Enlightenment* (Berkeley, Calif.,
1980), 91–112.

message to humanity. Thus clerical authority rested on the minister's intellectual qualifications to interpret the biblical text.[9] Fisher's defence of Quaker enthusiasm in terms of a rational, sceptical critique of the epistemological value of scriptural exegesis results in a curious yoking of reason with revelation, of concerted logical argument with celebration of the supra-rational workings of the inner light. Such a conjunction of the seemingly disparate discourses of rationalism and enthusiasm has previously been considered a late eighteenth-century phenomenon.[10] Writing at the moment of the Restoration, Fisher rejects the monolithic authority of the Bible by fusing his knowledge of post-Reformation developments in historical and textual criticism with epistemological arguments derived from his belief in the continuing revelations of the inner light. The peculiar bulk and repetitiveness of *Rusticus ad Academicos*—over 900 quarto pages, which must have made it a very expensive book, well beyond the means of 'rustics and artisans'—seems to be designed to parody the futility and circularity of biblical exegesis. *Rusticus* is in fact a fitting text on which to close two decades of pamphlet wars during which virtually all published statements of authority and assertions of truth were questioned, refuted, or parodied. Fisher's rejection of the sacred authority of the Bible is shaped not only by belief in the sufficiency of the wordless inner experience of the Spirit and by knowledge of the historical corruptions of the biblical text, but by an acute awareness of the materiality and plasticity of the printed word. If the 'textual exchange' of revolutionary England, much of which was framed in biblical terms, led to 'a greater cynicism' about the capacity of print to embody truth, then it was perhaps inevitable that the sanctified status of the Bible as a textual record of God's Word would itself come into question.[11]

SAMUEL FISHER'S 'LARGE CONTROVERSIES'

In the *DNB* entry on Fisher A. C. Bickley writes: 'Fisher's works show him to have been a man of considerable erudition and some literary skill, but they are disfigured by violence and coarseness. They were, however, Quaker textbooks for more than a century. He was skilful in argument,

---

[9] Heyd, *The Reaction to Enthusiasm in the Seventeenth and Early Eighteenth Centuries*, 38–9.

[10] On the relationship between William Blake's prophetic books and eighteenth-century biblical criticism see Mee, *Dangerous Enthusiasm*, esp. 161–213.

[11] Smith, *Literature and Revolution*, 44; see also Hill, *The English Bible*, 428–32.

had no little logical acumen, and great controversial powers.' The testimonies prefacing the collection of Fisher's Quaker writings published in 1679 all agree on his intellectual attainment. Ellis Hookes tells us that Fisher was considered at Oxford to be 'a Man of good natural Parts, [who] attained much outward Learning and Knowledge, in the Tongues, and Natural Arts and Sciences'. However, he became 'dissatisfyed and burthened with many Vain ceremonies and practises, then used at the *University*'. Luke Howard adds that Fisher 'accounted his Outward Learning abundently subordinate to the Grace of Life and Truth'. Such spiritual awareness 'made himme a Fisher of Men'.[12] One of the men whom Fisher played a part in converting was William Penn, whose testimony is interesting for the hints of reservation that are mixed with the expected praise. In comparison to Hookes and Howard, Penn seems oddly anxious to justify the place of Fisher's writings in the Quaker canon. Penn anticipates Bickley and Christopher Hill in dwelling on Fisher's polemical style:

his Part fell to be mostly controversial; in which, to carry a Clear Mind, and an even Hand, is very difficult; however, allowing him in some passages the freedom of the Prophet Elijah against the Prophets of Baal (1 King 18: 27) some times exposing absurd things by vulgar Terms and Proverbs to derision in the view of [the] Ingenious Reader; Yet all that kind of Rhetorik and Learning he had so low an esteem of it . . .

Penn points out the conjunction of subtlety and coarseness, derision and ingenuity in Fisher's prose but, like Hookes and Howard, is keen to emphasize Fisher's disdain for 'all that kind of Rhetorik and Learning' in which he had once excelled. Fisher employs his educational resources in his pamphlets only to expose 'absurd things'. Penn goes on to raise the question of Fisher's obvious enjoyment of polemic and satire and comparative lack of concern for the Quaker expression of personal spiritual experience:

And though it pleased God to begin my Convictions by the Work of his own Spirit in my Heart, and that it was much more my Desire to feel my self enabled by his holy power and vertue of it to overcome the world therein, then to entertain my self with Large Controversies. Yet for as much as the Understanding must be convinced, as well as the Heart Experience the Operation and feel the Truth of a Principle; such Labours have been, are and will be useful to distinguish Truth from Falsehood and to invalidate the Works of Ignorance and Malice, that have either obscured or Misrepresented what we hold; and they had this good Effect

---

[12] Samuel Fisher, *The Testimony of Truth Exalted*, ed. William Penn (1679), sigs. A2ʳ, B2ᵛ.

with me in particular, that in perusing his *Rusticus ad Academicos*, I found the Objections of several considerable Opposers so closely handled, and so plainly enervated, that my Heart was not more affected than my understanding was clearly satisfied.[13]

Penn was a leading figure in the development of Quakerism as a respectable religious movement in the aftermath of the Restoration. He tells us that he prefers to concentrate upon 'the Work of [God's] own Spirit in my Heart' than to 'entertain my self with Large Controversies'. The note of vague disdain brings to mind Penn's better known prefatory discussion of literary style in the first edition of George Fox's *Journal*, where he apologized for an expression that 'might sound uncouth and unfashionable to nice ears'.[14] His desire to remove Quakerism from controversy seems to lead to his half-expressed doubts over republishing Fisher's 'Large Controversies', in which 'opposers' are 'closely handled' and exposed to 'derision' through the use of 'Vulgar Terms and Proverbs'. Penn prefers Quakers to 'overcome the world therein' than to take on the world without.

Penn's reservation is an important one. Fisher's writings are not characterized by forms of expression usually associated with early Quakerism: an intense metaphorical language of grace expressing the merging of individual and godhead, or the use of Scripture as an interior allegory, a charting of the internal operation of the light within. Nor do they exhibit the violent apocalyptic language often favoured by George Fox. In *Rusticus* Fisher initially insists that he would much rather keep his peace than be drawn into controversy: 'I make my self for a while more like them than (through mercy) I *Really am* . . . I my self had much rather be in this case wholly silent (much printing being as burdensom to mens purses, as much writing is to their Persons)'.[15] This assertion of aloofness is followed by 939 quarto pages of fierce polemical engagement, *ad hominem* satire, and anti-intellectual parody, composed in densely alliterative, punning, and sometimes coarsely colloquial language. Fisher describes *Rusticus ad Academicos* as a text in which arguments are

---

13 Fisher, *The Testimony of Truth Exalted*, ed. Penn, sig. C2ʳ.

14 Smith (ed.), Fox, *The Journal*, 499. For a recent discussion of Penn's role in 'gentrifying' Quakerism see N. H. Keeble, 'The Politic and the Polite in Quaker Prose: The Case of William Penn', in Loewenstein and Corns (eds.), *The Emergence of Quaker Writing*, 112–25.

15 Fisher, *Rusticus ad Academicos* (1660), 'First Apologetical and Expostulary Exercitation', 39. The text is divided into four of these 'exercitations'—a word that Fisher has derived from the Latin *exercitatio*, meaning exercise or experience. Presumably Fisher is presenting his spiritual experiences to his university opponents as mock academic exercises. All future references are to this edition unless otherwise noted.

'promiscuously and interchangeably carried on by way of entercourse' ('To the Reader', sig. B4ʳ). His prose, like Coppe's, is libertine in the sense of appropriating oppositional voices for the purposes of inversion, mockery, and the refutation of propriety, both disputational and textual. Despite Fisher's division of *Rusticus* into a preface, introduction, and four 'Apologetical and Expostulatory Exercitations' (followed by the sub-sequent publication in the same year of *An Additionall and Apolegeticall Apendix*, a summary of his arguments consisting of a further 100 quarto pages), he more or less ignores construction and sequent argument for a loose travesty of the anarchy of mind which is his subject.

In its encyclopaedic range, satirical repetitiveness, and sheer textual bulk *Rusticus ad Academicos* might be seen as a parodic version of the 'cornucopian text', the term ascribed by Terence Cave to Renaissance works which seek to fulfil the humanist literary ideal of *copia* in composi-tion and expression and so recreate the inexhaustible plenitude of the 'paradigm texts' of classical epic and Scripture. The term has also been applied to early modern English prose works such as Nashe's *Lenten Stuff* (1599), Burton's *Anatomy of Melancholy*, and Thomas Browne's *Pseudodoxia Epidemica* (1646). These texts paradoxically develop a 'richness of utterance' to represent human destitution, whether it be physical poverty, mental dysfunction, or intellectual error. Cave argues that many of the episodes in Rabelais's *Gargantua and Pantagruel* (1534–51) comically dramatize the process whereby the 'Utopian myth' of 'dynamic productivity' enshrined in the ideal of *copia* will 'sooner or later begin to appear, in the postlapsarian world, as an emptying out, or as mere flux or repetition'.[16] This is, as we shall see, exactly the picture of Protestant biblical scholarship that Fisher wishes to paint. The repeti-tious agglomeration of Fisher's text is designed to reflect not the supra-rational promptings of the inner light but the madness of clerical pedantry and the folly of academic religious dispute: 'Besides, 'tis the very life of Collegians and Clergy-Men, to busie themselves most in their *Musing-Places*, where they may have most *Book-room*, being apt to think all *lesser Papers Peddling*, and unfit for Them to find ought in, that may be answerable to the Vast Volumniousse *of their Inventions*'.[17]

Erasmian humanism was incorporated into the English curriculum in which Fisher had been schooled through pedagogic texts such as Lily's

---

[16] Terence Cave, *The Cornucopian Text: Problems of Writing in the French Renaissance* (Oxford, 1979), 183; Pooley, *English Prose of the Seventeenth Century*, 191–213 (191).

[17] Fisher, *Rusticus*, 'To the Reader', in *The Testimony of Truth*, 47. In some places the print in the 1660 copy of *Rusticus* in the Bodleian Library is unclear and consequently the reprint in *The Testimony of Truth* has occasionally been preferred.

Grammar, to which Erasmus' *De ratione studii* (1512) was attached throughout the sixteenth and seventeenth centuries. The Erasmian philosophy of education was an attempt to 'compensate for the imperfections of fallen language by relating it to a divine origin or model', directing linguistic and rhetorical education towards the ultimate goal of biblical philology.[18] Fisher, however, identifies the postlapsarian instability of language with the 'paradigm text' of Scripture itself. The true knowledge revealed to the Quakers, restored to the Adamic condition through their experience of the internally resurrected Christ or inner light, transcends the false intellectual constructs of the fallen imagination, which are epitomized for Fisher by the futile activity of biblical criticism. George Fox provides the classic statement of Quaker regeneration in the *Journal*: 'I knew nothing, but pureness, and innocency, and righteousness, being renewed up into the image of God by Christ Jesus; so that I say, was come into the state of Adam, which he was in, before he fell. The creation was opened to me: and it was showed to me, how all things had their names given them, according to their nature and virtue'. Possessed of 'that Light and Spirit which was, before Scripture was given forth', Fox becomes fluent in the perfect language of Adam, which reveals to him the divine patterns in creation. The experience convinced Fox that men are not made 'Christ's ministers' by scriptural study or 'by Hebrew, Greek, Latin and the seven arts, which all was but the teachings of the natural man . . . the whore and beast has power over the tongues and many languages which are in mystery Babylon, for they began at Babel'.[19] The fall of language at Babel is substituted for the Fall of Man at Eden. Fox's version of the Adamic language seems to bear no relationship with Hebrew, although Fox apparently burst into Hebrew while on trial in Lancashire in 1664 as an indication of the Spirit's workings within him. However, the Adamic language which Fox identifies with the Word of God seems to be not only supragrammatical but wordless, pointing to the role of silence in Quaker devotion: 'all Languages upon the earth is but Naturall, and makes none divine, but that which makes divine is the Word, which was before Languages, and Tongues were'.[20]

Fisher, similarly 'renewed' and possessed of the 'Light and Spirit' of

[18] Cave, *The Cornucopian Text*, 327; see also Grafton and Jardine, *From Humanism to the Humanities*, 136–46.

[19] *Journal*, 27, 32–3, 255–6.

[20] William Braithwaite, *The Beginnings of Quakerism*, (2nd edn., rev. Henry J. Cadbury, York, 1981), 302; I am grateful to Meiling Hazelton for bringing this reference to my attention. Fox, *A Battle-Door*, sig. A2ᵛ.

the Word, identifies the 'mere flux or repetition' of scriptural controversy and scholarly dispute with the endless recurrence of sin and the unregenerate nature of those who 'glory in *Fencer*-like Faculties of Disputing in *Form, Mood* and *Figure*, over the Quakers' ('Second Exercitation', 16). Fisher represents the circularity of their arguments as a pointless dance:

> *One while* it looks like *So*, not *No*,
> *Another while* like *No*, not *So*,
> *One way* it seems or *So*, or *No*,
> *Another way*, nor *No*, nor *So*,
> Some wayes it shewes both *So* and *No*,
> So its a meer endlesse *No*, and *So*.

The priests and professors are trapped in this logomachy because they remain '*lockt* up to a post by *Adams fall 6000* years before they were born, and never unloosed till this day'.[21] Yet despite Fisher's Quaker perfectionism, the text which most closely resembles *Rusticus* in style and theme in terms of the immediate post-Restoration period is not any contemporary Quaker tract but Samuel Butler's burlesque poem *Hudibras*, the first part of which appeared in 1662. Butler's ridicule of Puritan rhetoric as a Babel-like confusion of languages, personified in Sir Hudibras's quixotic application of his excessive learning, is couched in similar terms to Fisher's mockery of the Presbyterian and Independent identification of superior spiritual knowledge with formal education:

> He was in LOGICK a great Critick,
> Profoundly skill'd in Analytick;
> He could distinguish, and divide
> A Hair 'twixt South and South-West Side;
> On either which he wou'd dispute,
> Confute, change Hands, and still confute:
> He'd undertake to prove by Force
> Of Argument a Man's no Horse;
> He'd prove a Buzzard to be no Fowl,
> And that a Lord may be an Owl;
> A calf an Alderman, a Goose a Justice,
> And Rooks Committee-Men and Trustees.
> He'd run in debt by Disputation,
> And pay with Ratiocination.
> And all this by Syllogism, true
> In Mood and Figure, he wou'd do.

---

[21] Fisher, *An Additionall and Apologeticall Appendix* to *Rusticus ad Academicos* (1660), 47, 14.

Indeed Butler's hostility to biblical politics in *Hudibras*—representative of the post-Restoration mood—was echoed in his disbelief that the Bible, as a repeatedly transcribed and translated text, was the Word of God (although he preferred not to make public this latter opinion).[22]

In his earlier Quaker tracts Fisher asserts his prophetic authority to speak before Parliament and Cromwell in a more characteristically Quakerish idiom than he employs in the 'Large Controversies' of *Rusticus*. In *The Scorned Quaker's True and Honest Account* (1656) he describes how on 17 July 1656 'the Word of God came unto me, even unto me *Samuel Fisher*, at my own outward being at *Lid* in *Kent*' (1). In *The Scorned Quaker's Second Account*, published in the same year, he again represents his actions and writings as directly experienced divine 'movings', using the language of 'disclaiming locutions':

> I am again moved and made willing by the Lord at my departure hence to my own Outward Being (which as it had likely been ere this, if this Service had not been put upon me, so (if the Lord so please) may be so soon as performed) to unburden myself in writing of that heavy Burden of the Lord's Word, that lay upon me to have spoken it at the times and place forementioned . . . (11)[23]

Here is that 'combination of temporal and geographical accuracy, personal experience and revelation' which N. H. Keeble finds characteristic of 'the Quaker habit of presenting their writings as the irresistible and extemporaneous product of revelatory moments'. Yet in the moment of proclaiming that the Quakers of republican England are subject to the same revelations as were bestowed on the Old Testament prophets, Fisher parenthetically hints at his later concerns: 'for the Scripture is not his voice, but (so far as truly Translated) a Declaration of what he spake to, and by those holy men that were moved to write it, who heard his Voice within, and saw him in our Light within, as ye may do'.[24]

Fisher published these pamphlets because he was physically prevented from voicing his criticism before Parliament of the Protectorate's policy on religious toleration. He had been suffused with divine anger after hearing Cromwell state that to his knowledge no man had suffered unjust

[22] Samuel Butler, *Hudibras* (1662–77), ed. John Wilders (London, 1968), 2–3; Samuel Butler, *Prose Observations*, ed. H. de Quehen (Oxford, 1979), 124.

[23] 'Disclaiming locutions' is the phrase used by Peter Carlton to describe the rhetorical motif in prophetic writing by which 'thoughts and feelings [are constituted] as happenings . . . such statements transformed mental events into direct communications from God, making them implicitly authoritative' ('Bunyan: Language, Authority, Convention', *English Literary History*, 51 (1984), 17–32 (20)).

[24] Keeble, *The Literary Culture of Nonconformity*, 183; Fisher, *The Scorned Quakers Second Account* (1656), 13.

imprisonment on the grounds of religious belief under the Protectorate. In a letter sent to Parliament in August 1659 Fisher declared that he has 'a few words to speak to this parliament in the name and feare of the Lord, of moment as in reference to the worke of this Day, and am writing at the dores desirous to be admitted in for that purpose'. Fisher's personal experience of persecution seems only to have deepened his conviction of the necessity of universal liberty of conscience. In 1659 he was dragged by the hair out of St Margaret's Church, Westminster, while attempting to address the Members of Parliament and subsequently severely beaten. Immediately after the Restoration and the publication of *Rusticus* Fisher was confined to Newgate and then the Gatehouse at Westminster. In 1662 he spent a year in Newgate for refusing to take oaths, in a cell so small and crowded that only one prisoner could lie down at a time. Shortly after his release he was committed to the White Lion Prison in Southwark for a further two years. He died in 1665, having contracted the plague in prison.[25]

In his courting of persecution through sensational episodes of physical protest and prophetic gesture Fisher might be thought to be closer to the more extreme enthusiastic figures of early Quakerism—James Nayler, Robert Rich, John Perrot—who were persecuted by the Quaker hierarchy established by George Fox as well as by the religious and political authorities. Fox thought Perrot and Rich to follow 'not the Lambs Obedience but the Ranters'.[26] It is difficult to place Fisher in this spectrum of early Quaker practice. He seems to have been sympathetic to Perrot. In 1657 Perrot and five other Quakers had set out on a conversion mission, planning to convert the Sultan of Turkey before proceeding to Jerusalem. Having left Turkey without securing a meeting with the Sultan, Perrot and John Luffe ended up in Italy seeking an audience with Pope Alexander II. After disclosing their intentions to several Jesuits, the pair were imprisoned in Rome in 1658; Perrot spent the next three years in solitary confinement.[27] When Fisher set out on his mission with John

[25] Bodleian Library, MS Tanner 51, fo. 112; Joseph Besse, *A Collection of the Sufferings of the People called Quakers*, 2 vols. (1753), i. 289, 366.

[26] Robert Rich, *Hidden Things Brought to Light* (1680), 17; Rich cites a letter from Fox to Perrot. On Fox's expulsion of Perrot and Rich, and the distinctions of belief, behaviour, and expression in the early Quaker movement, see Nigel Smith, 'Hidden Things Brought to Light: Enthusiasm and Quaker Discourse', in Loewenstein and Corns (eds.), *The Emergence of Quaker Writing*, 57–69.

[27] For further details of Perrot's mission and discussion of his poetic response to this suffering see Nigel Smith, 'Exporting Enthusiasm: John Perrot and the Quaker Epic', in Thomas Healy and Jonathan Sawday (eds.), *Literature and the English Civil War* (Cambridge, 1990), 248–64.

Stubbs (who, along with William Caton, had converted Fisher in 1655), he tried to secure Perrot's release. In *Rusticus* he refers to this mission and to 'J. Parrot who is in Prison there still', accusing the English clergy of being no better than the Roman Church in their treatment of the Quakers ('First Exercitation', 52). On the other hand, Perrot refers to Fisher being present at one of his grim interrogations at the hands of Fox after he was freed and returned from Rome, although not to Fisher taking any active part.[28]

William Penn attacked Perrot for sporting a beard, which Nigel Smith speculates was 'an imitation on Perrot's part of Rabbinic appearance', indicating 'the very important connections between Quakers and Jews, both parties showing an interest in each other because of their shared millennial concerns'.[29] Perrot had discussions through third parties with the Jews in Livorno on the problems of persecution. According to the accounts by William Caton of Fisher's activities while at the Quaker mission in Amsterdam, Fisher debated at the homes of Dutch Jews and at the Amsterdam Synagogue, where

> they were pretty moderate towards him: (I meane they did not abuse him) but assented to much of what he spoke: he had some discourse with two or three of their Doctors in private at Amsterdam: and they seemd to owne in words the substance of that which he declared: but they were in bondage as people of other formes are . . .[30]

Fisher's facility in Latin and Hebrew allowed him to communicate directly with the Jewish 'Doctors' (and perhaps with Spinoza as well), and through these discussions he may have learnt something of the mystical and sceptical arguments of some Jewish philosophers. Nonetheless it seems an exaggeration to describe Fisher as 'almost a Judaized Christian' considering he attacked 'the idolatry of the *Torah*' in the synagogues that he visited during his expedition. Indeed he explicitly equated rabbinical doctrine and the Talmud with 'those *Absurdities, Self-Contradictions, Confusions, Riddles* and *Rounds*' of Puritan teaching on the Bible.[31]

Yet Fisher's exposure to the varieties of religious belief in other lands and cultures, combined with his own experience of persecution, seems to

[28] Rich, *Hidden Things Brought to Light*, 4; Rich quotes a letter from Perrot to Fox, a copy of which was sent to Rich by Perrot from Jamaica in 1664.

[29] Smith, 'Exporting Enthusiasm', 260.

[30] Friends Library, London, Caton MSS, fo. 507, letter from William Caton to Margaret Fell, 1658.

[31] R. H. Popkin, 'Introduction' to Popkin (ed.), *Jewish Christians and Christian Jews* (Leiden, 1994) 13; Fisher, *The Testimony of Truth*, 242.

have only confirmed his convictions concerning universal liberty of conscience, first articulated in his Baptist writings:

> If it be a question, and a brabble about *Heathenism, Turkism, Judaism, Christianism* and about *religion, worship,* and *faith* and *Jesus* and words, and names as *Antinomists, Arminians, Anabaptists, Pelagians, Socinians, Anti-Christians, Pedobaptists, Sectaries, the Ranting Prophet* . . . I humbly conceive the *Magistrate* may lawfully, and more acceptably to God than otherwise, save himself so much labour, as to let these matters alone.[32]

Fisher's response to his own suffering was very different from Perrot's attempt to 'refashion the signifying power of poetic language and of allegory' in his long poem *A Sea of the Seed's Suffering* (1661). Rather Fisher deploys his own considerable education to satirize and undermine the basis of those arguments which were used to justify his persecution. He does so through a playful and deeply provocative prose:

> I can truly say (having been at the *Pope's* Palace which stands in *Monte Caballino*) that *fonte labra Prolui Caballino: yet haud unquam me Prophetam somniasse tam altum memini; ut Repente sic Rabula prodirem* . . . Did not *Cardinal Bellarmine* hold some truths which thou holdest, as wel as some that I hold aginst thee, and that Christ is the Son of God, which we both hold? . . . the Jesuits and Fryars, in some points of doctrine, are more Reformed, I here give thee the advantage of saying the same ore again.[33]

This passage exemplifies the way in which Fisher transforms the meaning of classical allusions to express his prophetic status. He rewrites the first three lines of the 'Prologue' to the *Satires* of Persius, which was translated anonymously in 1614 as follows:

> Nec fonte labra prolui cabballino
> nec in bicipiti somniasse Parnaso
> memini, ut repente sic poeta prodirem.
>
> (I never wash't, that I could tell,
>   My lips in Cabalinus' well,
> Nor ever on Parnassus' tops
>   I ever dreamt of any hopes
> Whereby a poet I should be
>   To write on th' sudden as you see.)[34]

---

[32] Fisher, *Christianismus Redivivus*, 536.

[33] Smith, 'Exporting Enthusiasm', 253; Fisher, *Rusticus*, 'Second Exercitation', 29; 'First Exercitation', 66.

[34] Printed in *The Oxford Book of Classical Verse in Translation*, ed. Adrian Poole and Jeremy Maule (Oxford, 1995), 435.

Unlike Persius, Fisher has washed in Cabalinus' well but never dreamed that he would become a prophet. The classical categories of poetic inspiration are replaced by those of Old Testament prophecy.

This is an unexpected literary allusion to find in an early Quaker tract. John Stubbs, instrumental in converting Fisher, condemned the reading of the classics as 'contrary to the practice of the Saints'.[35] Yet Fisher's prose is full of such rewritten or adapted classical references which display his status as *litteratus* against those who would disqualify the Quakers from being heard on the grounds of their educational inadequacy. Fisher is replying here to the accusation that he is a covert papist, made by John Owen, Independent minister, Cromwell's vice-chancellor at Oxford from 1652–7, and one of the main subjects of Fisher's ridicule in *Rusticus*. Owen was a double target of Fisher's satire, for he had both specifically attacked Quaker beliefs in his Latin work *Pro Scripturis . . . Contra Fanaticos* (1658) and defended the inerrancy of the biblical text in two works published in 1659, *Of the Divine Originall, Authority, self-evidencing Light and Power of the Scriptures* and *Of the Integrity and Purity of the . . . Text of Scripture*. The charge of papistry was more than merely indiscriminate abuse on the part of Owen. When Fisher returned from his stay in Rome without having been persecuted or even warned by the authorities there he sported, according to Anthony Wood, a 'very genteel equipage'. This led to a rumour that he was now a Jesuit in the pay of the Pope. His previous citing of the Jesuit Cardinal Bellarmine—'who held many truths which must not be rejected because he held them'—in dispute with the Independent minister Thomas Danson at Sandwich in 1659 had allowed Danson to confirm this rumour. Danson disclosed that he had it on good authority that Fisher had told two men in Dunkirk that 'he looked upon the Jesuits and Fryars there [in Rome], to be sounder in Doctrine than those we call the Reformed Churches'.[36]

By boldly repeating this assertion and alluding to his visit to Rome, Fisher was trying to enact his arguments for toleration, to force his opponents to reconsider their reflex rejection of any belief associated with Catholicism or sectarianism as blasphemous. It is a method not dissimilar to Walwyn's deliberately provocative pleas for universal toleration in the guise of a Catholic in *A New Petition of the Papist*, although Walwyn published anonymously. Fisher would also have found in the writings of

---

[35] Stubbs, 'A Word to all such as Teaches their Children to Learn other Tongues', appended to Fox, *A Battle-Door*, seventh pagination, 4.

[36] Thomas Danson, *The Quakers Folly Made Manifest* (1659), 57–8; the anecdote is repeated more or less verbatim by Anthony Wood in *Athenae Oxonienses*, iii. 699–703.

Bellarmine and other Jesuits such as Veron the use of sceptical arguments about the reliability of the Bible as a rule of faith to undermine Calvinist doctrine, and he mocks Owen for his refusal to accept good scholarship merely because it comes from the pen of Jews (Elias Levitas), Catholics (Bellarmine), and Quakers (Fisher himself).[37] Walwyn employed his reading of Montaigne and Charron to make the language of Pyrrhonian scepticism undermine the strict taxonomies of persecution. The shared biblical scepticism of Fisher and Robert Rich, a follower of James Nayler exiled from the Quaker community in England for his opposition to Fox and another reader of Montaigne and Charron, will be discussed at the end of the chapter. It suffices for the moment to compare Rich's belief that the path to perfection is to 'receive Truth from any Man, or Sect . . . and I hope, *receive and hold fast that which is good in every man of all religions*' with the equilibrium and qualification of Fisher's statement of openness to argument: 'I was much more settled, strengthened and stablisht in the perfect truth, wherein I walk, and I trust shall walk in, unto the end, unless I receive more to the contrary'.[38]

REASON AND RHETORIC IN THE PHILOSOPHY OF A QUAKER

In *The Quakers Folly Made Manifest* (1659) Thomas Danson, Independent divine and Fellow of Magdalen College, Oxford, recounts how he would only agree to a second public disputation in Sandwich with the Quakers Richard Hubberthorn and George Whitehead if Fisher would also dispute, as he was 'well reputed for his gifts in this County'. '[S]eeing [Fisher] had more reason than the rest of that way', Danson hoped he 'would not let it be dormant, but awaken it into exercise, and make some use of it' (52). As a university man, Fisher was an anomaly in the development of early Quakerism. The son of a Northampton hatter, he matriculated at Trinity College, Oxford, in 1623, but, according to Anthony Wood, 'being puritannically inclined, he translated to New-Inn Hall', where he went on to take an MA in 1630. He held a lectureship in Lyd in Kent from 1632, where, 'under the character of a very powerful preacher, he lived in conformity (tho' continuing still in his puritanism) till about the year 1643', when he was ordained as a Presbyterian minister. Soon

---

[37] Popkin, *The History of Scepticism*, 68; Fisher, *An Additionall and Apologetical Appendix*, 47.

[38] Robert Rich, *The Epistle of Mr. Robert Rich to the Seven Churches* (1680), 12; Fisher, *Christianismus Redivivus*, 304.

after, he was converted by two itinerant Baptists, whom he had insisted should be allowed to preach despite strong local opposition. He held a General Baptist conventicle in Ashford, Kent, until convinced by two travelling Quakers, William Caton and John Stubbs, in early 1655. His conversion was clearly regarded as something of a coup by the Quakers; Caton describes Fisher as 'a very Eminent and able Pastor among the *Baptists*'. Wood tells us that Fisher became the 'Coryphaeus of the quakers'.[39]

Only when he is in dispute with Fisher does Danson resort to Greek etymologies of scriptural terms. Fisher's renowned learning made him a particularly problematic figure in terms of the hostile stereotyping of the heretic. In *Rusticus* Fisher makes much of his ability to read and counter the attacks on Quakerism in John Owen's Latin works, foiling the attempts of the 'Rabbies' to cloak their error 'within the *linnen shroud* of a dark language'.[40] Fisher employed his facility in Latin to publicize Quaker views to a learned readership in *Lux Christi emergens*, written in jail in 1661, which outlined Quaker beliefs in a parallel English and Latin text. Margaret Fell turned to Fisher when she wanted some of her writings translated into Hebrew, Greek, and Latin in order to reach a worldwide audience, and he was capable enough in Hebrew to append his own composition to the translation, possibly by Spinoza, of Fell's *A Loving Salutation*.[41] He had probably studied Hebrew intensively at Oxford in the 1620s: 'The seventeenth century was the heyday of [oriental studies] at Oxford . . . [d]uring this period the university became a truly major centre for Hebrew and Arabic'. There was a 'mushrooming' of Hebrew lectureships at Oxford in the first half of the seventeenth century. Yet it was precisely the development of Hebrew studies, intended to advance the understanding of the Bible, which led to doubts about the authority of the text which gravely concerned many Protestants.[42]

Fisher knew of recent developments in textual criticism, employing the arguments of the French Calvinist Louis Cappel, the celebrated Hebraist Johannes Buxtorf, and the German orientalist Christian Rave—another illustration of the attractions of Rave's *Discourse of the Orientall Tongues*

[39] William Caton, *A Journal of the Life of the Faithful Servant and Minister of Jesus Christ Will Caton* (1689), 16; Wood, *Athenae Oxonienses*, iii. 699–703.

[40] Danson, *The Quakers Folly Made Manifest*, 23, 44; Fisher, *Rusticus*, 'Second Exercitation', 14.

[41] Friends Library, London, Spence MSS, fo. 27, letter from Margaret Fell to Samuel Fisher, March 1656.

[42] Mordecai Feingold, 'Oriental Studies', in Nicholas Tyacke (ed.), *The History of the University of Oxford, iv. Seventeenth Century Oxford* (Oxford, 1997), 449–50 (458).

(1648) to a radical readership—against John Owen's defence of the inspired origin of the vowel points and punctuation of the Hebrew text of the Old Testament. In *Arcanum Punctuationis Revelatum* (1624) and *Critia Sacra* (1650) Cappel had shown that the vowel markings in the Hebrew script of contemporary copies of the Old Testament did not exist in the form of Hebrew used in the biblical period. Fisher maintained that this discrepancy exploded the Calvinist argument that the surviving texts of Scripture were the sanctified and infallible record of God's Word. Fisher may have come across Cappel's arguments at Oxford (Cappel taught at Oxford from 1610–13), or in the *Prae-Adamitae* of La Peyrère, who had consulted Cappel for textual evidence of the instability of the biblical texts. (Peter Sterry, for instance, recorded reading *Prae-Adamitae* in his commonplace book for 1659.) Fisher had also read the *Biblia Polyglotta*, the massive work of biblical scholarship issued in 1657 under the editorship of Brian Walton.[43] Printed in Latin, Greek, Hebrew, Arabic, Syriac, Chaldean, Ethiopian, and Persian, with two hundred pages of prefatory material, the *Biblia Polyglotta* embodies the philological pursuits which Fisher ridicules in *Rusticus*. However, in *The Divine Original . . . and Power of the Scriptures* Owen attacked Walton for publishing the various textual discrepancies in the different copies of Scripture, maintaining 'an ideal of scriptural transparency and self-evidencing power, in which "Light manifests itself" '.[44] Fisher, who internalized Owen's luminist metaphor as the risen Christ within the perfected bodies of the Quakers, found in the textual scholarship of the *Biblia Polyglotta* more grist to his anti-scriptural mill. As Danson's comments indicate, Fisher's opponents realized that they were dealing with an intellectual equal and consequently believed that they could reason with him. Much of the satirical irony of *Rusticus* is released by Fisher's manipulation of the disjunction between the polemical image of the Quakers as mad and stupid and the application of his learning in debate with his clerical opponents.

Near the beginning of *Rusticus* Fisher addresses John Owen in an apology for the work which is worth quoting in full for an exposition of his aims and methods:

So not to leave him wholly Unanswered, or yet Answered only by the halves (though in Answering him, I should make my self more like him therein I am) in

---

[43] Fisher, *Rusticus*, in *The Testimony of Truth*, 315–17; Popkin, *The History of Scepticism*, 221; Vivian de Sola Pinto, *Peter Sterry, Platonist and Puritan* (Cambridge, 1934), 57; de Sola Pinto was unable to identify Sterry's reference to 'Pre-Adamita 1655'.

[44] Kroll, *The Material Word*, 247.

his Flood of Folly, and *Absar'd Assertion* of the *necessity* of every *Tittle* of the *Greek* and *Hebrew Text* to the according among men of all Sured Saving Truth: This is the respect in which (though else my Life and Delight, lyes not at all in penning and printing ought about such Impertenicies as these) I had not only a Liberty lent me but also a certain load laid upon me from the *Lord*, which led me into so large an Examination of *J.O.'s lost Labour* about the *Letter*, and to become a Fool among the Fools at this time, so far, as to Busie myself with them in their Baubles, if by any means I might gain some of them to a sight of their *Vanity, Madness, and Folly* . . . to dwell not so much in the *seeing, knowing*, and *Talking of Trivial, Temporal Tittles*, as in walking in the *Eternal Truth*, which is the beginning of that Wisdom, which is the Folly to the Fools that yet walk in Darkness, but doth in Truth excel their *University Wisdom*. ('To the Reader', sig. B4^v)

Acutely aware that he is engaging John Owen in the very terms of '*University Wisdom*' which he condemns—making 'my self more like him therein I am'—Fisher (ironically) seeks authority in Scripture, specifically Proverbs 26: 5: 'Answer a fool according to his folly'. At the same time this rhetorical strategy licenses Fisher's indecorous, coarse style as merely mimicry of the foolish voices of his opponents. The first page of the first Martin Marprelate pamphlet, *The Epistle* (1588), had similarly justified the jesting, rustic persona of Martin through a mock-scholarly inversion of Horace's dramatic convention of *decorum personae*:

Again may it please you to give me leave to play the dunce for the nonce as well as he, otherwise dealing with my master I cannot keep *decorum personae* . . . I could not deal commendably with this booke [John Bridge's *A Defence of the Government Established in the Church of England* (1587)] unless I should be sometimes tediousy dunsticall and absurd . . .

Marprelate claims that he is merely mimicking the 'dunsticall' style of his episcopal opponents. The *decorum personae* convention required that a character should speak according to their social status, just as the Elizabethan bishops maintained that religious debate should be a function of education, ordination, and office.[45] Consequently it was a particularly suitable literary device for Marprelate to appropriate and invert as a sanction for his own unlicensed voice. As we have seen, Richard Overton revived the Marprelate style and turned it against the Presbyterians in the 1640s to attack their efforts to persecute sectarian lay preachers. Fisher

[45] Martin Marprelate, *The Marprelate Tracts, 1588–9*, ed. William Pierce (London, 1911), 17. In the *Ars Poetica* Horace advises the playwright to 'give the right kind of manners to characters of varying dispositions and years'. He blamed contemporary lapses in dramatic decorum on the diluted social composition of audiences: 'For what taste could be expected in a crowd of uneducated men enjoying a holiday from work, when country bumpkins rubbed shoulders with men of rank, and slum dwellers with men of rank?' (*Classical Literary Criticism*, trans. T. S. Dorsch (Harmondsworth, 1965), 84, 86).

defends the satirical style of Overton's Marpriest tracts, arguing that their flouting of religious decorum merely reflects the behaviour of the Puritan clergy: 'the Clergy need not find fault (as they do) with the Mar-Priests of these times, for in very deed the Clergy, Priests and Presbiters have been the truest Priest-biters, Claw-Clergies and Mar-Priests themselves'. Marprelate had maintained that 'jesting is lawful by circumstances, even in the greatest matters'. Fisher agrees, commenting from the margin, the favourite haunt of Marprelate's irreverent voices: 'where the actions are Satanical, the reproof cannot be too Satyrical to whom soever'.[46]

In *Rusticus* the motifs of popular festivity previously used by Marprelate and Overton to reduce the Elizabethan bishops and Presbyterian clergy respectively to the level of rustic simpletons are used by Fisher to diminish the solemnity of biblical exegesis and reverse the charge of idiocy directed at the Quakers: 'These 7 or 8 *pye-ball'd May premises* and *Humble-Bee Applications* whereof some are true and some false, may like so many *Roaring-Megs* and *Thundering-Canons*, make such a Hideous, *Rumbling noyse* in a *Country Church* (as they use to say) as to *frighten poor Folk* out of their senses'. The four main targets of his satire—Owen, Danson, Richard Baxter, and the Baptist John Tombes— are made to dance the 'hay' or the 'round' in a comic image of the end-lessly circular process of scriptural debate: 'J. O. dances the *Hay* up and down, in and out by himself alone . . . these foure *sometimes* confounding and contradicting each man himself: and in a word dancing the *Rounds* together in the *dark, tracing* to and fro, *crossing and capering, up and down, in and out*, and sometimes *round about*, in the *Wood* of their own *wonted wisdom*'. Fisher emphasizes the tiresomeness of answering their infinite repetitions and qualifications, playing on the meaning of 'round' as trap or snare: 'Then let us come to a new song (*to go round again*) . . . yet (*to go round again*) it can accomplish it neither in the world, nor that to come, and so not at all; and (*to go round again*) is imperfect . . . A *Net, Gin, Trap*, a Snare's in it . . . *O Rotas! To go round again!*' The futile circu-larity of scholarly discourse is crystallized in the Latin palindrome of the Cirencester word square: 'ROTAS/OPERA/TENET/AREPO/SATOR'. These words were popularly thought to represent the names of the five nails of Christ's Cross, so Fisher may be suggesting that the immersion of his opponents in the empty forms of academic controversy blinds them to the simple truth of Christ's resurrection in all men.[47]

---

[46] Marprelate, 'Hay Any Worke for Cooper' (1589), in *The Marprelate Tracts*, ed. Pierce, 239; Fisher, *Christianismus Redivivus*, 553, 630, marginal comment.

[47] Fisher, *Rusticus*, in *The Testimony of Truth*, 191; Fisher, *An Additionall Appendix*, 46, 12,

Fisher's anti-intellectual satire seems to have been directly influenced by the Marprelate style. While the Marprelate tracts have usually been associated with the world of popular ridicule, of skimmingtons, flytings, and village libel, Martin in fact borrowed his parodic use of the dramatic convention of *decorum personae* from the letter to Thomas More prefacing the *Encomium Moriae*, in which Erasmus disingenuously claims that the attacks of Folly on the false intellectual pride of the clergy are merely a consequence of preserving the decorum of his character's voice. The satirical style of the Marprelate tracts is more accurately characterized as Erasmian than popular in its association of academic discourse with clerical dishonesty; *Mineral and Metaphysical Schoolpoints* (1589), for example, is a parody of the university exercise of exhibiting a theme in Latin and then defending it according to the rules of formal logic.[48] Marprelate makes much of the various meanings of 'hay' in *Hay Any Worke for Cooper* (1589): Thomas Cooper, Bishop of Winchester, becomes literally a 'cooper', a barrel-maker, while 'hay' is at once the grass of the fields, a 'have at you' to the bishops, and the festive dance on which Martin leads his opponents. The *OED* records the first use of a slang term for argument, 'argle', in *Hay Any Work for Cooper*, which was republished in 1641 (as *Reformation No Enemie*) and 1642 (under its original title). Fisher ridicules Owen's defence of the infallible authority of the scriptural text in the Martinist manner, ironically suggesting his rustic naivety in the face of superior learning: 'in an *extravagent* way [he] *Argles* against the *Arguments* urged not only by the learned *Jews, and Jesuites, Elias Levita, Bellarminus*' (*An Additional Appendix*, 25).

On other occasions the *ad hominem* satire echoes Overton's Marpriest tracts by depicting the clerical critics of the Quakers as grotesquely dilated or diminished personae. In Overton's *The Araignement of Mr. Persecution* the allegorical characters of Sir Simon Synod and Sir John Presbiter battle it out between each other and with the religious radicals using 'classical clubs', transforming 'ecclesiastical debate into a kind of Punch and Judy show'. In *Martins Eccho* (1646) Presbiter is metamorphosed into a baby with the Whore of Babylon as his godmother,

---

22–3, 47. On the Cirencester word square see Donald Atkinson, 'The Origin and Date of the "Sator" Word Square', *Journal of Ecclesiastical History*, 2 (1951), 1–18.

[48] John S. Coolidge, 'Martin Marprelate, Marvell and *Decorum Personae* as a Satirical Theme', *Publications of the Modern Language Association of America*, 74 (1959), 526–32; see also Nicholas McDowell, 'Degrees of Divinity: The Intellectual Resources of the Radical Imagination, c.1630–1660', D.Phil. thesis (Oxford University, 2000), 85–8. The main author of the tracts was probably Job Throckmorton, an Oxford-educated Warwickshire gentleman.

sucking on a teething ring representing the Ordinance for Tithes.[49] In *Rusticus* Baxter and Tombes are bathetically depicted as twin babies, monstrously born from 'that *Babylonish Bawd*':

> In the nine Sermons of *John Tombs* B.D., which came piping hot from the Press, while this of mine to you two, put out by *R. Baxter*, which pair of blind Brethren, as much enmity, threatning, and Thunder without Lightning, as hath been between them hitherto aginst each other, are it seems, like *Herod* and *Pilate*, now made friends together against *Christs* Light, so as to make one Head, though two Horns, wherewith to thrust it down if they could, for which a Rod, a Rod in the Lords hand, is already ready for the back of *Baxter*, who, and his once Heretical and Heterodox, but now Reverend and Orthodox Brother *Tombs*, as two Twins that tumbled both out of one Belly, even one and the same womb of that *Babylonish Bawd*, are both to be tumbled into one and the same *Tomb*. ('To the Reader', sig. B1ᵛ)

Spiritually childish, Baxter and Tombes must 'begin again with the Quakers, at [their] A.B.C. in the things of God' ('Second Exercitation', 28). Recalling the polemical strategy of Coppe's preface to *Divine Teachings* and George Fox's *A Battle-Door*, Fisher reduces Owen's insistence on the divine integrity of the Hebrew vowel points to childish fascination with the typography of the ABC or 'cross-row': he 'Crosses *Christ* like some *cris* † *Crosse* in th' *Row*' (*An Additionall Appendix*, 47). The joke is emphasized by a learned pun on 'Puritan' and 'puerilis', 'belonging to childhood': *Rusticus* is written to keep '*J.O.'s Juniors . . . buseyed in at their Schooles* (where *Pueritam Puerilia tractant*)' ('To the Reader', sig. C4ʳ).

Fisher's depiction of Baxter and Tombes as monstrous infants who incontinently excrete their writings 'piping hot' recalls Rabelais's commentary on the humanist ideal of rhetorical plenitude through images of bodily prodigality, of anal and genital emission. Fisher similarly associates interpretation and defecation, reducing the flux of rhetoric in scriptural debate to the flux of the exegetes' bowels. Appropriately the academic and controversial texts of his opponents are useful only as toilet paper, echoing John Cleveland's comic renaming of the 1640s newsbook or diurnal as 'the urinal': the '*Bagg and baggage* fit for nothing more indeed than to follow in the *Reare* of such *pitifull Polemicals*, as in the two Pieces they are annexed to . . . a *sorry shift* of halfe a sheet (for 'tis no more, nor better) of (meer wast) paper' ('First Exercitation', 19).[50] There is also

---

[49] Smith, 'Richard Overton's Marpriest Tracts', 47, 50.

[50] Cave, *The Cornucopian Text*, 149–50; John Cleveland, *The Character of a London Diurnal-Maker* (1644), in *Character Writings of the Seventeenth Century*, ed. Henry Morley (London, 1891), 307.

the implication of unfruitful seminal flow in the disputational exchange which takes place in the academic cloisters, through Fisher's play upon the monkish use of Latin to attack the Quakers: 'ye lye in *Latin* together at ease, as in a *Bed*, wherein ye take your fill of *Lies*' ('Second Exercitation', 14). The Hebrew vowel points were known as 'pricks', providing Fisher with the opportunity to pun at Owen's expense on the term's other connotations of lewdness and 'mental vexation' in the manner of Marprelate's fun with the ambiguities of early modern typography (Martin occasionally spells 'Vicar' as 'Fycker'). Fisher's tracts do not exploit dialogue and the dramatic techniques which characterize the Marprelate and Marpriest tracts. It is the language of scholarly dispute that above all provides Fisher with the material of his satire, in line with his confessed purpose of answering his foolish opponents—'Four of their *Choicest Champions*'—according to their folly.[51]

Fisher assumes the Pauline persona of the holy fool which, as we have seen, licensed the juxtaposition of prophecy and irony in the writings of Abiezer Coppe. Despite the unsurprising absence of scriptural reference in *Rusticus*, a work dedicated to undermining the spiritual authority of the Bible, Fisher cites the scriptural locus of the Christian folly theme, 1 Corinthians 1: 18–28:

so He will provoke you to Jealousie by a *foolish Nation*, and weary you by such as *are no People in your Eyes*, and by *Base, Mean, Weak, Foolish Nothings*, Confound your Mighty things that are: So that it shall be said of the *Learned Linguists* and *Greeks* that seek after Wisdom, *where's the Scribe, where's the Disputer of this world? hath not God made foolish the wisdom of this world . . .?*

He includes himself amongst the foolish 'mechanicks' derided by the opponents of the Quakers: '*Marvel not that* My Self, *and* other men, Meddle *so much with the* Massy Matters *of your* Ministry *who* have so long Excluded all Mechanicks and Plain Country Creatures, *from the* Close Conclave *of your* Clerical *and* Collegian Counsells' ('To the Reader', sig. D3ᵛ). Yet Fisher reverses the stereotype of the heretic as *illitteratus* by declaring that it is the learned clergy who are spiritually ignorant, that it is 'Oxford and Cambridge [who] nourish up illiteracy'('Second Exercitation', 29–30). The *OED* in fact lists this as the first recorded use of the term 'illiteracy'. Fisher's reversal of the charge of educational inadequacy is particularly apposite because he shows his learned opponents to have an insufficient knowledge of the history of the Hebrew language. On the title

---

[51] Fisher, *The Testimony of Truth*, 316–17, 46. See the *OED* on the various meanings of 'prick' in the period.

page of his collection of Baptist writings, *Christianismus Redivivus* (1655), Fisher signs himself 'Samuel Fisher M.A.', while the academic qualification has been excised on the title page of *Rusticus*. Yet Fisher cannot resist asserting his intellectual equality:

> And howbeit (*Jure Academico*) by as much Right, as such men, as chuse to have it still done so to themselves, in token of their *Mastership of Arts*, had that Half penny piece of Honour of *M.A.* Printed to my name, as *T.*[homas] *D.*[anson] now hath, in Title-Pages . . . yet if *my self*, or any shall henceforth write or cause himself by Pen or Press, to be inscribed either *M.A.* or *D.D.* or *B.D.* and any Reader in his ignorance, not knowing well how to *Cypher* or cast account, shall happen to read *Mr. Ass* or *Dr. Dunce* or *Blind Divine*, the Affecter of those Trifling Titles of Mr. of *Arts*, Doctor in *Divinity* and Batchelor in *Divinity*, who is not more *Baccalaureus* than *Laurus sine baccis*. ('First Exercitation', 40)

Once, Fisher apologizes for his own use of languages: 'As to the Tongue wherein it treats (excepting here and there a little *Hebrew*, and (for shew sometimes more than sense) a penful or two of *Greek interlin'd* in both parts and now and then two or three licks of *latine* among the *English*)' ('To the Reader', B2ʳ). But this is evidently disingenuous. Fisher's considerable knowledge of Hebrew is displayed in his arguments about the unreliability of the biblical text, while his continual use of Latin and Greek functions to parody learned discourse, which is contrasted with the divinely instituted 'plain speech' of the Quakers:

> [The clergy] are more ignorant in one thing, then the poor unlearned *Quakers* (as they call them) are in their own Mother *Tongue*: for as little as the *Qua*. Do *ultra linguam vernaculam sapere*, and as little *latine* as they do understand as *J.*[ohn] *O.*[wen] sayes in his *latine* labours against them, yet they are both ken and keep to the *proper Idiom* of the *English Language*, in using that of *Thee* and *Thou*' ('First Exercitation', 41) . . .

The leading Fifth Monarchist John Rogers, educated at grammar school in Essex and at King's College, Cambridge, also took some pride in his facility in Hebrew, despite his elevation of the spiritual wisdom of the '*lowest* and *slowest* capacity' amongst the saints above the 'folly and fraud of the *State-Ministers*'. Relating how a crowd of Presbyterian ministers 'fell a rayling and *assaulting* me' he responds to their accusations of intellectual inferiority: 'And seeing they would insinuate my want of Abilities, which I confesse are many, yet I would they would get their Guide Mr. *Sangar* (if he can) to *construe* them this peece of *Hebrew*'. After quoting some Hebrew, he challenges the ministers, if they 'can read it', to '*preach* and *practise* it then better, to the very roots of it'. Similarly when Rogers advises his readers that 'you will finde me λόγῳ ἰδιώης rude in speech', his use of Greek displays his learning in the very moment of denying its value. Rogers, like Fisher, combines enthusiasm and irony by playing upon the stereotype of the heretic as ignoramus. He comically deflates the charge of the Presbyterians that he an 'illiterate erroneous man', responding in cod Latin to accept the charge that, in their terms, his heterodox ideas make him '*ignorans upstartis*'.[52]

The rhetorical strategy of both Rogers and Fisher is shaped by their facility with classical and oriental languages. Fisher writes in the preface to *Rusticus*: 'I come now ἄνευ πύου ἄγαν without much Preamble, or more ado *ad rem substratem*, to the Business and Work it self, as it lyes before me'. Much of the irony here stems from the fact that the 'preface' appears after an address 'To the Reader' of some forty pages, a bibliographical parody of academic procrastination. Fisher's inversion of the *decorum personae* convention is restated in terms of a parody of the rules of formal theological debate: 'It being a generally received *Maxime* among all *Schoolmen* that an argument, that flyes in one face with no more force than *forte ita*, requires to be no more than forcibly rebell'd then *forte non* Yea *forte ita semper sat bene solitur per forte non*'. The object of Fisher's ridicule is the scholastic disputation which was a major part of the academic exercises at Oxford and Cambridge in the seventeenth century. The nature of these disputations is succinctly described by Ann Hughes in her discussion of printed debates between ministers and radicals in revolutionary England:

Ideally, a disputation was formal, ritualized, precise and dignified. A respondent, given a question in advance, prepared and put forward arguments to support it; one or more opponents stated contrary positions, and attacked the respondent's reasoning; a moderator summed up the points on both sides, elucidated obscure and neglected aspects of the debate and made a decision . . . most academic disputations were about formal matters which did not matter one way or another.[53]

Rusticus ad Academicos is an extended parody of the academic disputation which is neither precise nor dignified. The debate concerns a matter that, as far as the redeemed Fisher is concerned, does not matter one way or the other—the spiritual authority of scriptural interpretation. Fisher

---

[52] John Rogers, *Ohel or Beth-Shemish. A Tabernacle for the Sun* (second, enlarged, edition 1653), 158, 54; John Rogers, *Sagrir. Or Doomes-day drawing nigh, with Thunder and Lightening to Lawyers* (1653), sig. C2ᵛ.

[53] Fisher, *Rusticus*, in *The Testimony of Truth*, 61 [69], 190; Hughes, 'The Pulpit Guarded', 35; see also M. H. Curtis, *Oxford and Cambridge in Transition, 1588–1642* (Oxford, 1959), 88–116.

points to the irony of the names of the Oxford and Cambridge colleges: 'O
ye *Quakers*, ye *Seers*, flee ye far away hence to *Rome*, to *Papists*, *Jesuites*,
Jews, *Turks*, *Heathens* . . . we are the Doctors, Deans, Principals, Provosts,
presidents, Wardens, Masters of *Magdalene*, *Christ-Church*, *Jesus*, *Trinity*,
Emmanuel [not the] *Universally* Erring, *University* Seducers' ('Second
Exercitation', 21). The true heirs to such names are not the academics who
hide within the cloisters of the college buildings and the sophistries of
scriptural exegesis, who '*crawl* and *creep* about a while in some *Collegian
Cells*', but the Quakers who 'are a thousand fold more (spiritually) dis-
cerning' and who travel around the world to discuss their beliefs with the
representatives of other faiths ('First Exercitation', 2; 'Second Exercitation', 17). Indeed Fisher's implication is that the society of 'Jesuits, Jews,
Turks and Heathens' is more beneficial to Christian improvement than
the senior common room. Owen's argument in *Of the Divine Originall
. . . and Power of the Scriptures* that denial of the inspired status of the
complete scriptural text will be 'the Root of much hidden Atheisme' is
made to seem of consequence only to All Souls College, not all souls: '*Sith
the* Stresse *of a Case of such* Dangerous Consequences *Stands upon it, that
All Souls (as* J. O. *sayes at least so Depend on It), as to have No* Means of
their Salvation' ('To the Reader', sig. E1ᵛ).

Owen's choice of Latin to attack the Quakers in *Pro Scripturis, Contra
Fanaticos* is condemned as cowardly and representative of the incestuous
world of academia: 'in thy *Latine Legend*, wherein thou lyest more at
liberty, then in thy two *English* pieces of *emptinesse*, and the more *securely*
by how much thou (to thy self at least) to lye more hidden, or more
obscurely, out of the reach of their *rebuke*, whom thou reproached in that
Latine Language then in the other'. Owen's book is designed more for 'thy
crude Theologicall Disputations, Determinations (*tumultuarie sane satis
conscriptas*) as thou callest them *ad lectorem*, than to confute the *Quakers
plainly and openly*' ('Second Exercitation', 11). In the moment of condemnation Fisher satirically exploits the language of the condemned. The
Latin here seems redundant to the argument, and so the development of
the prose satirically enacts the point being made. At the same time, Fisher
is happy to take Owen on in a Latin boxing match: 'Be not so merry J. O.
about the Mouth; for *De te (mutato nomine Quakers) Fabula narratur* . . .
be Judges between me and J. O. (an *Oxford* man) in this Case. Unless these
boarish, brutish gestures *cum multiis aliis quae nunc prescribere longum
est*' ('Second Exercitation', 50, 68). If there is a sense of dialogue in
Fisher's polemics, it derives from the rhetorical technique known as
animadversion. The quoting of opponents within Fisher's text and the

lifting of statements out of their original frame of reference is designed to expose their absurdity and is explicitly justified as a means of displaying truth: 'here's four *utter untruths* asserted together, nevertheless as they are *Tru-lies*, yet they are *true* enough to serve the *truth*, I here summon them in proof' ('Second Exercitation', 8).

A further aspect of Fisher's 'promiscuous' prose is the collapsing of papal, episcopal, and Presbyterian religious forms as mere disguises for the spirit of persecution, as metamorphoses of the Beast. Overton had identified Catholic and Presbyterian through allegorical personification, so that the form or dress of Sir John Presbiter is merely a disguise for the persecuting soul of the Catholic priest, conveyed from the body of one cleric to another through a grotesque process of metempsychosis. Fisher achieves this effect mainly through the use of alliteration. Coarse, alliterative vernacular had been used to undermine the Latinate culture of Catholicism from the earliest days of the English Reformation, but Fisher makes alliteration fulfil several functions simultaneously.[54] Alliteration is used first in *Rusticus* to express the endless 'rounds' of academic debate and to mock a logic that is made to seem purely linguistically associative rather than spiritually substantial, dependent on little more than phonetic resemblance. The vast size of Fisher's text and his repetitive arguments themselves fulfil a rhetorical function, for they are designed both to reflect the folly of his opponents and to 'weary these vain, wise wild Asses out of their *Academical Niceties* and *Punctilios* out of their *Acute Astuteness*, and *Astute Acuteness* out of their witty Wiles, and *wicked Wrestlings* against the truth of a *foolish* nation' ('Second Exercitation', 17). The second rhetorical function of Fisher's alliteration is explained by an index to his terms, presented in the form of a dictionary. Under 'P' he explains his reference to 'PPPresbiters' as signifying the co-existence of papist, priest, and Presbyterian under the one clerical cloak. The elision comes to encompass the Independents like Owen as well, and Fisher emphasizes the unnatural aberration of the metamorphosis by having to create a sprawling term to define it, 'the *Po-Prela-Presbyter-Independent Pastorality*'. This allows him to associate the Presbyterian and Independent rejection of liberty of conscience with the covert return of papistry: 'The Doctrine then of *persecution* as taught and learnt, to this day by our *English Reformadoes* from *Romish Rubbish*, is not only a retaining of much of, but an open doore, for the rest of the Popes *Baggage* to return by as the times turn'. Featley's *The Dippers Dipt* and Edwards's

---

[54] See e.g. John Bale, *A Mysterye of Inyquytie Contayned within the Heretycall Genealogyie of Ponce Pantolabus* (1545).

Gangraena are specifically named as merely versions of the *Legenda Aurea*, the mid-thirteenth century collection of Catholic legends. The persecutory spirit 'shift[s] from Form to Form, from a darker to a clearer . . . from the very Prelatick Party that reformed most immediately from the thick fog of *Romish* false worship, to the *Presbyterian* whom they persecuted, from them to the *Independent*, whom they persecuted, from them to the *Baptists*, whom they persecuted; and from them to the *Ranters*'.[55]

The 'PPPresbiter' also signifies 'The Triple Tower of BBBabel i.e. the threefold kingdome of Priests'; the priests, Episcopalians and Puritans have built a '*BBBabel*, a three-fold Fort of Tyrannical Churchlines . . . TTThou knowest what TTThou art of'. The Puritan immersion in Hebrew, Greek, and Latin to establish the authority of their interpretation of Scripture is merely the erection of another persecutory form, and so Fisher's constant alliterative play in *Rusticus*, satirizing the '*Collegian Calumnies* and *Clerical Cavils* of all who *Causelessly* Quarrel with the *Quakers*', represents both the tiresome futility of their debate and the divine curse which has entrapped them in a babble of tongues for their pride in learning. The regenerate Fisher, like George Fox, has transcended this Babel/Babylon and been restored to the perfect stasis of union with the divine: 'I am hid as in a Pavillion from the strife of Tongues'. He has become 'abstract' and claims he would rather 'please myself to sit down in silence'; silence of course became an integral aspect of Quaker devotional practice.[56] The Quaker was accused of talking in a '*Babylonish Rhetorik*', 'a *Rhapsody* of oft-repeated *Non-Sense*; and when he has darkened your understandings with a cloud of insignificant *Babble*, he cries, Ah! *Friends mind the Light*'.[57] Fisher once again reverses polemical stereotypes—the critics of the Quakers are the true babbling heretics.

It has been argued that the literary effect of the jesting style of the Marprelate tracts is to lower the temperature of religious controversy (although the historical effect was precisely the opposite).[58] All such disputes are reduced to the playing out of folly. Consequently Overton could adapt the Marprelate style to develop arguments for universal toleration. Fisher's anticlerical satire is designed to force a similar recognition and,

---

[55] Fisher, *Christianismus Redivivus*, sigs. A4ʳˉᵛ, 619, 580, 584; see also Fisher, *Rusticus*, 'First Exercitation', 51.

[56] Fisher, *Christianismus Redivivus*, 538; Fisher, *Rusticus*, 'First Exercitation', 2, 48.

[57] Samuel Austin, *Plus Ultra, or the Second Part of the Character of a Quaker* (1676), 8.

[58] Coolidge, 'Martin Marprelate, Marvell and *Decorum Personae* as a Satirical Theme', 532.

for all its parodic productivity, constitutes a plea for silence, as Fisher sometimes acknowledges. Religious controversy is merely a repetition of the scholastic disputation, in which nothing matters one way or the other:

Now concerning these which are the *grand subjects* in reference to which all that is said of any of them by either of us, in our *Disputation* about them, is but the *Predicate*; so contrary are we (as the Case yet stands between Thy Self and me) to each other in our *Assertions*, that very much, if not most of that which is determinated of them *respectively* by either of us, is absolutely gainsaid by the other . . . ('Second Exercitation', 1–2).

In the end, such religious disputes are a mere textual '*Tergiversation*', a making of conflicting statements, with final resolution only either in physical persecution or toleration. However, Fisher does set out to establish one central intellectual argument in *Rusticus ad Academicos*: the absurdity of the notion that the Bible provides a supreme and sufficient rule of faith. In the Westminster Confession of Faith of 1642, reaffirmed in 1658, the scriptural texts were declared to be 'immediately inspired by God and by his singular care and Providence kept pure in all Ages [and] are therefore Authentical'. In keeping with Calvinist orthodoxy, the Confession maintained that '[t]he infallible rule of Interpretation of Scripture is Scripture itself'.[59] In *Of the Divine Originall*, Owen had upheld this assertion against the textual criticism and historical relativism of commentators such as Louis Cappel. Fisher quotes Owen's insistence that the orthography of the text of Scripture as it had been handed down to the seventeenth century must be 'authentical', otherwise all revealed truth would be subject to doubt. Such scriptural scepticism would be the 'foundation of Mahumetisme, the chiefest and principal prop of Popery, the onely pretence of Fanaticall Anti-Scripturalists, and the Root of much hidden Atheisme' ('First Exercitation', 76). Fisher does not deny that the original prophets and apostles were divinely inspired. Yet if, as Owen himself maintained in his attacks on the Quakers, revelation has ceased since biblical times, how can the seventeenth-century text, having been transcribed and translated on hundreds and thousands of occasions, be taken for a rule of faith and a sufficient means of delivering the message of salvation? If the text is 'yielded to be Alterable in the very *Greek* and *Hebrew* copies of it', if 'the letters, Vowels, Accents and Iotas of it are liable to be chang'd in Sound and Shape at the Wills of the Criticks', then it must be treated as an historical rather than a divine document. Yet,

---

[59] *The Confession of Faith, together with the larger and lesser Catechismes, Composed by the Reverend Assembly of Divines Sitting at Westminster, Presented to both Houses of Parliament* (1658), ch. 1, art. viii, 6.

while the Bible is 'fallible by false Interpretation and translation', the inner light is 'infallible, and to be followed in what it speaks infallibly to the Conscience'. Fisher ridicules Owen for '*Pin*[ning] the Everlasting Gospel of God *on so* Tickelish a Point, *as Mens* Mistaking, or not Mistaking, in Writing *out the* Bare letter *of it*'. Far from Quakerism being the 'Root of much hidden Atheisme', he accuses Calvinist theologians of making '*your own* Graves *with your own* Hands *and pluck*[ing] *up your own* Religion *by the very Roots*', punning on their insistence on the infallibility of the Hebrew linguistic roots in the Old Testament texts.[60]

Fisher's argument is grounded upon the epistemological fallacy of identifying God's Word—the Light—with a material object. While the Quakers were accused of papistry for locating divine authority in the inner light rather than Scripture, Fisher compares Calvinist idolatry of the Bible with the Catholic cult of the Virgin Mary. They worship 'the bare *back-side* of that *Book*, which contains the *Scripture*, called *the Bible*, [as] if to *blesse* it, and adorn and adore the naked *Body* of it, [as] if to do by it little lesse, then all that the *Papists* do, in way of *honour* and *exaltation* of it, to lead to the *dead Body* of their *Great Godesse the Virgin Mary*' ('Second Exercitation', 50). They '*overlay* [the Bible] with Gold and *curious colours*, [as] if to make *Images, Pictures* of it [as] if to spare no cost in Printing, Re-Printing, Binding, Beautifying'. Scripture 'came forth from' the Word, but is now 'a *copy* and *declaration* or *Images* of it, as much in dignity below it, as the *painted Picture* of a *face* or a *man* on a Wall is to the true *Face* or *person* which they do but outwardly represent' ('Second Exercitation', 51, 57). Puritans sought to replace material images which they associated with Catholic idolatry—pictures, statues—with arrangements of words, whether the text of Scripture or the diagrams of Ramist logic.[61] In rejecting the Bible as a graven image, Fisher represents himself as continuing the process of Reformation iconoclasm to destroy the idol of textuality.

The seventeenth-century text is but 'the Remote issue and Product, at the hundredth hand perhaps of God's voice in the Prophets, yea but Remote Transcripts of fallible men from the handy-work or manuscripts of the first Penmen . . . the Letter is Changeable, Alterable, Flexable, Passing, Perishing, Corruptible at mans will, who may mis-transcribe'. To emphasize his point, Fisher generalizes his argument about the fallibility of the transcribed text of Scripture by comparison with the instability of all texts in the process from written to printed page. This is

---

60 Fisher, *The Testimony of Truth*, 49; Fisher, *Rusticus*, 'First Exercitation', sig. E1ʳ.

61 Margaret Aston, *England's Iconoclasts*, i. *Laws Against Images* (Oxford, 1988), 452–66.

graphically depicted through parody of the bibliographical convention of listing the errata made in the printing of *Rusticus*. 'A List of the *Typographicall Mistakes*' near the beginning becomes an opportunity to express satirically his reduction of Scripture to a material and historical document:

> Though (in J. O.'s blind judgement) it seems to border on *Atheism* to say the *same fate* (as to Mistakes) hath attended the *Hebrew and Greek* Text of *Scripture*, in its *Transcribing* as hath done other Books, yet it seems to me, upon that but *Running Review* I have yet taken thereof, that the same Fate in that kind, hath attended this of mine; which hath ever attended both the *Scripture*, and His, and J. T.'s and all other Books (of any Bulk) in their passage through the Press.

Fisher includes mistaken Greek and Hebrew characters in his errata, in a visual echo of the lists in the *Biblia Polyglotta* of the thousands of textual variants in the Greek and Hebrew of the various copies of the scriptural texts. He goes on to accept the possibility of many more mistakes which have gone unnoticed:

> Sundry more *Typographical Errors* probably there are uncorrected, then I can on a sudden cast my eyes on, by some of which *possibly* the sense is interrupted, but of all that are, I may safely say (with J. O. in his Vindication of the Entireness to a Tittle of the *Originall* Texts) bare all such as are *Evident Mistakes, consisting only on superfluity and redundancy of unnecessary, or deficiency of words necessary to the sense of the place*, that is to say *All* of that sort soever, and then there will be few or none at all.[62]

The bibliographical parody serves to reduce the Bible to the status of a text like any other, and as such it is inherently prone to error and distortion. The 'faults' in *Rusticus* expose the faults in Scripture and also the faults of Owen and the Puritans in erecting their faith on such shifting foundations. Fisher would have found an example of this use of the apparatus of publishing for the purposes of religious satire in the Marprelate tracts. In Marprelate's first pamphlet the errata, instead of listing typographical errors, list the errors of the bishops.[63]

For Fisher the Bible is tainted, like any other printed text, by the uncertainties inherent in the process of typesetting and publication. The problem of who decides which books of the Bible are canonical is up to the publisher as much as the councils of the clergy. Fisher raises the question of who deems some texts apocryphal and others orthodox, as well as the possibility of '*the loss even of whole Epistles* and Prophecies *of*

---

[62] Fisher, *The Testimony of Truth*, 521; Fisher, *Rusticus*, 'To the Reader', sig. G2ᵛ.
[63] *The Marprelate Tracts*, ed. Pierce, 172.

inspired men, the Copies of *which are not by* the Clergy Canoniz'd, *nor by* the Bible-sellers *bound up in that* Bulk, and compasse of *their* modern Bibles' ('First Exercitation', sig. A3ʳ). Fisher points out that all nations have 'many sorts of *Chirography* and *Brachography*' and various typographies. But who invented them? Might not the typographies used for 'cutting and setting and stamping' the letters of the biblical text have been composed by 'men moved merely with love of money and hope of gain? in which way the Bible comes out lyable to the common fate of all other books, as to matter of *falsification* by *misprinting*'. Fisher was sufficiently in touch with developments in 1650s Oxford to be aware of the efforts of John Wilkins and Seth Ward to compose 'an universal character'. These efforts finally produced Wilkins's *An essay towards a real character and a philosophical language* (1668), sponsored by the fledging Royal Society, in which the invention of a language which perfectly reflected and communicated the structure of nature was presented as a means of preventing religious differences and exposing errors such as enthusiasm. Fisher responds by arguing that because 'J.[ohn] O.[wen] denyes *Wilkins Ward* or any man else in these dayes to be inspired or guided by *the Infallible Spirit*', such attempts to remove ambiguity from any form of script are futile.[64] The wordless inner light is the only true universal character. There is evidently a disputational sleight of hand on Fisher's part here: he appropriates Owen's denial of the possibility of divine inspiration to undermine arguments for the infallibility of the biblical text while simultaneously maintaining that the Quakers are subject to revelations of the same nature and authority as those experienced by the prophets and apostles.

Fisher's attitude towards the Bible as an emphatically material collection of printed letters rather than a linguistic manifestation of spiritual truth seems to be related to a developing scepticism about the authority of print which developed with the flood of controversial publishing in revolutionary England. 'Received notions of authorship' were undermined in the 1640s as texts were 'anatomized, split up, and reused in an opponent's animadversion'.[65] For Fisher, the status of the biblical text as a material entity makes it vulnerable not only to men's fallibility or self-interested interpretation, but to physical damage: 'in every way uncertain, most uncertain, liable to be altered, falsified, corrupted, to be

---

[64] Fisher, *An Additionall Appendix*, 27. On Wilkins's real character as a reaction to the religious conflict of the 1640s see Achinstein, 'The Politics of Babel in the English Revolution'.

[65] Smith, *Literature and Revolution*, 42.

mis-transcribed, mistranslated, wrested this way and that, to moulder away, to perish, be torn to pieces, burned, and many wayes brought to nothing . . . witness the written rule of *Jeremiah's* prophecy which *Zedekiah* cut away with a pen knife, and consumed in the fire'. Fisher distinguishes between 'the *Writing* of the *Word*, and the *Word* it self written of'. He summons Hebrew etymology to demonstrate that 'Scripture' signifies 'letters legible to our bodily Eyes, however extant upon what ever outward matter capable to receive their impression, *Tables of Stones, Walls, Skins, Parchment* [by] *Cutting, Graving, Stamping, Printing*'. The Bible is reduced to a merely literal 'script'.[66]

Radicals may have been the most obvious beneficiaries of the press freedoms of the 1640s but 'they were also its first victims'.[67] Fisher continually complains about the polemical distortion of Quaker texts or of his own words in the same terms in which he calls the accuracy of the Bible into question: 'thy *Additions* to our words are not by far so *Volumnious* as thy *Ablations* from them are . . . our discourses to thee, whilst thy own to us are repeated generally by the *dative*, are rendered mostly by the *Ablative* case, being rehearsed well nigh totally all away'. The 'Billingsgate Rhetorik' of which the Quakers are accused is in fact the true idiom of their critics, who scramble in 'much petty Businesses as *Muscles and Cockel-shells*, meer mouldering writings, *Externall Texts*, trifling *Transcripts, Letters, pedling points, Syllables, Triviall Tittles and Iotas*' ('First Exercitation', 10). Fisher describes the Bible as 'a Mouldering and Muldered Writing', so that it assumes a status equivalent to 'the light chaffy leaves of the whistling *News-Books*' that circulate 'false constructions' of the Quakers, 'laying down things in their Names, they never did speak, or diminishing from their words' ('First Exercitation', 1, 7, 12). Fisher is equally sensitive to the rhetorical power of the printed image. In his Baptist writings he blames the 'brazen fac't front' of Featley's *The Dippers Dipt* and Ephraim Pagit's *Heresiography* (1645), which depicted sectarian conventicles engaging in naked frolics, for the popular association of heterodox belief with libertinism. The reader is 'deceived in believing such things, by giving credit unto them, without a surer ground, than because they are come forth in Print to a Publike view'. Consequently Fisher does not have a very high opinion of his potential readership: 'they are *Extempore stupified* into a *Satisfaction* that they see the same, whether they see it yea or nay'.[68]

[66] Fisher, *The Testimony of Truth*, 547; Fisher, *Rusticus*, 'Second Exercitation', 5–7.
[67] Smith, *Literature and Revolution*, 42.
[68] Fisher, *Christianismus Redivivus*, 410; Fisher, *Rusticus*, 'First Exercitation', 9, 32.

Milton was deeply upset by the 'repeated bastardization in print' of his arguments in *The Doctrine and Discipline of Divorce*. At the same time he was one of the most effective 'animadverters' of the 1640s.[69] The same ambivalent response to the textual exchange of the period is evident in *Rusticus*, although Fisher claims to be merely satirically imitating the logomachy of his clerical critics. Fisher realized that the reader of his vast text may lose the sense of parody:

And as to the *Bigness of the Book* which calls for so much the more Cost from him that Buyes it, and so much the more pains from him thats willing to Busie himself in it: if that Trouble any one, it shall not trouble me . . . He that likes not the length of it, hath enough of the same to make it shorter to himself . . .

Fisher actually recommends that readers should cut *Rusticus* into pieces if they find it too tiresome. If the pamphlet wars of the 1640s led to a greater awareness of 'the insecurity of the printed medium as a channel of communication' and consequently to a lack of faith in 'the idea of "text" as concurrent with divine order', then Fisher's rejection of the spiritual authority of the Bible as the 'pure text' on the grounds of its unstable textuality is the logical consequence of these anxieties.[70] At the same time Fisher gives us insights into his obvious enjoyment of controversial exchange, a characteristic of his prose which Penn was anxious about in republishing his writings in 1679. In a Burtonian insight into the mental processes of composition, we see Fisher writing to the moment as each new polemic arrives on his desk: ''Tis time to return to talk on with the *Pope* and the *priesthood* to whom I have almost forgotten what more I was about to say, being put by it by ones presentment of these proposals to me *inter scribendum*, which draw'd me on this long Parenthesis, and off from my present purpose'. Anthony Wood had heard it said that Fisher defended outrageous opinions *'disputia gratia,* to hold an argument for discourse sake'.[71] Certainly Fisher applied his rhetorical and disputational training at Oxford to hold an argument which overturned the logocentric basis of an English Protestant culture in which accounts of 'what constituted creditable scripture (and what idolatrous forgery), how it should be represented and read (and by whom), and what effects it could have on the reader or hearer (and what effects it *should* have on them) . . . lay at the heart of religious conflict'.[72]

[69] Miller, 'Print and Textuality in the 1640s', 27; see also James Grantham Turner, 'The Poetics of Engagement', in Loewenstein and Turner (eds.), *Politics, Poetics, and Hermeneutics in Milton's Prose*, 257–75.

[70] Fisher, *The Testimony of Truth*, 46–7; Miller, 'Print and Textuality in the 1640s', 38.

[71] Fisher, *Christianismus Redivivus*, 578; Wood, *Athenae Oxonienses*, iii. 703.

[72] Adrian Johns, 'The Physiology of Reading and the Anatomy of Enthusiasm', in

SCEPTICISM AND PERFECTION

One feature of Fisher's refusal to have the light of God 'bound up' in 'hide-bound Bibles' is his expulsion of Spirit from Scripture in the language of Epicurean atomism: 'so that there's a talk in them of *grammar* and *rules of art*, and the *world of points* not coming together by chance, and of the *Chaldee Paraphrast* and many mere matters, yet they seem to me to be *a world created by a casual concurrence of Antick Atomes*'. The text of Scripture has not been 'kept pure in all Ages [and] therefore Authentical' by providence, following the decree of the Westminster Assembly, but is the result of a purely natural and historical process of compilation which Fisher compares to the collision of spiritless atoms. Fisher is echoed in Swift's parody of Hobbesian materialism in 'Ode to the Athenian Society' (1692). For Swift, 'Hobbism' reduces the world to the effect of:

> a *Crowd of Atoms* justling in a heap,
> Which from Eternal seeds begun,
> Justling some thousand years till ripen'd by the Sun.[73]

Hobbes's nominalism and materialism function to deny the existence of any Spirit in the material world, abolishing both the spiritual authority of the clergy and the possibility of divine immanence in man. Thus Hobbes could reduce enthusiastic claims to revelation to a physiological condition of madness or overheated passion. Yet Fisher's rejection of the Calvinist identification of the Spirit's workings with the scriptural text combined with his representation of the Bible as merely the physical substance of print and page results in the adoption of a Hobbesian, materializing rhetoric. Indeed Fisher's view of the biblical text as 'a world created by a casual concurrence of Antick Atomes' echoes Hobbes's criticism of those who derive religious arguments only from the interpretation of 'single Texts' of Scripture 'without considering the main Designe': '[They] can derive no thing from them cleerly; but rather by casting atomes of Scripture, as dust before mens eyes, make every thing more obscure than it is; an ordinary artifice of those that seek not the truth, but their own advantage'.[74]

O. P. Grell and A. Cunningham (eds.), *Religio Medici: Religion and Medicine in Seventeenth Century England*, (Aldershot, 1996), 136–70 (141). For a discussion of these issues in the post-Restoration period see Kroll, *The Material Word*, esp. 239–74.

[73] Fisher, *The Testimony of Truth*, 307; Jonathan Swift, *The Complete Poems*, ed. Pat Rogers (Harmondsworth, 1983), 50, ll. 127–9.

[74] Thomas Hobbes, *Leviathan* (1651), ed. Richard Tuck (Cambridge, 1991), 415.

These are sentiments with which Fisher would have agreed. They are the final lines of Part 3 of *Leviathan*. Part 4 of the text, 'Of the Kingdome of Darknesse', is characterized by a virulent anticlericalism and ridicule of the metaphysical premisses and absurd language of scholastic theology. The school divines 'take from young men the use of Reason, by certain Charms, compounded of Metaphysiques, and Miracles, and Traditions, and Abused Scripture, whereby they are good for nothing else, but to execute what they command them'.[75] The opening chapter of Part 4 of *Leviathan* is entitled '*Of Spirituall Darknesse from* Misinterpretation *of Scripture*'. Fisher pointed to the end of Deuteronomy to illustrate the internal inconsistencies of the biblical texts: did Moses '*write of his own Death and Burial* and of Israels *Mourning for him, after he was dead*'? Hobbes had raised this problem in *Leviathan* but preferred to back away from its consequences for the status of Scripture as an 'Authentical' and 'pure' text:

For it were a strange interpretation, to say Moses spake of his own sepulcher (though by Prophecy) . . . It is therefore sufficiently evident, that the five Books of Moses were written after his time, though how long after it be not so manifest . . . But though Moses did not compile those Books entirely, and in the form we have them; yet he wrote all that which he is there said to have written . . .[76]

We do not know for sure if Fisher read Hobbes, but the 'Naylerite' Quaker Robert Rich claimed to have. In *Love Without Dissimulation* (1666) he provides an extensive list of his reading in honour of 'the Spirits of certain Friends to the Bridegroom, who longed to see this day of the Son in Man'. This includes, as expected, the 'innocent and patient' James Nayler and John Perrot. Also named are 'dear' John Saltmarsh, 'honest' William Erbery, William 'Doomesday' Sedgwick, 'Divine' John Webster, 'Noble' Sir Henry Vane, John Warr, Richard Coppin, Giles Calvert, and Samuel How, the Continental mystics Nicholas of Cusa, Hendrik Niclaes, and Jacob Boehme, translators of these spiritualist works such as John Everard, Giles Randall, and John Pordage, the self-proclaimed 'King of the Jews' Thomas Tany, and the Ranters Abiezer Coppe and Joseph Salmon. It is a comprehensive reading list of the radical speculation of the English revolution. A less predictable name on the list is 'Brave Mr. Hobbs'.[77] There may be an important connection between Rich and Fisher. Rich was a reasonably wealthy London merchant. After hearing of the Great Fire of London while in self-imposed exile in Barbados, he

75 Hobbes, *Leviathan*, 481.
76 Fisher, *The Testimony of Truth*, 265; Hobbes, *Leviathan*, 261–2.
77 Robert Rich, *Love Without Dissimulation* (1666), 6–7.

demonstrated his ecumenical spirit by donating thirty pounds to the 'Catholics, Episcopal Protestants, Presbyterians, Independents, Baptists and Quakers' to help them rebuild their churches. According to Thomas Danson, one rumour concerning Fisher's 'genteel equipage' when he returned from Rome and Constantinople was his receipt of 'great Bills of exchange from a quaking *London* Merchant'.[78] Could this have been Rich?

Rich's attitudes towards Scripture bear some comparison with those of Fisher, although Rich did not have much formal education; a good deal of his prose is composed of quotations from contemporary texts and translations and his ideas seem to be mostly derived from his independent reading. Rich thought Scripture a 'nose of wax' in which he could place 'no more stress and confidence'. This scepticism stemmed from his discovery of the alterations and distortions of translation which the text had suffered since it was 'first written and uncorrupted'. He found this information in Robert Gell's work on the errors of current translations: 'Dr. *Gell*, a pious man, and well read in the *Orientall Tongues*, who hath writ a book in *Folio*, printed *Anno* 1659, entituled, *An essay towards an amendment of the last English Translation of the Bible*, wherein many faults are found, and amended by him'. Gell, who had impressive intellectual credentials as a former Fellow of Christ's College, Cambridge, claimed to have discovered 676 pages of errors in the Authorized Version. His *Remaines* were posthumously issued in 1676 by Robert Bacon, named by Rich as one 'of my old Acquaintance[s]' in *Love Without Dissimulation*.[79] As with Walwyn, Rich's financial means enabled him to amass a considerable and diverse library, and his heterodox beliefs were similarly shaped by his literacy and access to translations in London bookshops. In an address to the Catholic Church Rich declared that he 'approved of many of your Books' including '*Charoone* of Wisdom' and 'the *Essays* of Lord *Michael Montaigne*'. The unprejudiced reading of both Walwyn and Rich put into practice their belief in universal religious toleration, and reading the French sceptics seems to have had a similar effect on both men. Rich sounds very like Walwyn in his desire to promote 'universal love amongst all sorts of People, without respect of persons, Parties or Sects' and in his belief that 'a Man should receive Truth from any Man, or Sect, *try all things*, and I hope, *receive and hold fast that which is good in*

---

[78] See Rich, *The Epistle of Robert Rich* (1680); Danson, *The Quakers Folly Made Manifest*, 57.

[79] Rich, *The Epistle of Robert Rich*, 84; Rich, *Love Without Dissimulation*, 5; on Gell's reputation as a perfectionist see Smith, *Perfection Proclaimed*, 99 n. 80.

every man of all Religions. Rich also put his money where his mouth was, giving money to Catholic, Anglican, Presbyterian, Independent, Baptist, and Quaker Churches alike because 'God teacheth and leadeth his people diversely, now after this manner, and another after another manner . . . there are diversity of Gifts, different Administrations and Operations, but all wrought by one and the same Spirit'. The 'Light' gave Rich the 'freedom to look into all manner of *Opinions* and *Religions*'. The persecutory spirit, however, inhabits George Fox, who desires 'preheminence, and to have Dominion over the faith of others; and that glory in making Proselytes, and to have a Multitude follow, calling you Masters or Teachers'.[80] Walwyn had rejected enthusiasm and appealed to grace vouchsafed as natural reason as the sufficient means by which an individual could come to his or her own inner knowledge of religious truth. The effect of Rich's use of Montaigne and Charron is a rather blurred differentiation between the dictates of the inner light and the processes of reason. Truth is 'ever the universal spirit of Love and right Reason, the true *Elixir* and Philosophers Stone . . . I leave to the light of Right reason in every man to judge'.[81]

Whether or not Fisher and Spinoza exchanged ideas in Amsterdam in 1658, Fisher's rejection of the Bible as a revealed rule of faith had a contemporary English context in the incorporation of modes of sceptical thought into radical religious speculation of the revolutionary period. Spinoza treated the Bible as a historical document and maintained that 'rational people at any time or place could find the Divine law', with or without Scripture. For Spinoza, 'the ultimate "rule of faith" was rationality . . . and moral improvement can be codified as a rational process'. For Fisher, the ultimate rule of faith was the inner light which was self-sufficient and self-revealing to all, of whatever religion or race: 'Is the Light in *America* then any more insufficient to lead its Followers to God, than the Light in Europe, Asia, Africa?'.[82] The inner light, the manifestation of the Word within man, operates above rationality, and it is this bathetic clash between the Quakers and the clergy, the yokels and the professors, divine light and 'humane' logic, which releases much of the satirical humour of Fisher's prose. Yet for all his parody of academic disputation, Fisher summons his considerable education to appeal to the rational proofs of evidence, historical context, and linguistic change

---

[80] Rich, *The Epistle of Robert Rich*, 10–12, 79; Robert Rich, *A Testimony to the Truth* (1679), 1; *Mr Robert Rich His Second Letters from Barbadoes* (1669), 8, 20.

[81] Robert Rich, *Mr Robert Rich His Second Letters from Barbadoes*, 12.

[82] Popkin, 'Spinoza and Samuel Fisher', 230–1; Fisher, *The Testimony of Truth*, 696.

against the Puritans' blind faith in Scripture. Through force of reason Fisher proves the Bible cannot be identified with the Word. In response to those such as Henry More and John Owen who depicted Quaker enthusiasm as a 'misconceit of being inspired' caused by excess passion and a credulous imagination, Fisher insists that the inner light is not subjective fancy but a universal character, 'the Common Light and Publick Spirit of God, which is one and the same in all'. This recalls Rich's reference to the 'light of Right Reason in every man'. The question of distinguishing between the inner light and natural reason is one which clearly occupied Fisher, for he explicitly denies any identification, of which he had apparently been accused. He writes only 'of which Light and its universality and sufficiency to save such as seek God in it, and how its a supernatural, spirituall gift, and grace of God to all men, where it is, and not the naturall faculty of mans understanding'.[83] Popkin argues that for Fisher understanding of the divine is achieved through 'spiritual refinement and devotion, not necessarily involving any intellectual process'. Yet at the same time Fisher describes the light within as 'such a *Substantive*, as is well able, if let alone, and in the midst of not a little interruption, to stand by itself in *reason* before any . . . [it] stand[s] by itself to shew its *reason* or *signification* to such as soberly reason with it'. The workings of the inner light are held here to be entirely compatible with rational argument.[84]

The Quaker missionaries in Amsterdam fell out in the early 1660s with the Collegiant sect, whose spiritualist doctrines they had recognized as similar to their own, over the rationalistic direction in which Collegiant thought was developing, partly through the influence of Spinoza. In 1661–2 William Ames, leader of the Dutch Quakers, became engaged in a dispute with Pieter Balling, leading Collegiant and close friend of Spinoza, over the nature of the inner light. This dispute resulted in Balling writing a tract, *Het Licht op den Kandelaar* (1662) in which he conceived, like the Quakers, of the inner light as superior in authority to all other sources, including Scripture; however, he did so 'in terms that would permit either a rationalistic or spiritualistic interpretation', producing a concept of the natural light of reason as an infallible source of

---

[83] Henry More, *Enthusiasmus Triumphatus, or, A Discourse of the Nature, Causes, Kinds, and Cure, of Enthusiasme* (1656), 2; Fisher, *The Testimony of Truth*, 546; Fisher, *Rusticus*, 'To the Reader', B4';

[84] Fisher, *Rusticus*, 'First Exercitation', 72; Popkin, 'Spinoza and Samuel Fisher', 232. So Nigel Smith is not quite right to argue that Fisher's 'placing of all divine knowledge in the category of the spirit enables him to disregard the validity of any role which reason might play'; *Perfection Proclaimed*, 297.

truth.[85] While the Collegiant fusion of reason with the indwelling Spirit has thus been seen as originating in a reaction to the extreme spiritualism of the Quakers, an embryonic notion of the rational inner light is already apparent by 1660 in the antiscriptural writings of Samuel Fisher. Whether Fisher influenced the Collegiants or vice versa, or whether they were both influenced by Spinoza, or whether Fisher influenced Spinoza who influenced the Collegiants, remains a matter for conjecture. What becomes clear is that Fisher stands as the founder of a learned strand of Quakerism which developed in the sectarian melting pot of mid-seventeenth-century Holland and which subjected the Christian tradition to rational and sceptical critique. The learned Quaker bibliophile Benjamin Furly, who hosted such figures as John Locke, John Toland, and the third Earl of Shaftesbury at his great library in Rotterdam, immediately translated Balling's tract on the rational inner light into English as *The Light Upon the Candlestick* (1663), making no adverse comment upon its ideas.[86]

J. G. A. Pocock has described how the post-Restoration Church of England 'had to steer its way between three menacing figures: Giant Pope, Giant Hobbes and Giant Enthusiast, the last a many-headed figure to be identified with no individual in particular, but with the individual himself or herself'. However, Spinoza 'came to be considered the philosopher of atheism and enthusiasm', because of his monistic metaphysics in which 'God and universe, mind and matter' were held 'to be of one substance and indistinguishable'. Pocock argues that although Hobbes was the enemy of enthusiasm

in the sense that he denied the existence of any spirit that might pervade the material world; it would be hard to say of what nature he supposed Christ to be, and his atheism seemed to many to consist in his reduction of God to infinitely tenuous material substance. But this was not so far from enthusiasm as it might seem; if God, the mind, and material universe were all of one substance, thinking matter might have the weight of the whole universe behind its thoughts and authorizing its actions.[87]

It seems unlikely that Quaker enthusiasts such as Rich or even Fisher would have come to such conclusions from reading 'Brave Mr. *Hobbs*'. Rather they would have been attracted to the materialist and historicist

---

[85] Andrew C. Fix, *Prophecy and Reason: The Dutch Collegiants in the Early Enlightenment* (Princeton, NJ, 1991), esp. 192–205 (202).

[86] On Furly see *BDBR*; on his translation of Balling's text see Popkin, 'Spinoza's Relations with the Quakers', 27 n. 45.

[87] Pocock, 'Within the Margins: The Definitions of Orthodoxy', 43.

analysis which he applied to abolish the *jure divino* authority of the Catholic, Anglican, and Presbyterian clergy, all of whom by 'wresting of Scripture' falsely tried to 'prove that the Kingdom of God . . . is the present Church'. For Hobbes, clerical power was maintained by inculcating superstition and instilling fear in the people. He attacked academic jargon ('names that signifie nothing') and school divinity for its futile circularity and emptiness of meaning. Clerics and university men are the most numerous inhabitants of the Kingdom of Darkness in Book 4 of *Leviathan* and, as Quentin Skinner has shown, Hobbes uses the full array of satirical tropes recommended in humanist textbooks to ridicule their strained and partisan interpretations of Scripture.[88] As we have seen, Fisher and Rich would also have found in *Leviathan* some of the most sceptical discussions of the textual and historical integrity of the scriptural text that had so far been published in English. Yet equally Hobbes turns the force of his scornful rhetoric on sectarian claims to revelation: '[if] there were nothing else that betrayed their madnesse; yet that very arrogating inspiration to themselves, is argument enough' (55). Moreover Hobbesian civil science, in which the absolute sovereign enforces strict obedience to all laws, religious as well as civil, and acts, in the absence of certainty, as the supreme exegete of Scripture, looks like the diametric opposite of Fisher's vision of the State as a purely secular institution whose only religious role is to ensure liberty of conscience (a vision shared by the Levellers Overton and Walwyn).

There is, however, a possible link between Fisher and versions of Hobbesian philosophy. Fisher was apparently familiar with the attacks of Henry Stubbe the Younger on the academic regime of 1650s Oxford in *A Light Shining out of Darkness* (1659; 2nd, enlarged, edn. 1659): 'yet when the *Game* begins again (as here it doth between thee and the Quakers, as it hath between thee and some of thy own Fellows *of thy own society* who have already entered the Lists and taken thee to do viz. *Henry Stubbs*)'.[89] As this tract was published anonymously, Fisher seems to have been well informed. Stubbe issued *A Light Shining out of Darkness* amongst a series of defences of the 'Good Old Cause' of republicanism. He was at this stage Second Keeper at the Bodleian Library and studying for an MA at Christ Church. Anthony Wood describes him as the 'most noted Latinist and Grecian of his age'. He also served an anticlerical and republican patron, Sir Henry Vane the Younger—the 'Noble' Sir Henry Vane whose

---

[88] Hobbes, *Leviathan*, 419; Quentin Skinner, *Reason and Rhetoric in the Philosophy of Hobbes* (Cambridge, 1996), esp. 395–400.
[89] Fisher, *Rusticus*, 'Second Exercitation', 15.

mystically inclined writings are listed by Rich in his radical reading list. In
A Light Shining out of Darkness Stubbe attacked the clerical identification
of formal education with spiritual authority. He turned on his former
associate John Owen, who had just stepped down as Vice-Chancellor of
Oxford, engaging with Owen's attacks on the preaching of the 'illiterate'
amongst the Quakers in *Pro Scripturis... Contra Fanaticos* (1658). Charles
Webster contends that Stubbe had an oblique 'double purpose' in ridiculing the religious application of the forms of institutional learning in
which he himself had excelled. Webster argues that Stubbe sought to 'stir
up anxieties about religious or educational reform and to frighten his
audience into renewing their faith in Anglican and scholastic values'.
Stubbe's submerged 'satirical purpose' is revealed in 'his long quotations
from the most celebrated critics of classical learning ... given in such a
way as to underline their degree of familiarity with pagan writing and
classical languages'.[90] These 'critics' include Cicero, Cardinal Bellarmine,
and John Selden, as well as Erasmus in the *Encomium Moriae*. Webster's
interpretation ignores the polemical and biographical context of Stubbe's
pamphlet. Stubbe issued at least six pamphlets in 1659–60 in which he
championed the original republican spirit of the early 1650s that had
succeeded in 'overturning', as he put it, the monarchy and the established
Church. He also defended the virtue of Vane against the criticism of
'court parasites', condemned the spiritual tyranny of Presbyterianism
and the concept of a tithe-funded clergy, and called for the toleration of
sectarianism on the grounds that 'the magistrate's intermeddling with
Christ's power over the judgements of men' is 'the mystery of iniquity
working in men of a legal conscience'.[91] If *A Light Shining out of Darkness*
was a satire designed to exhibit Stubbe's own 'social and religious conservatism', it was so oblique that nobody got the joke: Stubbe was dismissed from his post at the Bodleian and sent down from Oxford.[92]
Moreover, we have seen how learned radicals in this period displayed
their learning in the moment of ridiculing its spiritual value, allowing
them to appropriate and subvert the pervasive stereotype of the heretic as
illitteratus.

   More convincing is James R. Jacob's definition of Stubbe as a 'radical
Independent' who applied the anticlerical arguments of his friend
Thomas Hobbes in *A Light Shining out of Darkness* to reach anti-
Hobbesian political conclusions. Stubbe was a good friend of Hobbes in

   [90] Webster, *The Great Instauration*, 173–7 (174, 177).
   [91] [Henry Stubbe], *Malice Rebuked* (1659), 5, 7–10; see also Christopher Hill, *The
Experience of Defeat: Milton and Some Contemporaries* (London, 1984), 254–8.
   [92] Webster, *The Great Instauration*, 173.

the 1650s, as their correspondence testifies, and had begun to translate *Leviathan* into Latin. Jacob shows that one of Stubbe's aims in *A Light Shining out of Darkness* was to 'subject to criticism the claims of Presbyterian and Anglican clergy that their powers and privileges came from God's commands [in Scripture]. In this enterprise his principal tool was Hobbes's own materialist, historicist analysis of established religion, worked out in the last parts of *Leviathan* and elsewhere.' Stubbe used Hobbes's anticlerical arguments, as well as John Selden's historical analysis of the ideological origins of the tithe system, *History of Tithes* (1617), to 'separate the realm of spiritual conduct from all human supervision, whether by church or state'.[93] Stubbe accused John Owen of going back on his own Independent beliefs by condemning lay preaching and calling for State persecution of the Quakers. He includes a 'brief Apologie for the Quakers, that they are not inconsistent with a Magistracy', invoking the linguistic studies of Erasmus to defend Quaker pronominal usage of 'thou' and 'you', adding that 'we always bestowe [thou] upon God in prayer'. To the argument that the Quakers are insufficiently educated to preach and interpret Scripture, Stubbe delivered a provocative reply: 'Is not the gospell of *John* as bad *Greeke* as any *Quaker's English*? I say nothing of the difference in the Old Testament betwixt *Isaiah* and *Jeremiah*'. Although Stubbe had read 'divers reports . . . concerning severall enormous acts and miscarriages of some *Quakers*', he claimed to be 'so well acquainted with the stratagems' of anti-heretical polemic that he could give such sensational accounts little credit. Stubbe in fact develops his argument for religious toleration around a defence of Quaker practice: 'As for my part, since I am not sensible of the convictions or emotions of the Spirit under which another lies, so I dare not condemn the *Quaker*, whether he reprove openly, or walk naked through the streets, denouncing woes and menaces: it is sufficient argument for me, that what God bids, is not undecent'.[94] The only religious role that Stubbe ascribed to the civil magistrate was to ensure the absence of persecution.

Jacob argues that Stubbe 'assimilated Quaker ideas to his own brand of Independency' and that he viewed Quaker inner light as equivalent to the radical Independent doctrine of 'the holy spirit informing the individual Christian and making everyone his own priest', a view compatible with 'his republican political vision of a polity of autonomous and sociable

[93] James R. Jacob, *Henry Stubbe, Radical Protestantism and the Early Enlightenment* (Cambridge, 1983), 34, 36. For the extant correspondence between Hobbes and Stubbe see *The Correspondence of Thomas Hobbes*, ed. Noel Malcom, 2 vols. (Oxford, 1994).

[94] Henry Stubbe, *A Light Shining out of Darkness* (2nd, enlarged, edn. 1659), 87, 89, 91.

men'. At one point in his discussion of Quakerism Stubbe wondered if the
Quakers might not, however, be mistaking '*nature* for *grace*, and esteem
of that to be *taught of Christ* which is a *light of nature*'.[95] After the
Restoration Stubbe was best known as the foremost critic of the Royal
Society but he also composed an unpublished work entitled 'An Account
of the Rise and Progress of Mahometanism' (first published, 1911). By
means of comparative historical and cultural analysis, Stubbe reduced the
principles of religious belief to those held in common by Jews, Muslims,
and the primitive Christians. Stubbe argued that Christian criticisms of
the Koran 'may be urged with the same strength against our Bible' and
that the episodes in the Koran may be compared with 'the popish legends,
or the fables recorded in our Fathers and believed by the primitive
Christians'. He declared that '[o]ur notions on the torments of the wicked
in a lake of fire and brimstone somewhere underground' are as 'absurd as
fables of the Mahometans'. In responding to Owen's accusation that
denial of the ahistorical purity of the scriptural texts would be 'the
foundation of Mahumetisme', Fisher argued that Protestant identification of the Spirit with the corrupted texts of the Bible was indistinguishable from Islamic reliance on the fables of the Koran or Catholic
ascription of divine authority to the '*treasury of Traditions* that lyes lockt
up in the *Popes Breast*'. We might also recall that Fisher was condemned
as a Jesuit for asking of his Presbyterian and Independent critics: 'Didst
not *Cardinal Bellarmine* hold some truths which thou holdest, as well as
some that I hold against thee, and that Christ is the Son of God, which we
both hold?'.[96]

'The Rise and Progress of Mahometanism' circulated in manuscript in
late seventeenth-century England, and the deist Charles Blount refers to
it in a letter to Rochester in 1678.[97] The objective of Stubbe, like that of
Blount and Spinoza, was to replace the notion of a true Church served by
an ordained ministry, who derived their exclusive spiritual authority to
preach and interpret Scripture from Apostolic succession, with a civil
religion which conformed to the principles of man's innate reason. His
comments in *A Light Shining out of Darkness* suggest that he considered
the Quaker inner light, which Fisher defined in opposition to the
uncertain external evidence of the Bible, to be a version of this innate

95 Jacob, *Henry Stubbe*, 38–9; Stubbe, *A Light Shining*, 84.

96 Stubbe, *The Rise and Progress of Mahometanism*, ed. Hafiz Mahumed Khan (London,
1911), 155, 159, 167; see also Jacob, *Henry Stubbe*, ch. 4. Fisher, *Rusticus*, 'Second Exercitation',
185; 'First Exercitation', 75, 65.

97 *The Letters of John Wilmot, Earl of Rochester*, ed. Jeremy Treglown (Oxford, 1980),
206–16.

natural reason which established the fundamental principles of religious belief; to be what Rich called the 'light of Right Reason in every man'. There are other instances of convergence between Quakerism and deism in the later seventeenth century. In 1685 William Penn was accused of indoctrinating George Villiers, second Duke of Buckingham, in the deistical arguments that Buckingham outlined in his controversial pamphlet in favour of religious toleration, *A Short Discourse upon the Reasonableness of Men's Having a Religion* (1685). In 1674 the Quaker and Aberdeen graduate George Keith translated the medieval Islamic fable of Ibn Tufayl which depicts a child stranded on a desert island arriving at the basic truths of religion by means of his innate instincts. Keith's translation is obviously designed to represent the inner light as a universal, natural truth which all men can discover if removed from the impositions of official religious structures, but it also dramatizes Stubbe's depiction of a universal and natural religion in 'An Account of the Rise and Progress of Mahometanism'.[98]

In his study of the various attacks of deists and freethinkers on the Church of England in the Restoration and early eighteenth century J. A. I. Champion has noted that they set about their task by 'rewriting the history of religion . . . radicals like Charles Blount and John Toland sidestepped propositional debates about the existence of God and proposed alternative histories of the Christian past'. Central to these debates were discussions of the authority of the Scriptures, the chronology of the Old Testament and the nature of biblical history.[99] The rejection of the Bible as a revealed rule of faith through textual, historical, and comparative analysis by Samuel Fisher, the most learned of the early Quakers, heralds the deist controversy which was to occupy the minds and pens of the orthodox at the turn of the century. Fisher's subversion of biblical authority, arguments for universal toleration, and location of religious truth in a 'Common Light' which 'stand[s] by itself in *reason* before any' lend credence to J. G. A. Pocock's argument that 'there was little need of Voltairean *philosophes*' in late seventeenth-century England—and perhaps no need of an 'English Enlightenment' at all—because the deist

---

[98] For Penn's response to these accusations see his *Defence of the Duke of Buckingham's Book of Religion* (1685). On Keith's translation see David A. Pailin, *Attitudes Towards Other Religions: Comparative Religion in Seventeenth and Eighteenth Century Britain* (Manchester, 1984), 25.

[99] J. A. I. Champion, *The Pillars of Priestcraft Shaken: The Church of England and its Enemies, 1660–1730* (Cambridge, 1992), 100. See also Gerard Reedy, SJ, *The Bible and Reason: Anglicans and Scripture in Late Seventeenth Century England* (Phila., 1985), 20–45; Joseph M. Levine, 'Deists and Anglicans: The Ancient Wisdom and the Idea of Progress', in Lund (ed.), *The Margins of Orthodoxy*, 219–39.

ideas of Blount and Toland represented 'the secularization of elements in revolutionary Puritanism' such as the 'spiritualist materialism' of Gerrard Winstanley, who may have died a Quaker.[100] The importance of textual and historical criticism of the Bible to deist arguments is evident in the questions which Toland posed of the clerical exegetes of the Church of England. Toland asked

how the immediat Successors and Disciples of the Apostles could so grossly confound the genuin Writings of their Masters, with such as were falsely attributed to them; or since they were in the dark about these Matters so early how came such as follow'd them by a better Light; why all those Books which are cited by Clemens and the rest should not be counted equally Authentic; and what stress should be laid on the Testimony of those Fathers, who not only contradict one another, but are often inconsistent with themselves.

Wondering in his life of Milton how so many of the English people could have believed the *Eikon Basilike* to be the authentic work of Charles I, Toland wrote: 'I cease to wonder any longer how so many suppositious pieces under the name of Christ, the Apostles, and other great Persons, should be publish'd and approved in those primitive times, when it was of so much importance to have 'em believed'.[101] As Pocock points out, the belief that 'Christ was in the people, the congregation or the individual . . . contained de-Christianizing implications once it was asserted that Christ was in them in the form of their reason'. Although William Blake's incorporation of eighteenth-century developments in the rational and historical treatment of Scripture into an enthusiastic cosmology warns against the acceptance of a Whig narrative of inevitable progress towards enlightenment, the de-Christianizing implications of Fisher's rational attack on the sanctified status of Scripture are encapsulated by Thomas Paine in *The Age of Reason* (1794–5): 'Take away from Genesis the belief that Moses was the author, on which only the strange belief that is the word of God has stood, and there remains nothing of Genesis, but an anonymous book of stories, fables and traditionary or invented absurdities and downright lies'.[102]

100 Pocock, 'Post-Puritan England and the Problem of the Enlightenment', 96–7, 105. There is no mention of Fisher in either Israel's *Radical Enlightenment* or in the essays in Timothy Morton and Nigel Smith (eds.), *Radicalism in British Literary Culture, 1650–1830: From Revolution to Revolution* (Cambridge, 2002).

101 Toland, *Amyntor, or a Defence of Milton's Life* (1699), quoted in Reedy, *The Bible and Reason*, 93; Toland, *The Life of John Milton* (1698), in *The Early Lives of Milton*, ed. Helen Darbishire (1965), 150.

102 Pocock, 'Within the Margins: The Definitions of Orthodoxy', 41; Paine, *The Age of Reason, Part the Second, being an Investigation of True and Fabulous Theology* (1795), 14.

Epilogue:
Milton and the Radical Imagination

In a stirring but rarely quoted passage in the *Pro Se Defensio* (1655) Milton envisages his fellow grammar-school boys as the natural heroes of the English republic and urges them to translate their humanist training into vigorous civic and martial action:

We, who as boys are accustomed under so many masters to sweat out eloquence in the shade and who are convinced that the force of demonstrative oratory is in vituperation scarcely less than in praise, may indeed bravely and safely scourge the names of ancient tyrants. And as it happens, we kill Mezentius over again in stale antitheses; or, in the rueful bellowing of enthymemes, we roast, with a daintiness more exquisite than in his own bull, the Agrigentine Phalaris. I allude to those who were trained in the grammar schools: for such are the men, whom, in a republic, we most delight to honor and adore—such we fondly style most potent, and most magnificent, and most august! But yet it was expected that those who thus spent a good part of their youth in literary exercises in the shade, should, at some after period, when the country, when the republic stood in need of their services, throw aside their foils, and dare the sun, the dust and the field; that they should at last have the courage to use in their contests hands and arms of flesh and blood, to brandish real weapons, to encounter a real enemy. We persecute with no small hostility indeed, some, the Suffenuses and Sophists; some, the Pharisees, the Simons, the Hymanaeuses, the Alexanders: for all these are ancients. But when we find them brought to life again, and appearing in the modern church, we praise them in eulogies, we honour them with professorships and stipends, as patterns of all excellence, as prodigies of learning, as mirrors of sanctity . . . My way of thinking is, I confess, far enough removed from this, as I have shown in my conduct on more occasion than one.[1]

The radical writers who have been the subject of this book agreed with Milton that the 'modern church' was populated by tyrants who falsely represented themselves as 'prodigies of learning' and 'mirrors of sanctity' to preserve their positions of power in society. Yet those radicals who had undergone the linguistic and rhetorical training eulogized by Milton saw humanist culture not as the key to the spiritual regeneration of an England corrupted by the monarchy and the Church, but as a bulwark of

---

[1] The Columbia translation is preferred here: *The Works of John Milton*, ed. Frank A. Patterson et al., 18 vols. (Columbia, 1931–8), ix. 223–7.

that antichristian tyranny. The Leveller Richard Overton identified the use of the humanist curriculum to divide society into literate elite and illiterate multitude with the dehumanization, exploitation, and, eventually, the damnation of the common people. The 'Ranter' Abiezer Coppe and the Quaker Samuel Fisher equated formal education with the subjection to religious and moral law from which they had been liberated, and mockingly opposed the empty forms of linguistic knowledge valorized by the clergy to the divine insights revealed by the internal workings of the spirit. They satirically applied their humanist education to reject the religious, political, and cultural values which they associated with that education. Ironically it was the Leveller autodidact William Walwyn who came closest to embodying the Miltonic vision of political and religious liberty achieved through the application of humanist study. Humphrey Brooke provides us with an insight into how Walwyn read classical anti-tyrannical texts in translation:

Lucian was taken off a shelf either by me, or Mr. Walwyn, I can't say which, and . . . we read one of the Dialogues, which was the Tyrant, or Megapenthes; and afterwards commended it as very useful in the time he lived; when by setting forth the foulenesse and deformity of Tyrannie in a third person, he informed the people of the wickednesse of such under whom they lived . . .[2]

Yet Walwyn thought Cicero, whom Milton places at the centre of his ideal curriculum in *Of Education* and to whom he proudly compares himself in the *Pro Populo Anglicano Defensio* (1651), to be 'a verbal and vain-glorious Writer'. Whereas Milton blamed the corruption of the clergy upon the failure of the universities to provide the nation's youth with sufficient linguistic and rhetorical expertise, Walwyn felt that the humanist curriculum bred men to be 'artificial and crafty, rather than truly wise and honest, to be Sophisters and Pedantick Disputers, and Wranglers about words' (410).[3] While Milton's 'medium and message coalesce' in his defences of the republic, with his pristine Ciceronian Latin embodying the restoration of 'humanist civility' to both the political and cultural life of England, the Fifth Monarchist republican John Rogers hoped that his 'rude' style would demonstrate to his readers that he was 'the more a *Christian*, though the less a *Ciceronian*' (54).[4] Yet Rogers was

---

[2] Brooke, *The Charity of Church-Men*, in *LT*, 334.

[3] *Walwyns Just Defence*, in *WWW*, 410. On Milton and the failure of the universities to provide a proper humanist education, see Martin Dzelzainis, 'Milton's Classical Republicanism', in David Armitage, Armand Himy, and Quentin Skinner (eds.), *Milton and Republicanism* (Cambridge, 1995), 3–24. On Milton as an English Cicero see Milton, *Political Writings*, ed. Martin Dzelzainis (Cambridge, 1991), 86–7, 253.

[4] Norbrook, *Writing the English Republic*, 209–11; Rogers, *Ohel or Beth-Shemesh*, 54.

another of those classically trained men whom Milton exhorted to act in defence of the republican values in which they had been educated. Rogers was thrown out of his home in Essex in 1643 by his father, a Laudian minister, for his Puritan convictions. He returned to Cambridge, where he had begun to study as a servitor at King's College; he had been forced to leave by the intensification of the Civil War. In Cambridge he 'sought from College to Colledge to be but a sizar or poor scholar' but without success; he was forced to eat leather, discarded quills, and grass. He was even tempted to eat his own fingers. Poverty again drove him to the point of suicide but, 'prepared for the act' and about to plunge a knife into his chest, a friend burst into his garret to reveal that Rogers had been offered the position of tutor to the children of a Huntingdon gentleman. For Rogers this was an event of cosmic significance, which revealed his sanctified status and prophetic vocation. Rogers's experience of conversion then took the form of progressive revelation in dreams. In the pivotal dream in his conversion narrative he dreamed about the Bible, 'the *letter which killed me*', and awoke to realize that the free grace of Christ 'by faith made mine, did excel the righteousness of the scribes and Pharisees . . . I was so much changed I was amazed at myself'. Rogers was certain that he was not 'filled with a *fancy*' but had been granted '*assurance of salvation*'. For the first time he began to 'plainly see *my self* (and by my self others)'.[5]

Subject to extreme bouts of religious despair from the age of ten brought on by listening to Calvinist preachers describing the torments of the damned, Rogers had been an obsessive reader in his youth, writing down and memorizing every sermon that he heard, repeating his 'little Catechism' to himself like a kind of magic charm, and reading the Bible 'over and over and over again'. All was to no avail: 'the more I read the more I *roar'd* in the *black gulf* of *despair*'. After his conversion, however, he found that books and reading had become irrelevant and that knowledge was infused through the 'sweet and secret *soule-whisperings*, and spirit-*breathings*, by which the *soul* and the *spirit* converse together . . . which is not an enthusiastical fancy or *illusion*, but a *reall* truth which every Saint hath a *taste* of, being *inspirations*'.[6] He now viewed redemption as a physical condition that was apparent from empirical observation but could not be discovered through any text, including the Bible:

---

[5] Rogers's conversion narrative, one of the finest of the genre, is in *Ohel*, 419–38.

[6] Rogers, *Ohel*, 27. For a similar insight into the psychological effects of Calvinist doctrine on the young, see Coppe's account of how as a teenager he kept 'a daily register of my sins, and set them down in a Book'. For several years from the age of thirteen Coppe tried to memorize daily up to nine chapters of the Bible (*CRW*, 134).

Now as the *Physitian* findes some secrets (and oftentimes excellent things) by his *practice* and *experience* which hee could never *attain* unto by reading or search, or study *out of books* . . . the greatest Rabbies or *Learnedest* alive can not acquire or attaine [the knowledge of free grace] by reading *books, scriptures* or the like, so that experience teaches more, and better . . . (*Ohel*, 384).

Anatomizing the spiritual experiences of the members of the Independent congregation over which he presided in Dublin in 1652, he found 'Prophetick symptomes . . . bubbling and broyling' within them as they became as Adam was: '*Redire in prius: pium suum*, before perfect' (36–7). There is an anticipation here of Rogers's career after the Restoration: he gained degrees in medicine from Oxford and Utrecht and wrote a medical treatise in Latin, *Analecta inauguralia* (1664). Coppe also saw out his days practising physic; the attraction of medicine to the radical prophets is explained by George Fox's disclosure that after he had 'come into the state of Adam, which he was in, before he fell', he was unsure 'whether I should practise physick for the good of mankind, seeing the nature and virtues of the creatures were so opened unto me by the Lord'.[7]

Rogers had a dispute with James Harrington in 1659 over the original form of the Mosaic State, which they both believed should provide the model for an English republic.[8] The opposing attitudes of Milton and Rogers towards books and knowledge can be illuminated by comparing them to the opposing philosophies of Harrington and Hobbes. The epistemological basis of *The Commonwealth of Oceana* (1656), the fullest expression of Harrington's republican vision, is that truth can be discovered 'within the body of past knowledge' through reading and study. At the centre of *Oceana* is a 'humanist process of self-education'. Harrington was responding to the anti-humanist political science of *Leviathan*, where Hobbes 'replaces *auctoritas* with "experience" derived

---

[7] Smith (ed.), Fox, *The Journal*, 27. Walwyn also practised medicine and published four tracts on the subject after 1649, while the Oxford-educated army chaplain and antinomian Henry Pinnell translated Paracelsian tracts in the 1650s. For discussions of the relationship between free grace, physic, and Paracelsianism see Peter Elmer, 'Medicine, Religion, and the Puritan Revolution', in *The Medical Revolution of the Seventeenth Century* (Cambridge, 1989), 10–45; McDowell, 'Degrees of Divinity', 201–11.

[8] James Harrington, *A Parallel of the Spirit of the People, with the Spirit of Mr Rogers* (1659); Rogers, *Mr Harrington's Parallel Unparallel'd* (1659); Pocock, 'Post-Puritan England and the Problem of Enlightenment', 96–8. The main point of dissension was over Harrington's claim that the Fifth Monarchist proposal for rule by a spiritual elite of saints was merely another attempt to establish a clerical monopoly over religious knowledge in the manner of Catholic, episcopalian, and Presbyterian church governments.

from sense perceptions'.[9] Rogers's conversion similarly leads him to reject *auctoritas*, the accumulated body of wisdom stored in sacred and classical texts, in favour of simple *sapientia*, the certain knowledge derived from the physical experience of the Spirit: 'we are *matter* enough afforded us in the *historical* and *demonstrable* part of [the saints'] *Experiences*' (355). Consequently the classical books which Rogers had studied are deployed without concern for their context or textual integrity. He reads the classics, as he now reads all texts, as commentaries on his personal spiritual experience. Puritan divines had preached that biblical hermeneutics would become redundant in the millennium, when the real presence of the divine would render all systems of signification irrelevant; for Rogers, the internalized apocalypse had already abolished textuality.[10] Milton used Cicero's analysis of fortitude in the *De Officiis*, 'the Bible of the humanists', as his blueprint in *Of Education* for a reformed curriculum which would conform more closely to the humanist ideal of a linguistic and rhetorical education as a training for virtuous public service.[11] The *De Officiis* was one of Rogers's favourite texts. Citing '*Tullins Offices lib. 8 & 9 de invent. Ante finem libri*', Rogers transforms the Ciceronian identification of moral virtue with civic duty into an analysis of the effects of free grace and a defence of the separation of the perfected saints in gathered Churches from those who remain 'under the law internally'. Cicero, 'a meer *Moralist*', is invoked to distinguish 'Discipline' and 'Politie': the redeemed live voluntarily under the discipline of the congregation, while the unregenerate live according to the 'outward lawes' of the civil and ecclesiastical polity. While 'Politie' has 'no higher *principle* than *reason*', 'Discipline' is 'absolutely above, and yet in nothing *against pure reason*'.[12] Rogers's internalization of the classical values of liberty and virtue within the sanctified body of the saint and the congregation—values which Milton sought to establish as the basis of a republican polity—is further illustrated in his transformation of the sense of classical exempla, as in this anecdote from Plutarch's *Lives*: 'When *Cyneas* the Ambassador of *Pyrrhus*, after his return from *Rome*, was asked by his *Master*, what he thought of the City and State, answered; 'O Sir! It

---

[9] Smith, *Literature and Revolution*, 166; Norbrook, *Writing the English Republic*, 359–60.

[10] For a discussion of language and Puritan millenarianism which refers to Rogers see Crawford Gribben, *The Puritan Millennium: Literature and Theology 1550–1682* (Dublin, 2000), 167–71.

[11] Skinner, *Reason and Rhetoric in the Philosophy of Hobbes*, 292; Dzelzainis, 'Milton's Classical Republicanism', 12–13.

[12] Rogers, *Ohel*, 3, 7–8, 378; for Rogers's use of *De Officiis* see also Rogers, *Sagrir. Or Doomsday drawing nigh* (1653), 5, 45, 103, 105.

is *Respublica Regum,* a Commonwealth of Kings, and a State of States-
men: And so is the Church' (*Ohel,* 182).

Rogers reads the classical texts in which he had been educated in the
same way that many radical prophets used Scripture, as an allegorical
account of inner spiritual states. The story of '*Dyonisius* a *Stoick*' (perhaps
Dionysius of Syracuse, an account of whom is given in Plutarch's *Lives*)
becomes an illustration of how experience exposes and undermines the
false knowledge disseminated by books:

And, as I remember, I have read of *Dyonisius* a *Stoick,* who wrote a *book* that paine
was nothing but a *fancy,* and an *imagination;* but falling fearfully ill of the *stone*
(not long after) and feeling the *torture* of it, then he roars out; Oh! all that he had
written was false! all was false! for now he had found *paine* more then a fancy; and
so surely experience teaches ingenuously and truly. And such as *know Christ,* and
the *love of God* by experience, can say [as much] of their former conceptions, and
apprehensions of him as an *austeer Master* to please, exacting duties, and a *severe
Judge,* hasty to condemn, and damn . . . (383–4)

The residual influence of Rogers's youthful despair is evident in the
opposition of the antinomian God who releases men from sin and the law
to the Calvinist God, the '*severe Judge*' invoked by the hellfire preachers
who terrified him as a child. Rogers uses the anecdote to emphasize the
physical reality of the experience of grace, so reversing the accusation that
claims of inspiration are 'nothing but a *fancy,* and an *imagination*'. Indeed
'fancy' is associated with the faulty intellectual constructs of bookish
study. So this classical exemplum in which Stoic notions of self-
sufficiency are almost comically undermined by physical experience is
interpreted as a lesson in the folly of human pretensions to wisdom
through learning. In ridiculing the antinomian and perfectionist beliefs
abroad in revolutionary England, the cleric Francis Fulwood suggested
that new theories of philosophy were being invented daily which outdid
the discoveries of Socrates, Plato, and Aristotle.[13] Of course Fulwood was
being sarcastic—invoking the stereotype of the heretic as *illitteratus* in
associating the radicals with forms of knowledge of which he believed
them to have no conception. Fulwood's mocking opposition of classical
and sectarian theories of knowledge was not entirely fanciful. Some
learned radicals deliberately sought to break down the classical structures
of knowledge in which they had been educated and to transform their
sense according to the claims of the Spirit.

---

[13] Francis Fulwood, *Vindiciae mediorum & mediatoris* (1651), 86. On Fulwood's scorn for
the learning of his opponents in printed accounts of his public disputations with radicals see
Hughes, 'The Pulpit Guarded'.

The tension between 'humanism' and 'radical Puritanism' in Milton's mind has of course been the subject of much critical debate. The cultural tensions between humanism and radical Puritanism in English society in the age of Milton have received rather less attention, if we define humanism accurately as the dominant educational philosophy of the period rather than vaguely and misleadingly as an aristocratic tradition of letters. Critics have tended rather to translate 'the political conflicts that organized Milton's world and the cultural conflicts that consequently organized his work, into . . . the psychology of internal conflict'.[14] While offering the 'popular heretical culture' as a new context for Milton's thought, Christopher Hill nonetheless came to the old conclusion that the mind of Milton was divided. Milton lived 'in a state of permanent dialogue with radical ideas which he could not wholly accept' because, as an 'elitist Puritan scholar', he had little respect for opinions which were espoused by artisan radicals and circulated amongst the unlettered multitude.[15] Hence his bestial characterization in 'On the Detraction which followed upon my Writing Certain Treatises' of those who lacked the education to understand that his ideas on divorce were a manifesto for liberty, not licence. Yet if we accept that Milton was finally contemptuous of the arguments of 'illiterate Mechanick persons' (despite his momentary vision in *Areopagitica* of London sectarians as 'wise and faithful labourers'), how do we relate Milton to the university-educated, humanistic radicals that have been the subject of this book? We need to consider whether the evolution of Milton's heretical ideas about free will, monism, materialism, and antitrinitarianism can be connected with this native tradition of learned radicalism that developed in England in the 1640s and 1650s. In *Tetrachordon* (1645) Milton quotes Daniel Featley's attack in *The Dippers Dipt* on his arguments about divorce, so Milton certainly knew of Overton's *Mans Mortalitie*, to which *The Doctrine and Discipline of Divorce* is compared by Featley. *Mans Mortalitie* appeared at the end of 1643 or the beginning of 1644, just as Milton was revising and enlarging *The Doctrine and Discipline of Divorce*, the second edition of which appeared no later than February 1644. Might the emergent monism that has been identified in this revised version have been shaped by reading Overton's learned arguments for the indivisibility of spirit and

[14] Nancy Armstrong and Leonard Tennenhouse, *The Imaginary Puritan: Literature, Intellectual Labour and the Origins of Personal Life* (Berkeley, Calif., 1992; paperback edn., 1994), 27–46 (28). On the meanings of 'humanism' in early modern England see Pincombe, *Elizabethan Humanism*, 3–9.

[15] *Milton and the English Revolution*, 113, 248–9.

flesh?[16] It seems less incredible that Milton might have read and even enjoyed the anti-intellectual writings of Abiezer Coppe once we recognize Coppe's satirical treatment of collegiate traditions; Milton had himself presided over a 'feast of fools' at Cambridge, one of the end-of-term festivities during which the academic curriculum was subject to comic inversion and parody.[17] Coppe's point, which Milton might well have appreciated given the anger in his early prose at the abuse of learning in the universities, is that the nonsense and absurdity of the feast of fools is the real world of academic study, not its parodic reflection. Recognition of the learning of a figure such as John Biddle, Oxford Fellow and translator of Virgil and Juvenal as well as antitrinitarian tracts, allows us to look afresh at Milton's involvement in the licensing of heretical books during the 1650s. The argument that Milton licensed Biddle's translation of *The Racovian Catechism* (1652), condemned by Parliament as 'blasphemous, erroneous, and scandalous', becomes more persuasive if we assume that Milton was particularly attracted to radical beliefs disseminated by those with whom he shared a learned, humanist background. The incident of *The Racovian Catechism* 'raises the intriguing possibility', as Dobranski observes, that Milton was involved with licensing and commenting on other heretical books.[18]

At the same time, the radicals who have featured in the preceding chapters held beliefs quite clearly at odds with Milton's heroic vision in the *Pro Se Defensio* of a republic founded and defended on the humanist values instilled in the classroom. In the writings of Coppe, Fisher, and John Rogers classical texts no longer provide access to a political and cultural tradition; rather they are transformed into expressions of personal prophetic virtue which merely reflect and articulate the saving presence of the spirit within. Yet the enthusiastic repudiation of learning and textuality was nevertheless a position that Milton understood. One of the prefatory poems to *Ohel or Beth-Shemesh* celebrates John Rogers's prophetic charisma as a transcendence of the classical categories of literary inspiration:

> And *Vates* be in strife
> Whether *Prophet* or *Poet* he shall be;

---

[16] *CPWM*, ii. 583; on the emergent monism in the revised edition of *The Doctrine and Discipline of Divorce* see Fallon, 'The Metaphysics of Milton's Divorce Tracts'.

[17] R. Richek, 'Thomas Randolph's *Salting* (1627), its Text, and Milton's Sixth Prolusion as Another Salting', *English Literary Renaissance*, 12 (1982), 102–31.

[18] In his detailed reconstruction of Milton's involvement with the licensing of *The Racovian Catechism* Stephen B. Dobranski does not mention Biddle; for Parliament's verdict on the tract see Dobranski, 'Licensing Milton's Heresy', 143–4.

> But yet at last agree.
> For *Sions* sake, and *Sions* sons (which doth
> Fill full my Pen and Pencil) to be both
>
> .   .   .   .   .   .
>
> Tis not *Minerva*, *Pallas* whom some fain
> The daughter of *Joves* brain:
> Nor *Clio*, nor *Melpomene* indites,
> But tis the *Spirit* which writes.

This representation of Rogers's prophetic status in terms of an opposition between Hebraic and classical conceptions of inspiration is an appropriate anticipation of his treatment of humanist culture in *Ohel or Beth-Shemesh*. How different in its meaning and message, though, is this poem from the most famous invocation in English literature, in which Milton calls on the Holy Spirit to act as his muse and to illuminate 'what in me is dark' in the manner of Moses and the Old Testament prophets, so empowering him to pursue '[t]hings unattempted yet in prose or rhyme'?[19] A perfect apprehension of all learning is of course Satan's last temptation to Christ in *Paradise Regained* (1671). Christ, perhaps voicing Milton's disillusionment with humanist values after the failure of the republic, declares that those who are 'from God inspired', no matter how lowly and unlearned, possess a greater knowledge than can ever be derived from humane learning. This is, as we have seen, the traditional defence of the heretic against the charge of ignorance by the clerical representatives of orthodoxy. Christ concludes his rejection of the classical philosophies with Stoicism, arguing that the Stoics' misconceived pride in their intellectual perfection makes them ignorant of their degenerate nature and so ignorant of the redemptive knowledge of grace; just as Rogers recounts how '*Dyonisius a Stoick*' discovered through bitter experience that 'Oh! all that he had written was false!':

> The Stoic last in philosophic pride,
> By him called virtue; and his virtuous man,
> Wise, perfect in himself, and all possessing,
> Equal to God, oft shames not to prefer,
> As fearing God nor man, contemning all
> Wealth, pleasure, pain or torment, death and life,
> Which then he lists, he leaves, or boasts he can,
> For all his tedious talk is but vain boast,
> Or subtle shifts conviction to evade.
> Alas what can they teach, and not mislead;

---

[19] Milton, *Paradise Lost*, ed. Fowler, i. 6–26; Rogers, *Ohel*, 83–4.

Ignorant of themselves, of God much more,
And how the world began, and how man fell
Degraded by himself, on grace depending?[20]

---

[20] Milton, *Complete Shorter Poems*, ed. Carey, 505–6 (IV. 300–12). David Loewenstein has persuasively connected the representation of Christ in *Paradise Regained* with Quaker testimonies of suffering (*Representing Revolution in Milton and his Contemporaries: Religion, Politics, and Polemics in Radical Puritanism* (Cambridge, 2001), 242–68.

Bibliography

MANUSCRIPTS

Bodleian Library, Oxford

MS Rawlinson, A. 26, fos. 239, 252: account of John Rogers's treatment and behaviour while confined in Windsor Castle, May 1655.
MS Rawlinson, A. 47, fo. 25: notes on life and opinions of John Rogers, 1655.
MS Rawlinson, C. 409, fo. 76: account of Samuel Fisher, Baptist.
MS Tanner, 51, fo. 112: letter from Samuel Fisher to Parliament, August 1659.

British Library

Add. MS 4365, fo. 172: letter from Christian Rave to Samuel Hartlib concerning a Hebrew academy in England.
Add. MS 23146: diary of Thomas Dugard, 1632–42.

Friends House Library, London

MS Caton, fo. 507: letter from William Caton to Margaret Fell, 1658.
MS Spence, fo. 27: letter from Margaret Fell to Samuel Fisher, March 1656.

UNPUBLISHED THESES

LAURENCE, ANNE, 'Parliamentary Army Chaplains, 1642–1651', D.Phil. thesis, 2 vols. (Oxford University, 1981).
McDOWELL, NICHOLAS, 'Degrees of Divinity: The Intellectual Resources of the Radical Imagination in England, c.1630–1660', D.Phil. thesis (Oxford University, 2000).
McGREGOR, J. F., 'The Ranters: A Study in the Free Spirit in English Sectarian Religion, 1648–1660', B.Litt. thesis (Oxford University, 1968).
RIGNEY, JAMES, 'The English Sermon, 1640–1660: Consuming the Fire', D.Phil. thesis (Oxford University, 1994).

PRINTED SOURCES

Primary Works

AUSTIN, SAMUEL, *Plus Ultra, or the Second Part of the Character of a Quaker* (1676).
BALE, JOHN, *A Mysterye of Inyquytie Contayned within the Heretycall Genealoygie of Ponce Pantobalus* (1545).

[BALLING, PETER], *The Light Upon the Candlestick*, trans. B.[enjamin] F.[urly] (1663).

BAXTER, RICHARD, *Saints Everlasting Rest* (1650).

—— *Plain Scripture Proof of Infants Church Membership* (1651).

—— *Relinquiae Baxterianae*, ed. Matthew Sylvester (1696).

BESSE, JOSEPH, *A Collection of the Sufferings of the People called Quakers*, 2 vols. (1753).

A Blow at the Root (1650), repr. in appendix to Davis, *Fear, Myth and History: The Ranters and the Historians* (Cambridge, 1986).

BOEHME, JACOB, *Signatura Rerum, or the Signature of all Things, shewing the Sign, and Signification of the several Forms and Shapes in the Creation*, trans. John Ellistone (1651).

BRAYNE, JOHN, *An Exposition Upon the Canticles* (1651).

—— *The New Earth or, The True Magna Charta* (1653).

BRINSLEY, JOHN, *The posing of the parts; or, A most plaine and easie way of examining the accidence and grammar* (1611; 7th edn. 1630).

—— *Ludus Literarius, or the Grammar Schoole* (1612), ed. E. T. Campagnac (Liverpool, 1917).

BROOKE, HUMPHREY, *The Charity of Church-Men* (1649), in *LT*.

BROWNE, ROBERT, *A Treatise on the 23. of Matthewe* (Middelburg, 1582).

BURTON, ROBERT, *The Anatomy of Melancholy*, ed. Thomas C. Faulkner, Nicola J. Keissling, and Rhonda L. Blair, 3 vols. (Oxford, 1989–94).

BUTLER, SAMUEL, *Hudibras* (1662–77), ed. John Wilder (London, 1968).

—— *Prose Observations*, ed. H. de Quehen (Oxford, 1979).

CARDWELL, EDWARD (ed.), *Documentary Annals of the Reformed Church of England*, 2 vols. (1844).

CAREW, RICHARD, *The True and Readie Way to Learne the Latine Tongue*, ed. Samuel Hartlib (1654).

Catalogus Liborum Bibliothecis Selectissimus Doctorissimorum Virorum (1681).

CATON, WILLIAM, *A Journal of the Life of the Faithful Servant and Minister of Jesus Christ Will Caton* (1689).

CHARRON, PIERRE, *Of Wisdome*, trans. Samson Lennard (1606).

CLARKSON, LAURENCE, *A General Charge, or Impeachment of High-Treason, in the name of Justice, Equity, against the Communality of England* (1646).

—— *A Single Eye All Light, no Darkness* (1650), in *CRW*.

—— *The Lost Sheep Found* (1660), in *CRW*.

CLEVELAND, JOHN, *The Character of a London Diurnal-Maker* (1644), in *Character Writings of the Seventeenth Century*, ed. Henry Morley (London, 1891).

The Confession of Faith, together with the larger and lesser Catechismes, Composed by the Reverend Assembly of Divines Sitting at Westminster, Presented to both Houses of Parliament (1658).

COPPE, ABIEZER, preface to *John the Divines Divinity* (1648), in *CRW*.

—— *Some Sweet Sips, of Some Spiritual Wine* (1649), in *CRW*.

—— 'An Additional and Preambular Hint', preface to Richard Coppin, *Divine Teachings* (1649), in *CRW*.

—— *A Fiery Flying Roll* (1649), in *CRW*.

—— *A Remonstrance of the Sincere and Zealous Protestation of Abiezer Coppe* (1651), in *CRW*.

—— *Copps Return to the Wayes of Truth* (1651), in *CRW*.

—— *Divine Fire-Works* (1657).

COPPIN, RICHARD, *Anti-Christ in Man* (1649).

—— *The Exaltation of all Things in Christ* (1649).

—— *Divine Teachings* (1649; 2nd edn. 1653).

—— *Truths Testimony and A Testimony of Truths Appearing* (1655).

CRASHAW, RICHARD, *Poetical Works*, ed. L. C. Martin (2nd edn., Oxford, 1957).

CULPEPER, NICHOLAS, *A Physical Directory* (1650).

DANSON, THOMAS, *The Quakers Folly Made Manifest* (1659).

DELL, WILLIAM, *The Stumbling Stone* (1653).

—— *The Trial of Spirits* (1653).

—— *Several Sermons and Discourses* (1709).

A Description of the Sect called the Familie of Love (1641).

DONNE, JOHN, *The Complete English Poems*, ed. A. J. Smith (Harmondsworth, 1971; repr. 1986).

EDWARDS, THOMAS, *Gangraena; Or a Catalogue and Discovery of many of the Errours, Heresies, Blasphemies and pernicious Practices of the Sectaries of this time, vented and acted in England in the last four years*, 3 pts. (1646).

Englands Warning by Germanies Woe; or An Historical Narration of the Originall, Progresse, Tenets, Names, and Severall Sects of the Anabaptists in Germany and the Low Countries (1646).

ERASMUS, DESIDERIUS, *Praise of Folly*, ed. A. H. T. Levi, trans. Betty Radice (Harmondsworth, 1971).

EVERARD, JOHN, *The Gospel-Treasury Opened*, 2 pts. (1657).

F., I., *John the Divine's Divinity* (1648).

FEATLEY, DANIEL, *The Dippers Dipt* (1645; 5th edn. 1647).

FISHER, SAMUEL, *Christianismus Redivivus* (1655).

—— *The Scorned Quakers True and Honest Account* (1656).

—— *The Scorned Quakers Second Account* (1656).

—— *Rusticus ad Academicos* (1660).

—— *An Additionall and Apologetical Appendix to Rusticus and Academicos* (1660).

—— *Lux Christi emergens* (1661).

—— *The Testimony of Truth Exalted*, ed. William Penn (1679).

[FORSET, EDWARD], *Pedantius* (1631), ed. G. C. Moore-Smith (Louvain, 1905).

FOSTER, GEORGE, *The Sounding of the Last Trumpet* (1650).

FOSTER, JOSEPH (ed.), *Alumni Oxonienses: The Members of the University of Oxford, 1500–1714* (Oxford, 1891–2).

FOWLER, CHRISTOPHER, *Daemonium Meridianum*, 2 pts. (1655, 1656).

FOX, GEORGE, *A Battle-Door for Teachers and Professors To Learn Singular and Plural* (1660).

—— *Journal*, ed. J. L. Nickalls (Cambridge, 1952).

—— *The Journal* (1694), ed. Nigel Smith (Harmondsworth, 1998).

FRY, JOHN, *The Clergy in their Colours* (1650).

FULWOOD, FRANCIS, *Vindiciae mediorum & mediatoris* (1651).

GELL, ROBERT, *An Essay Towards an Amendment of the last English Translation of the Bible* (1659).

—— *Gells Remaines*, ed. Robert Bacon (1676).

GODWIN, THOMAS, *Moses and Aaron. Civil and Ecclesiastical Rites, Used by the Ancient Hebrewes* (1634).

HAINE, WILLIAM, *Lillies Rules Construed* (1638).

HALL, THOMAS, *Vindiciae Literarum, The Schools Guarded: or, The excellency and usefulnesse of Arts, Sciences, History, and all Sorts of humane Learning, in subordination to Divinity, and Preparation for the Mynistry* (1654).

HARRINGTON, JAMES, *A Parallel of the Spirit of the People, with the Spirit of Mr. Rogers* (1659).

Heteroclitanomalonomia (n.d.), in *Jacobean Academic Plays: Malone Society Collections, xiv*, ed. Suzanne Gossett and Thomas L. Berger (Oxford, 1988), 57–97.

HOBBES, THOMAS, *Leviathan* (1651), ed. Richard Tuck (Cambridge, 1991).

—— *The Correspondence of Thomas Hobbes*, ed. Noel Malcom, 2 vols. (Oxford, 1994).

HOOKER, RICHARD, *Of the Laws of Ecclesiastical Polity*, ed. Arthur Stephen MacGrade (Cambridge, 1989).

HORACE, *Ars Poetica*, in *Classical Literary Criticism*, trans. T. S. Dorsch (Harmondsworth, 1965).

HOSKINS, JOHN, *Direccions for Speech and Style* (1599).

HOW, SAMUEL, *The Sufficiencie of the Spirits Teaching without Humane Learning* (1640).

A Justification of the Mad Crew (1650), repr. in appendix to Davis, *Fear, Myth and History*.

LILY, WILLIAM, and COLET, JOHN, *A Short Introduction of Grammar; Brevissima Institutio seu Ratio Grammaticae* (1624 edn.).

MARPRELATE, MARTIN, *The Marprelate Tracts, 1588–9*, ed. William Pierce (London, 1911)

MARLOWE, CHRISTOPHER, *Dr Faustus: The A-Text*, ed. Roma Gill (2nd edn., London, 1989).

MERRIOT, THOMAS, *Grammatical Miscellanies* (1660).

MILTON, JOHN, *The Works of John Milton*, ed. Frank A. Patterson et al., 18 vols. (Columbia, 1931–8).

—— *Complete Prose Works*, ed. D. M. Wolfe et al., 8 vols. (New Haven, Conn., 1953–82).

—— *Complete Shorter Poems*, ed. John Carey (Harlow, 1971; 8th repr. 1992).

—— *Paradise Lost*, ed. Alastair Fowler (Harlow, 1971; 14th repr. 1991).

—— *Political Writings*, ed. Martin Dzelzainis (Cambridge, 1991).

Momus Elenctius (Oxford, 1654).

MONTAIGNE, MICHEL DE, *The Complete Essays*, trans. M. A. Screech (Harmondsworth, 1993).

MORE, HENRY, *Enthusiasmus Triumphatus, or, A Discourse of the Nature, Causes, Kinds, and Cure, of Enthusiasme* (1656).

Musarum Oxoniensium (Oxford, 1654).

NASHE, THOMAS, *The Unfortunate Traveller and Other Works*, ed. J. B. Steane (Harmondsworth, 1985).

NEDHAM, MARCHAMONT, *A Discourse Concerning Schools and Schoolmasters* (1663).

Norton Anthology of English Literature, ed. M. H. Abrams et al., 2 vols. (6th edn., New York, 1993).

NORWOOD, RICHARD, 'Confessions' (written 1639–40), in *Grace Abounding: With Other Spiritual Autobiographies*, ed. John Stachniewski with Anita Pacheo (Oxford, 1998).

OSBORN, JOHN, *The World to Come* (1651).

OVERTON, RICHARD, *Mans Mortalitie* (1643), ed. Harold Fisch (Liverpool, 1968).

—— *The Arraignement of Mr. Persecution* (1645).

—— *Divine Observations* (1646).

—— *An Arrow Against All Tyrants and Tyranny* (1646).

—— *A Defiance Against All Arbitrary Usurpations* (1646).

—— *The Commoners Complaint* (1647).

—— *Man Wholly Mortal* (1655).

OVID, *Metamorphoses*, trans. Mary Innes (Harmondsworth, 1955).

The Oxford Book of Classical Verse in Translation, ed. Adrian Poole and Jeremy Maule (Oxford, 1995).

OWEN, JOHN, *Of the Divine Originall, Authority, Self-Evidencing Light and Power of the Scriptures* (1659).

PAINE, THOMAS, *The Age of Reason, Part the Second, being an Investigation of True and Fabulous Theology* (1795).

PENN, WILLIAM, *Defence of the Duke of Buckingham's Book of Religion* (1685).

PERKINS, WILLIAM, *The Works of William Perkins* (Cambridge, 1605).

PEYRÈRE, ISAAC LA, *Men Before Adam* (1656).

[PHILALETHES], *An Answer to Doctor Chamberlaines Scandalous and False Papers* (1650).

PRICE, JOHN, *Walwins Wiles* (1649), in *LT*.

The Ranters Religion (1650), repr. in appendix to Davis, *Fear, Myth and History*.

RAVE, CHRISTIAN, *Discourse of the Orientall Tongues* (1648; 2nd edn. 1649).

General Grammar for the Ready Attaining of the Ebrew, Samaritan, Calde, Syriac, Arabic, and Ethiopic Languages (1649).

RICH, ROBERT, *Love Without Dissimulation* (1666).

—— *Mr Robert Rich His Second Letters from Barbadoes* (1669).

—— *A Testimony to the Truth* (1679).

—— *Hidden Things Brought to Light* (1680).

—— *The Epistle of Mr. Robert Rich to the Seven Churches* (1680).

ROBERTSON, WILLIAM, *A Gate or Door to the Holy Tongue* (1653).

ROGERS, EDWARD, *Some Account of the Life and Opinions of a Fifth Monarchy Man* (London, 1867).

ROGERS, JOHN, *Ohel or Beth-Shemesh. A Tabernacle for the Sun* (1653).

—— *Sagrir. Or Doomes-day drawing nigh, with Thunder and Lightening to Lawyers* (1653).

—— *Jegar-Sahadutha. An Oyled Pillar. Set up for posterity, against Present wickednesses, hypocrisies, blasphemies, persecutions & cruelties of this serpent power in England* (1657).

—— *Mr. Harrington's Parallel Unparallel'd* (1659).

—— *Analecta Inauguralia* (1664).

ROUS, FRANCIS, *The Diseases of the Time Attended by their Remedies* (1622).

RUTHERFORD, SAMUEL, *A Survey of the Spirituall Antichrist, opening the secrets of Familisme and Antinomianisme*, 2 pts. (1648).

SALTMARSH, JOHN, *Free Grace; or, The Flowings of Christ's Blood Freely to Sinners* (1645).

SELDEN, JOHN, *Uxor Ebraica* (1646), trans. Jonathan R. Ziskind (Leiden, 1991).

Several Proceedings in Parliament, xvi (January 1650).

SHAKESPEARE, WILLIAM, *The Riverside Shakespeare*, ed. G. Blakemore Evans (Boston, Mass., 1974).

A Short Historie of the Anabaptists of High and Low Germany (1642).

SPENCER, JOHN, *A Discourse Concerning Vulgar Prophecies* (1665).

STERRY, PETER, *The Comings Forth of Christ* (1650).

—— *Free Grace Exalted* (1670).

—— *Discourse of the Freedom of the Will* (1675).

[STUBBE, HENRY], *Malice Rebuked* (1659).

—— *A Light Shining out of Darkness* (2nd, enlarged, edn. 1659).

—— *The Rise and Progress of Mahometanism*, ed. Hafiz Mahumed Kahn (London, 1911).

STUBBS, JOHN, 'A Word to all such as Teaches their Children to Learn other Tongues', appendix to Fox, *A Battle-Door for Teachers and Professors* (1660).

SWIFT, JONATHAN, *The Complete Poems*, ed. Pat Rogers (Harmondsworth, 1983).

TANY, THOMAS, *Theauraujohn High Priest To the Jewes* (1652), in *The Writings of Thomas Tany*, ed. Andrew Hopton (London, 1988).

TAYLOR, JOHN, *A Swarme of Schismatiques and Sectaries* (1641).

—— *The Anatomy of Separatists, alias Brownists* (1642).

Theologia Germanica, trans. Giles Randall (1646).

TICKELL, JOHN, *The Bottomlesse Pit Smoaking in Familisme* (Oxford, 1651; 2nd edn. 1652).

TOLAND, JOHN, *The Life of John Milton* (1698), in *The Early Lives of John Milton*, ed. Helen Darbishire (London, 1965).

TRAPNELL, ANNA, *A Legacy for Saints* (1654).

VENN, J., and VENN, J. A., *Alumni Cantabrigienses . . . to 1751*, 4 vols. (Cambridge, 1922–7).

WALKER, CLEMENT, *Anarchia Anglicana: Or, The History of Independency*, 2 pts. (1649; 2nd edn. 1661).

WALWYN, WILLIAM, *A New Petition of the Papists* (1641), in *WWW*.

—— *The Power of Love* (1643), in *WWW*.

—— *The Compassionate Samaritane* (1644), in *WWW*.

—— *Toleration Justified and Persecution Condemned* (1645), in *WWW*.

—— *A Parable or Consultation of Physitians Upon Master Edwards* (1646), in *WWW*.

—— *A Prediction of Mr. Edwards His Conversion and Recantation* (1646), in *WWW*.

—— *A Whisper in the Eare of Mr. Thomas Edwards* (1646), in *WWW*.

—— *A Still and Soft Voice* (1647), in *WWW*.

—— *Vanitie of the Present Churches* (1649), in *LT*.

—— *Walwyns Just Defence* (1649), in *WWW*.

[WARD, SETH, and WILKINS, JOHN], *Vindiciae Academiarum* (Oxford, 1654).

WEBSTER, JOHN, *The Judgement Set* (1654).

—— *Academiarum Examen* (1654).

WILMOT, JOHN, *The Letters of John Wilmot, Earl of Rochester*, ed. Jeremy Treglown (Oxford, 1980).

WINSTANLEY, GERRARD, *A New-Yeeres Gift for the Parliament and Armie* (1650), in *Divine Right and Democracy: An Anthology of Political Writings in Stuart England*, ed. David Wootton (Harmondsworth, 1986).

—— *The Works of Gerrard Winstanley*, ed. G. H. Sabine (New York, 1941).

—— *The Law of Freedom and Other Writings*, ed. Christopher Hill (Cambridge, 1983).

WOOD, ANTHONY, *Athenae Oxonienses*, ed. Philip Bliss, 4 vols. (Oxford, 1813–20).

—— *The Life and Times of Anthony Wood, Antiquary, of Oxford, 1632–1695, as Described by Himself*, ed. A. Clark, 5 vols. (Oxford, 1891–1900).

WRITER, CLEMENT, *The Jus Divinum of Presbyterie* (1646; 2nd edn. 1655).

—— *Fides Divina* (1657).

—— *An Apologetical Narration* (2nd edn., 1658).

SECONDARY WORKS

ACHINSTEIN, SHARON, 'The Politics of Babel in the English Revolution', in James Holstun (ed.), *Pamphlet Wars: Rhetoric in the English Revolution* (London, 1992), 14–44.

ALSOP, J. D., 'Gerrard Winstanley: Religion and Respectability', *Historical Journal*, 28 (1985), 705–9.

ANDERS, H., 'The Elizabethan ABC with Catechism', *The Library*, 4th ser. 16 (1936), 32–48.

ARMSTRONG, NANCY, and TENNENHOUSE, LEONARD, *The Imaginary Puritan: Literature, Intellectual Labour and the Origins of Personal Life* (Berkeley, Calif., 1992; paperback edn., 1994).

ASHCROFT, RICHARD, 'Anticlericalism and Authority in Lockean Political Thought', in Roger D. Lund (ed.), *The Margins of Orthodoxy: Heterodox Writing and Cultural Response, 1660–1750* (Cambridge, 1995), 73–96.

ASTON, MARGARET, *England's Iconoclasts, i. Laws Against Images* (Oxford, 1988).

ATKINSON, DONALD, 'The Origin and Date of the "Sator" Word Square', *Journal of Ecclesiastical History*, 2 (1951), 1–18.

AYLMER, GERALD, 'Gentleman Levellers?', *Past and Present*, 49 (1970), 120–5.

—— *The Levellers in the English Revolution* (London, 1975).

BAKER, DAVID WEIL, *Divulging Utopia: Radical Humanism in Sixteenth Century England* (Amherst, Mass., 1999).

BARRY, JONATHAN, 'Literacy and Literature in Popular Culture: Reading and Writing in Historical Perspective', in Tim Harris (ed.), *Popular Culture in England, c.1500–1850* (London, 1995), 69–94.

BAUMAN, RICHARD, *Let Your Words Be Few: Symbolism of Speaking and Silence Among Seventeenth-Century Quakers* (Cambridge, 1983).

BILLER, PETER, 'The *Topos* and Reality of the Heretic as *Illitteratus*', in D. Harmening (ed.), *Religiöse Laienbilding und Ketzerabwehr in Mittlealter* (Wurzburg, 1994), 1–27.

—— 'Heresy and Literacy: Earlier History of the Theme', in Peter Biller and Anne Hudson (eds.), *Heresy and Literacy, 1000–1530* (Cambridge, 1994), 1–18.

BINNS, J. W., *Intellectual Culture in Elizabethan and Jacobean England: The Latin Writings of the Age* (Leeds, 1990).

BOAS, F. S., 'University Plays', in Sir A. Ward and A. R. Waller (eds.), *The Cambridge History of English Literature, vi. The Drama to 1642, Part Two* (Cambridge, 1910; repr. 1969).

BRAITHWAITE, WILLIAM, *The Beginnings of Quakerism* (2nd edn., rev. Henry J. Cadbury, York, 1981).

BURGESS, GLEN, 'The Impact on Political Thought: Rhetorics for Troubled Times', in John Morrill (ed.), *The Impact of the English Civil War* (London, 1991), 67–83.

BURKE, PETER, *Popular Culture in Early Modern Europe* (1978; rev. edn. 1994).

—— 'Popular Culture in Seventeenth Century London', in Barry Reay (ed.), *Popular Culture in Seventeenth Century England* (1985), 31–58.

—— 'William Dell, the Universities and the Radical Tradition', in G. Eley, and W. Hunt (eds.), *Reviving the English Revolution: Reflections and Elaborations on the Work of Christopher Hill* (London, 1988), 181–9.

—— 'Tacitism, Scepticism and Reason of State', in J. H. Burns (ed.), with the assistance of Mark Goldie, *The Cambridge History of Political Thought 1450–1700* (Cambridge, 1991; paperback edn., 1996), 479–98.

BURNS, NORMAN T., *Christian Mortalism from Tyndale to Milton* (Camb., Mass., 1972).

BURRAGE, CHAMPLAIN, *The Early English Dissenters*, 2 vols. (Cambridge, 1912).

CALDWELL, PATRICIA, *The Puritan Conversion Narrative* (Cambridge, 1983).

CAPP, BERNARD, *The Fifth Monarchy Men: A Study in Seventeenth Century English Millenarianism* (1972).

CAREY, JOHN, *John Donne: Life, Mind, and Art* (London, 1981).

CARLTON, PETER, 'Bunyan: Language, Authority, Convention', *English Literary History* 51 (1984), 17–32.

CASSIRER, ERNST, KRISTELLER, PAUL OSKAR, and RANDELL, JOHN HERMANN, (eds.), *The Renaissance Philosophy of Man* (Chicago, Ill., 1965).

CAVE, TERENCE, *The Cornucopian Text: Problems of Writing in the French Renaissance* (Oxford, 1979).

CHAMPION, J. A. I., *The Pillars of Priestcraft Shaken: The Church of England and its Enemies, 1660–1730* (Cambridge, 1992).

CHARTIER, ROGER, *The Cultural Uses of Print in Early Modern France*, trans. Lydia C. Cochrane (Princeton, NJ, 1987).

—— *Cultural History: Between Practices and Representations*, trans. Lydia C. Cochrane (Cambridge, 1988).

CHRISTIANSON, PAUL, *Reformers and Babylon: English Apocalyptic Visions from the Reformation to the Eve of the Civil War* (Toronto, 1978).

CLARK, DONALD LEMEN, *John Milton at St Paul's School: A Study of Ancient Rhetoric in English Renaissance Education* (New York, 1948).

CLUCAS, STEPHEN, 'Samuel Hartlib's "Ephemerides", 1635–59, and the Pursuit of Scientific and Philosophical Manuscripts: The Religious Ethos of an Intelligencer', *The Seventeenth Century*, 6 (1991), 33–55.

COLLINS, R. W., *Calvin and the Libertines of Geneva*, ed. F. D. Blackley (Toronto, 1988).

COOLIDGE, JOHN S., 'Martin Marprelate, Marvell and *Decorum Personae* as a Satirical Theme', *Publications of the Modern Language Association of America*, 74 (1959), 526–32.

CORNS, THOMAS N., 'Milton's Quest for Respectability', *Modern Language Review*, 77 (1982), 769–79.

—— *Uncloistered Virtue: English Political Literature, 1640–1660* (Oxford, 1992).

COWARD, BARRY, *The Stuart Age: A History of England 1603–1714* (London, 1980).

CRANE, MARY THOMAS, *Framing Authority: Sayings, Self, and Society in Sixteenth Century England* (Princeton, NJ, 1993).

CRESSY, DAVID, *Literacy and the Social Order: Reading and Writing in Tudor and Stuart England* (Cambridge, 1980).

CUDDON, J. A., *A Dictionary of Literary Terms* (1977; rev. edn. Harmondsworth, 1987).

CURTIS, M. H., *Oxford and Cambridge in Transition, 1588–1642* (Oxford, 1959).

—— 'The Alienated Intellectuals of Early Stuart England', *Past and Present*, 23 (1962), 25–43.

CUST, RICHARD, and HUGHES, ANN (eds.), *Conflict in Early Stuart England: Studies in Religion and Politics 1603–42* (Harlow, 1989).

DAVIS, J. C., *Fear, Myth and History: The Ranters and the Historians* (Cambridge, 1986).

—— 'Fear, Myth and Furore: Reappraising the "Ranters" ', *Past and Present*, 129 (1990), 79–103.

—— 'Puritanism and Revolution: Themes, Methods, Categories and Conclusions', *Historical Journal*, 33 (1990), 693–7.

—— 'Religion and the Struggle for Freedom in the English Revolution', *Historical Journal*, 35 (1992), 507–30.

DEBUS, A. G. (ed.), *Science and Education in the Seventeenth Century: The Webster–Ward Debate* (New York, 1970).

DOBRANSKI, STEPHEN J., 'Licensing Milton's Heresy', in Stephen J. Dobranski and John P. Rumrich (eds.), *Milton and Heresy* (Cambridge, 1998), 139–58.

DOLLIMORE, JONATHAN, *Radical Tragedy: Religion, Ideology, and Power in the Drama of Shakespeare and his Contemporaries* (Hemel Hempstead, 1984; 2nd edn. 1989).

DOW, F. D., *Radicalism in the English Revolution 1640–1660* (Oxford, 1985).

DZELZAINIS, MARTIN, 'Milton's Classical Republicanism', in David Armitage, Armand Himy, and Quentin Skinner (eds.), *Milton and Republicanism* (Cambridge, 1995), 3–24.

ECCLES, MARK, 'Francis Beaumont's *Grammar Lecture*', *Review of English Studies*, 16 (1940), 402–14.

ELMER, PETER, 'Medicine, Religion, and the Puritan Revolution', in Roger French and Andrew Wear (eds.), *The Medical Revolution of the Seventeenth Century* (Cambridge, 1989), 10–45.

ELSKY, MARTIN, *Authorizing Words: Speech, Writing and Print in the English Renaissance* (Ithaca, NY, 1989).

FALLON, STEPHEN, 'The Metaphysics of Milton's Divorce Tracts', in David Loewenstein and James Grantham Turner (eds.), *Politics, Poetics and Hermeneutics in Milton's Prose* (Cambridge, 1990), 69–83.

—— *Milton among the Philosophers: Poetry and Materialism in the Seventeenth Century* (Ithaca, NY, 1991).

FERRY, ANNE, *The Art of Naming* (Chicago, Ill., 1988).

FIX, ANDREW C., *Prophecy and Reason: The Dutch Collegiants in the Early Enlightenment* (Princeton, NJ, 1991).

FLETCHER, HARRIS FRANCIS, *The Intellectual Development of John Milton*, 2 vols. (Urbana, Ill., 1956).

FLINKER, NOAM, 'Milton and the Ranters on Canticles', in Mary A. Maleski (ed.), *Fine Tuning: Studies in the Religious Poetry of Herbert and Milton* (New York, 1989), 273–99.

FORCE, J. E., and POPKIN, R. H., (eds.), *The Books of Nature and the Books of Scripture* (Dordrecht, 1994).

FRANK, JOSEPH, *The Levellers* (Cambridge, Mass., 1955).

FUDGE, ERICA, *Perceiving Animals: Humans and Beasts in Early Modern English Culture* (Hampshire, 2000).

GIBBONS, B. J., 'Richard Overton and the Secularism of the Interregnum Radicals', *The Seventeenth Century*, 10 (1995), 63–75.

GIMELFARB-BRACK, MARIE, *Liberté, egalité, fraternié, justice! La vie et l'oeuvre de Richard Overton, niveleur* (Berne, 1979).

GLOVER, S. D., 'The Putney Debates: Popular versus Elitist Republicanism', *Past and Present*, 164 (1999), 47–80.

GRAFTON, ANTHONY, and JARDINE, LISA, *From Humanism to the Humanities: Education and the Liberal Arts in Fifteenth and Sixteenth Century Europe* (Cambridge, Mass., 1986).

GREAVES, RICHARD, *The Puritan Revolution and Educational Thought* (New Jersey, 1969).

GREEN, IAN, '"For Children in Yeeres and Children in Understanding": The Emergence of the English Catechism under Elizabeth and the Early Stuarts', *Journal of Ecclesiastical History*, 37 (1986), 397–425.

—— *The Christian's ABC: Catechisms and Religious Instruction in England, c.1530–1740* (Oxford, 1996).

GRIBBEN, CRAWFORD, *The Puritan Millennium: Literature and Theology 1550–1682* (Dublin, 2000).

GURNEY, JOHN, 'Gerrard Winstanley and the Digger Movement in Walton and Cobham', *Historical Journal*, 37 (1994), 775–802.

HALLER, WILLIAM, *Liberty and Reformation in the Puritan Revolution* (New York, 1955)

HALPERN, RICHARD, *The Poetics of Primitive Accumulation: English Renaissance Culture and the Genealogy of Capital* (New York, 1991).

HARRIS, TIM, 'Problematizing Popular Culture', in Tim Harris (ed.), *Popular Culture in England, c.1500–1850* (London, 1995), 1–27.

HAWES, CLEMENT, *Mania and Literary Style: The Rhetoric of Enthusiasm from the Ranters to Christopher Smart* (Cambridge, 1996).

HAYES, T. WILSON, 'John Everard and the Familist Tradition', in Margaret Jacob and James Jacob (eds.), *The Origins of Anglo American Radicalism* (London, 1984), 60–9.

HEINEMANN, MARGOT, 'Popular Drama and Leveller Style—Richard Overton and John Harris', in Maurice Cornforth (ed.), *Rebels and Their Causes: Essays in Honour of A. L. Morton* (London, 1978), 69–92.

—— *Puritanism and Theatre: Thomas Middleton and Oppositional Drama under the Early Stuarts* (Cambridge, 1980).

HERENDEEN, WYMAN, 'Milton's *Accidence Commenc't Grammar* and the Deconstruction of Grammatical Tyranny', in P. G. Stanwood (ed.), *Of Poetry and Politics: New Essays on Milton and his World* (New York, 1995), 297–312.

HEYD, MICHAEL, *'Be Sober and Reasonable': The Reaction to Enthusiasm in the Seventeenth and Early Eighteenth Centuries* (Leiden, 1995).

HILL, CHRISTOPHER, *Intellectual Origins of the English Revolution* (Oxford, 1965).

—— *The World Turned Upside Down: Radical Ideas in the English Revolution* (1972; repr. Harmondsworth, 1991).

—— *Milton and the English Revolution* (London, 1977).

—— 'Radical Prose in Seventeenth-Century England: From Marprelate to the Levellers', *Essays in Criticism*, 32 (1982), 95–118.

—— *The Experience of Defeat: Milton and Some Contemporaries* (London, 1984).

—— *Collected Essays of Christopher Hill, i. Writing and Revolution in Seventeenth Century England* (Brighton, 1985).

—— *Collected Essays of Christopher Hill, ii. Religion and Politics in Seventeenth Century England* (Brighton, 1986; repr. 1988).

—— *A Nation of Change and Novelty: Radical Politics, Religion and Literature in Seventeenth Century England* (1990; repr. 1993).

—— *The English Bible and the Seventeenth Century Revolution* (1993; Harmondsworth, 1994).

—— 'Freethinking and Libertinism: The Legacy of the English Revolution', in Roger D. Lund (ed.), *The Margins of Orthodoxy: Heterodox Writing and Cultural Response, 1660–1750* (Cambridge, 1995), 54–72.

HILL, W. SPEED, (ed.), *Studies in Richard Hooker* (Cleveland, Ohio, 1972).

HINDS, HILARY, *Gods Englishwomen: Seventeenth Century Radical Sectarian Writing and Feminist Criticism* (Manchester, 1996).

HOBBY, ELAINE, *Virtue of Necessity: English Women's Writing 1649–88* (London, 1988).

HOLDEN, W. P., *Anti-Puritan Satire 1572–1642* (New Haven, Conn., 1954).

HOLSTUN, JAMES, 'Ranting at the New Historicism', *English Literary Renaissance*, 19 (1989), 189–225.

HOWELL, W. S., *Logic and Rhetoric in England, 1500–1700* (Princeton, NJ, 1956).

HUDSON, ANNE, '*Laicus Litteratus*: The Paradox of Lollardy', in Peter Biller and Anne Hudson (eds.), *Heresy and Literacy, 1000–1530* (Cambridge, 1994), 222–36.

HUEHNS, GERTRUDE, *Antinomianism in English History: With Special Reference to the Period 1640–1660* (London, 1951).

HUGHES, ANN, 'Thomas Dugard and his Circle in the 1630s: A "Parliamentary–Puritan" Connexion?', *Historical Journal*, 29 (1986), 771–93.

—— *Politics, Society and Civil War in Warwickshire, 1620–1660* (Cambridge, 1987).

—— 'The Pulpit Guarded: Confrontations Between Orthodox and Radicals in

Revolutionary England', in Anne Laurence, W. R. Owens, and Stuart Sim (eds.), *John Bunyan and his England, 1628–88* (London, 1990), 31–50.

—— 'Early Quakerism: A Historian's Afterword', in David Loewenstein and Thomas N. Corns (eds.), *The Emergence of Quaker Writing: Dissenting Literature in Seventeenth Century England*, (London, 1995), 141–5.

—— 'Gender and Politics in Leveller Literature', in Susan D. Amussen and Mark A. Kishlansky (eds.), *Political Culture and Cultural Politics in Early Modern England* (Manchester, 1995).

HUNT, LYNN, 'History, Culture, Text', in Lynn Hunt (ed.), *The New Cultural History* (Berkeley, Calif., 1989), 1–24.

HUNTER, MICHAEL, 'The Problem of "Atheism" in Early Modern Europe', *Transactions of the Royal Historical Society*, 35 (1985), 135–57.

ISRAEL, JONATHAN I., *Radical Enlightenment: Philosophy and the Making of Modernity 1650–1750* (Oxford, 2001).

JACOB, JAMES R., *Henry Stubbe, Radical Protestantism and the Early Enlightenment* (Cambridge, 1982).

JEWELL, HELEN M., *Education in Early Modern England* (London, 1998).

JOHNS, ADRIAN, 'The Physiology of Reading and the Anatomy of Enthusiasm', in O. P. Grell and A. Cunningham (eds.), *Religio Medici: Medicine and Religion in Seventeenth Century England* (Aldershot, 1996), 136–70.

KATZ, DAVID S., *Philo-semitism and the Re-admission of the Jews to England, 1603–55* (Oxford, 1982).

KEEBLE, N. H., *The Literary Culture of Nonconformity in Later Seventeenth Century England* (Leicester, 1987).

—— 'The Politic and the Polite in Quaker Prose: The Case of William Penn', in David Loewenstein and Thomas N. Corns (eds.), *The Emergence of Quaker Writing: Dissenting Literature in Seventeenth Century England* (London, 1995), 112–25.

—— 'Introduction', in N. H. Keeble (ed.), *The Cambridge Companion to Writing of the English Revolution* (Cambridge, 2001).

KENDALL, R. T., *Calvin and English Calvinism to 1649* (Oxford, 1979).

KIBBEY, ANNE, *The Interpretation of Material Shapes in Puritanism: A Study of Rhetoric, Prejudice and Violence* (Cambridge, 1986).

KNOTT, JOHN R., *Discourses of Martyrdom in English Literature, 1563–1694* (Cambridge, 1993).

KROLL, R. W. F., *The Material Word: Literate Culture in the Restoration and Early Eighteenth Century* (Baltimore, Md., 1991).

LAKE, PETER, 'Calvinism and the English Church', *Past and Present*, 114 (1987), 32–76.

—— and SHARPE, KEVIN, 'Introduction', in Peter Lake and Kevin Sharpe (eds.), *Culture and Politics in Early Stuart England* (Stanford, 1994), 1–16.

LAURENCE, ANNE, *Parliamentary Army Chaplains 1642–1651* (Suffolk, 1990).

LESLIE, MICHAEL, 'The Spiritual Husbandry of John Beale', in Michael Leslie and

Timothy Raylor (eds.), *Culture and Cultivation in Early Modern England* (Leicester, 1992), 151–72.

LEVINE, JOSEPH M., 'Deists and Anglicans: The Ancient Wisdom and the Idea of Progress', in Roger D. Lund (ed.), *The Margins of Orthodoxy: Heterodox Writing and Cultural Response 1660–1750* (Cambridge, 1995), 219–39.

LINDLEY, KEITH, *Popular Politics and Religion in the English Civil War* (London, 1997).

LOEWENSTEIN, DAVID, *Representing Revolution in Milton and his Contemporaries: Religion, Politics, and Polemics in Radical Puritanism* (Cambridge, 2001).

McDOWELL, NICHOLAS, review of David Loewenstein, *Representing Revolution in Milton and his Contemporaries: Religion, Politics, and Polemics in Radical Puritanism* (Cambridge, 2001), in *Notes and Queries*, NS, 49 (2002), 524–5.

McGREGOR, J. F., 'The Baptists: Fount of All Heresy', in J. F. McGregor and B. Reay (eds.), *Radical Religion in the English Revolution* (Oxford, 1984), 23–64.

—— 'Seekers and Ranters', in J. F. McGregor and B. Reay (eds.), *Radical Religion in the English Revolution* (Oxford, 1984), 121–40.

—— et al., 'Debate. Fear, Myth and Furore: Reappraising the Ranters', *Past and Present*, 140 (August 1993), 155–210.

MACK, PHYLLIS, *Visionary Women: Ecstatic Prophecy in Seventeenth Century England* (Berkeley, Calif., 1992).

McLACHLAN, H. J., *Socinianism in Seventeenth Century England* (Oxford, 1951).

MACLACHLIN, ALASTAIR, *The Rise and Fall of Revolutionary England: An Essay on the Fabrication of Seventeenth Century History* (1996).

MALCOM, NOEL, *The Origins of English Nonsense* (London, 1997).

MARSH, CHRISTOPHER, *The Family of Love in English Society, 1550–1630* (Cambridge, 1994).

MATAR, N. I., 'Peter Sterry and the Ranters', *Notes and Queries*, NS, 29 (1982), 504–6.

MEE, JOHN, *Dangerous Enthusiasm: William Blake and the Culture of Radicalism in the 1790s* (Oxford, 1992).

MILLER, LUCASTA, ' "The Shattered *Violl*": Print and Textuality in the 1640s', in *Essays and Studies, (Literature and Censorship)* 46 (1993), 23–38.

MILLER, PERRY, *The New England Mind: The Seventeenth Century* (Cambridge, Mass., 1954).

MILWARD, PETER (ed.), *Religious Controversies of the Jacobean Age* (London, 1978).

MOORE-SMITH, G. C., *College Plays Performed in the University of Cambridge* (Cambridge, 1923).

MORGAN, JOHN, *Godly Learning: Puritan Attitudes towards Reason, Learning and Education 1560–1640* (Cambridge, 1986).

MORRILL, JOHN, *The Nature of the English Revolution: Essays by John Morrill* (London, 1993).

MORTON, A. L., *The World of the Ranters: Religious Radicalism in the English Revolution* (London, 1970).

MORTON, TIMOTHY, and SMITH, NIGEL (eds.), *Radicalism in British Literary Culture, 1650–1830: From Revolution to Revolution* (Cambridge, 2002).

MOSS, J. D., 'The Family of Love and its English Critics', *Sixteenth Century Journal*, 6 (1975), 35–52.

MULLETT, MICHAEL, *Radical Religious Movements in Early Modern Europe* (London, 1980).

MULLIGAN, LOTTE, 'The Religious Roots of William Walwyn's Radicalism', *Journal of Religious History*, 12 (1982), 162–79.

NELSON, BYRON, 'The Ranters and the Limits of Language', in James Holstun (ed.), *Pamphlet Wars: Rhetoric in the English Revolution* (London, 1992), 61–76.

NORBROOK, DAVID, *Writing the English Republic: Poetry, Rhetoric, and Politics, 1627–1660* (Cambridge, 1999).

Norton Anthology of English Literature, ed. M. H. Abrams et al., 6th edn., 2 vols. (New York, 1993), vol. i.

NUTTALL, A. D., *The Alternative Trinity: Gnostic Heresy in Marlowe, Milton, and Blake* (Oxford, 1998).

NUTTALL, G. F., *The Holy Spirit in Puritan Faith and Experience* (Oxford, 1946).

—— *Visible Saints: The Congregational Way, 1640–1660* (Oxford, 1957).

O'DAY, ROSEMARY, *Education and Society, 1500–1800: The Social Foundations of Education in Early Modern Britain* (1982).

ONG, WALTER, *Romance, Rhetoric and Technology: Studies in the Interpretation of Expression and Culture* (Ithaca, NY, 1971).

ORME, NICHOLAS, 'Schools and Schoolbooks, 1400–1550', in Lotte Hellinga and J. B. Trapp (eds.), *The Cambridge History of the Book in Britain, iii. 1400–1557* (Cambridge, 1999), 449–69.

OYER, JOHN S., *Lutheran Reformers Against Anabaptists* (The Hague, 1964).

PADLEY, G. A., *Grammatical Theory in Western Europe 1500–1700: The Latin Tradition* (Cambridge, 1976).

PAILIN, DAVID A., *Attitudes Towards Other Religions: Comparative Religion in Seventeenth and Eighteenth Century Britain* (Manchester, 1984).

PARKER, PATRICIA, ' "Rude Mechanicals" ', in Margreta De Grazia, Maureen Quilligan, and Peter Stallybrass (eds.), *Subject and Object in Renaissance Culture* (Cambridge, 1986), 43–82.

PATRIDES, C. A., and WITTERICH, JOSEPH (eds.), *The Apocalypse in English Renaissance Thought and Literature* (Ithaca, NY, 1984).

PINCOMBE, MIKE, *Elizabethan Humanism: Literature and Learning in the Later Sixteenth Century* (Harlow, 2001).

PINTO, VIVIAN DE SOLA, *Peter Sterry, Platonist and Puritan* (Cambridge, 1934).

POCOCK, J. G. A., *Politics, Language and Time: Essays in Political Thought and History* (London, 1972).

—— 'Post-Puritan England and the Problem of the Enlightenment', in Perez

Zagorin (ed.), *Culture and Politics from Puritanism to the Enlightenment* (London, 1980), 91–111.

POCOCK, J. G. A., 'Within the Margins: The Definitions of Orthodoxy', in Roger D. Lund (ed.), *The Margins of Orthodoxy: Heterodox Writing and Cultural Response, 1660–1750* (Cambridge, 1995), 33–53.

POOLE, KRISTEN, *Radical Religion from Shakespeare to Milton: Figures of Nonconformity in Early Modern England* (Cambridge, 2000).

POOLEY, ROGER, *English Prose of the Seventeenth Century, 1590–1700* (Harlow, 1992).

POPKIN, R. H., *The History of Scepticism from Erasmus to Spinoza* (Berkeley, Calif., 1979).

—— 'Spinoza's Relations with the Quakers', *Quaker History*, 73 (1984), 14–28.

—— 'Spinoza and Samuel Fisher', *Philosophia*, 15 (December 1985), 219–36.

—— and SIGNER, MICHAEL J., (eds.), *Spinoza's Earliest Publication? The Hebrew Translation of Margaret Fell's 'A Loving Salutation'* (London, 1987).

—— 'Theories of Knowledge', in C. B. Schmitt with Q. Skinner (eds.), *The Cambridge History of Renaissance Philosophy*, (Cambridge, 1988, repr. 1996), 668–84.

—— and VANDERJAGT, ARGO, (eds.), *Scepticism and Irreligion in the Seventeenth and Eighteenth Centuries* (Leiden, 1993).

– — (ed.), *Jewish Christians and Christian Jews* (Leiden, 1994).

POTTER, G. R., (ed.), *Hudrich Zwingli* (London, 1978).

REAY, BARRY, 'Laurence Clarkson: An Artisan and the English Revolution', in Christopher Hill, Barry Reay, and William Lamont (eds.), *The World of the Muggletonians* (London, 1983), ch. 6.

—— 'Popular Culture in Early Modern England', in Barry Reay (ed.), *Popular Culture in Seventeenth Century England* (London, 1985), 1–30.

—— 'Radicalism and Religion in the English Revolution', in J. F. McGregor and B. Reay (eds.), *Radical Religion in the English Revolution* (Oxford, 1984), 1–22.

—— 'Quakerism and Society', in J. F. McGregor and B. Reay (eds.), *Radical Religion in the English Revolution* (Oxford, 1984), 141–64.

—— 'Popular Religion', in Barry Reay (ed.), *Popular Culture in Seventeenth Century England* (London, 1985), 91–128.

—— *The Quakers and the English Revolution* (London, 1985).

—— 'The World Turned Upside Down: A Retrospect', in G. Eley and W. Hunt (eds.), *Reviving the English Revolution: Reflections and Elaborations on the Work of Christopher Hill* (London, 1988), 53–72.

REEDY, GERARD SJ, *The Bible and Reason: Anglicans and Scripture in Late Seventeenth Century England* (Phila., 1985).

RICHEK, R., 'Thomas Randolph's *Salting* (1627), its Text, and Milton's Sixth Prolusion as Another Salting', *English Literary Renaissance*, 12 (1982), 102–31.

ROGERS, JOHN, *The Matter of Revolution: Science, Poetry, and Politics in the Age of Milton* (Ithaca, NY, 1996; paperback edn. 1998).

SAURAT, DENNIS, *Milton: Man and Thinker* (1925; 2nd edn. 1946).

SCHOLEM, GERSHOM H., *On the Kabbalah and its Symbolism* (Boston, Mass., 1965).

SCOTT, JONATHAN, *England's Troubles: Seventeenth Century Political Instability in a European Context* (Cambridge, 2000).

SCREECH, M. A., *Erasmus: Ecstasy and the Praise of Folly* (1980; repr. Harmonds-worth, 1988).

SCRIBNER, BOB, 'Is a History of Popular Culture Possible?', *History of European Ideas*, 10 (1989), 175–91.

—— 'Heterodoxy, Literacy, and Print in the Early German Reformation', in Peter Biller and Anne Hudson (eds.), *Heresy and Literacy 1000–1530* (Cambridge, 1994), 255–78.

SHAW, HOWARD, *The Levellers* (1968; 2nd edn. 1971).

SHUGER, DEBRA, *Habits of Thought in the English Renaissance: Religion, Politics and the Dominant Culture* (Berkeley, Calif., 1990).

SIMON, JOAN, *Education and Society in Tudor England* (Cambridge, 1967).

SKINNER, QUENTIN, *Reason and Rhetoric in the Philosophy of Hobbes* (Cambridge, 1996).

SMITH, NIGEL, 'Richard Overton's Marpriest Tracts: Towards a History of Leveller Style', in T. N. Corns (ed.), *The Literature of Controversy: Polemical Strategy from Milton to Junius* (London, 1987), 39–66.

—— *Perfection Proclaimed: Language and Literature in English Radical Religion, 1640–1660* (Oxford, 1989).

—— 'Exporting Enthusiasm: John Perrot and the Quaker Epic', in Tom Healy and Jonathan Sawday (eds.), *Literature and the English Civil War* (Cambridge, 1990), 248–64.

—— '*Areopagitica*: Voicing Contexts, 1643–5', in David Loewenstein and James Grantham Turner, (eds.), *Politics, Poetics, and Hermeneutics in Milton's Prose*, (Cambridge, 1990), 103–22.

—— 'The Uses of Hebrew in the English Revolution', in Peter Burke and Roy Porter (eds.), *Language, Self, and Society* (Oxford, 1991), 50–71.

—— 'The Charge of Atheism and the Language of Radical Speculation, 1640–1660', in Michael Hunter and David Wootton (eds.), *Atheism from the Reformation to the Enlightenment* (Oxford, 1992), 131–58.

—— *Literature and Revolution in England, 1640–1660* (New Haven, Conn., and London, 1994; paperback edn. 1997).

—— 'Hidden Things Brought to Light: Enthusiasm and Quaker Discourse', in David Loewenstein and Thomas N. Corns (eds.), *The Emergence of Quaker Writing: Dissenting Literature in Seventeenth Century England* (London, 1995), 57–69.

—— review of Clement Hawes, *Mania and Literary Style: The Rhetoric of Enthusiasm from the Ranters to Christopher Smart* (Cambridge, 1996), in *Modern Philology*, 97 (1999), 277–80.

SOLT, L. F., 'Anti-intellectualism in the Puritan Revolution', *Church History*, 25 (1956), 306–16.

SPUFFORD, MARGARET, 'First Steps in Literacy: The Reading and Writing Experiences of the Humblest Seventeenth Century Autobiographers', *Social History*, 4 (1979), 407–35.

—— 'The Importance of Religion in the Sixteenth and Seventeenth Centuries', in Margaret Spufford (ed.), *The World of the Rural Dissenters, 1520–1725* (Cambridge, 1995), 1–102.

STACHNIEWSKI, JOHN, *The Persecutory Imagination: English Puritanism and the Literature of Religious Despair* (Oxford, 1991).

STEWART, ALAN, *Close Readers: Humanism and Sodomy in Early Modern England* (Princeton, NJ, 1997).

SWANSON, R. N., 'Literacy, Heresy, History, and Orthodoxy: Perspectives and Permutations for the Late Middle Ages', in Peter Biller and Anne Hudson (eds.), *Heresy and Literacy, 1000–1530* (Cambridge, 1994), 279–93.

SYLVESTER, D. W., *Educational Documents 800–1816* (London, 1970).

THOMAS, KEITH, 'Women and the Civil War Sects', *Past and Present*, 13 (1958), 42–62.

—— *Religion and the Decline of Magic: Popular Beliefs in Sixteenth and Seventeenth Century England* (1971; repr. Harmondsworth, 1991).

—— 'The Meaning of Literacy in Early Modern England', in Gerd Baumann (ed.), *The Written Word: Literacy in Transition* (Oxford, 1986), 97–131.

TODD, MARGO, 'Seneca and the Protestant Mind: The Influence of Stoicism on Puritan Ethics', *Archiv für Reformationgeschichte*, 74 (1983), 182–99.

—— (ed.), *Reformation to Revolution: Politics and Religion in Early Modern England* (London, 1995).

TOLMIE, MURRAY, *The Triumph of the Saints: The Separate Churches of England, 1616–49* (Cambridge, 1977).

TRUBOWITZ, RACHAEL, 'Female Preachers and Male Wives: Gender and Authority in Civil War England', in James Holstun (ed.), *Pamphlet Wars: Rhetoric in the English Revolution* (London, 1992), 112–33.

TUCK, RICHARD, *Natural Rights Theories* (Cambridge, 1979).

—— *Philosophy and Government 1572–1651* (Cambridge, 1993).

TUER, A. W., *History of the Horn-Book* (London, 1897).

TURNER, JAMES GRANTHAM, *One Flesh: Paradisal Marriage and Sexual Relations in the Age of Milton* (Oxford, 1987).

—— 'The Poetics of Engagement', in David Loewenstein and James Grantham Turner (eds.), *Politics, Poetics, and Hermeneutics in Milton's Prose* (Cambridge, 1990), 257–75.

TYACKE, NICHOLAS, 'Puritanism, Arminianism, and Counter Revolution', in Conrad Russell (ed.), *The Origins of the English Civil War* (London, 1973), 119–43.

—— (ed.), *The History of the University of Oxford, iv: Seventeenth Century Oxford* (Oxford, 1997).

WALKER, D. P., *The Decline of Hell: Seventeenth Century Discussions of Eternal Torment* (London, 1964).

WALL, WENDY, ' "Household Stuff": The Sexual Politics of Domesticity and the Advent of English Comedy', *English Literary History*, 65 (London, 1998), 1–45.

WALTER, JOHN, 'The Impact on Society: A World Turned Upside Down?', in John Morrill (ed.), *The Impact of the English Civil War* (London, 1991), 104–22.

WATKINS, OWEN C., *The Puritan Experience* (London, 1972).

WATSON, FOSTER, *The English Grammar Schools to 1660* (1908).

WATT, TESSA, *Cheap Print and Popular Piety, 1550–1640* (Cambridge, 1991; paperback edn. 1994).

WATTS, MICHAEL R., *The Dissenters: From the Reformation to the French Revolution* (Oxford, 1978).

WEBBER, JOAN, *The Eloquent 'I': Style and Self in Seventeenth Century Prose* (Madison, Wisc., 1968).

WEBSTER, CHARLES, *The Great Instauration: Science, Medicine and Reform, 1626–1660* (London, 1975).

WEIMANN, ROBERT, *Authority and Representation in Early Modern Discourse* (Baltimore, Md., 1996).

WILDING, MICHAEL, 'Milton's *Areopagitica*: Liberty for the Sects', in T. N. Corns (ed.), *The Literature of Controversy* (London, 1987), 7–38.

WILLIAMS, G. H., *The Radical Reformation* (Phila., 1962).

WILLIAMS, RAYMOND, *Keywords: A Vocabulary of Culture and Society* (London, 1976).

WILLIAMSON, GEORGE, *Seventeenth Century Contexts* (London, 1963).

WISEMAN, SUSAN, *Drama and Politics in the English Civil War* (Cambridge, 1998).

WOOTTON, DAVID (ed.), *Divine Right and Democracy: An Anthology of Political Writings in Stuart England* (Harmondsworth, 1986).

—— 'Leveller Democracy and the Puritan Revolution', in J. H. Burns (ed.), with the assistance of Mark Goldie, *The Cambridge History of Political Thought 1450–1700* (Cambridge, 1991; paperback edn. 1996), 412–442.

WORDEN, BLAIR, *The Rump Parliament* (1974; 2nd edn. Cambridge, 1977).

WRIGHTSON, KEITH, *English Society, 1580–1680* (London, 1982).

ZAGORIN, PEREZ, 'The Authorship of *Mans Mortalitie*', *The Library*, 5th ser., 5 (1950), 179–83.

Index